THE

OTHER HALF OF THE GLOBE

SKETCHES AND PHOTOGRAPHS

FROM THE

SOUTHERN HEMISPHERE

BY

D. L. MILLER

Author of "Eternal Verities," "Girdling the Globe," Etc.

SIXTH EDITION—TWELVE THOUSAND.

The earth is said to be among the smallest of the
planets, and yet a hundred and fifty thousand miles of
travel makes one acquainted with but a small portion of it

ELGIN, ILL.:
THE BRETHREN PUBLISHING HOUSE
1907

Photograph of Our Party under the Temple Platform at Jerusalem in What is Known as Solomon's Stables, Taken in 1904.

THIS BOOK

IS AFFECTIONATELY DEDICATED TO MY

KINDEST AND BEST FRIENDS,

THE READERS OF

THE GOSPEL MESSENGER

PREFACE

THIS book was written and is printed with a distinct purpose and for a special class of readers. The writer had in mind the increase of the circulation of the *Gospel Messenger,* and it was written for the readers of that most excellent Christian journal. It is not to be placed on the market for sale, and at the present time the only way to secure a copy is to subscribe for the paper.

The actual cost of making the book is borne by the Brethren Publishing House. No compensation is received for the writing and no profit is to accrue to any one save those, possibly, who receive and read it. An increased list of subscribers will widen the opportunity for doing good. I have a hope also that the book in itself may do good in the world. Thus two opportunities are afforded to accomplish good.

" The Other Half " was planned several years before it was written and printed. It involved an absence from home of nearly two years and a tour over the face of the earth in which a distance of sixty-four thousand five hundred miles was traveled. Under God's blessing the miles have been traveled, the book made, and it is yours. It comes from the heart of the author, with deep gratitude to God, and with love and esteem to the readers.

Elder Wilbur B. Stover, of Bulsar, India, who traveled with me to South Africa, and did his full part toward making the trip both pleasant and profitable, has his say. He very kindly prepared the chapters dealing biographically with Livingstone and Mackay.

Maijee, the Gujerati name of my wife, who has always been my best help and constant companion, traveled with me on all the tours save one. She remained at Bulsar while we visited South Africa. We have finished the greater part of life's voyage together. We have had smooth sailing, for God has wonderfully blessed us. Some storms we have met, but met them trusting in our Great Captain. And now the voyage will soon be over. One of these days we shall enter the haven of eternal rest. The storms will be over, quarantines will have all been passed and there will be joy, and peace, and rest.

D. L. Miller.

TABLE OF CONTENTS.

PART ONE.

CHAPTER I.

TABLE OF CONTENTS.

PART TWO.

CHAPTER I.

CHAPTER II.

CHAPTER III.

CHAPTER IV.

CHAPTER V.

The Other Half of the Globe

CHAPTER I.

Off for Northern Europe, France and Switzerland—A Cruise on the Mediterranean—A Call at Constantinople, Smyrna, Samos and Beirut—Our Sixth Visit to Jerusalem—A Successful Dragoman—The Dead Sea and the Jordan—An Embarkation at Joppa—The Russian Fleet in the Suez Canal—All Aboard for " Dear Old India."

THE journeyings of which this book is a brief record began at Bulsar, India, where the author and Maijee, my wife's India name, had been making our home for some time. We had a most pleasant and delightful time in association with our own missionaries, visiting the stations, not only our own but others as well, so that we might become the better acquainted with this important field of labor now being so successfully occupied by the Brethren church. It was a labor of love, if such pleasant experiences may be called labor, and was most thoroughly enjoyed. It is now a pleasant memory, but one we would fain keep green while life lasts.

We had left our Mt. Morris, Illinois, home on the fourth of August, 1904, with the avowed purpose, if the Lord blessed us with health and strength, to be away at least two years or more. The old home has grown dear to us, for here we have spent a quarter of a century in life's activities, and in these years we have found a large number of warm-hearted friends who have always been very kind to us. Separations are never pleasant, and this is especially true when old friends

11

take the parting hand. A few weeks were spent visiting among
the churches in Eastern Pennsylvania, where we had a very
enjoyable season holding meetings with the people of God.
Then came a short stay in Brooklyn, where we are now doing
a good work for the Lord, and we were ready to sail on the
Deutschland for Hamburg, Germany. Before sailing we were
joined at New York by Elder I. B. Trout, our Sunday-school
editor, Brother W. R. Miller, so long pastor of the Chicago
church where he laid the foundation for the successful work
now going on there, Brother and Sister Berkebile, of Ohio,
missionaries to India, and Brother M. R. Murray, of Kansas.
This made up our little company, and as a matter of course
we had a good time. Fine weather and smooth seas were the
order for the most part of the voyage. One or two days of
rough sea tried the sailor qualities of those unacquainted
with the ocean, but no one suffered seriously.

At Hamburg, Germany, we were met by Brother and Sister Vaniman, our missionaries in Scandinavia, a meeting very
much enjoyed by all who took part in it. Several weeks were
spent among the churches in Scandinavia, and another two
weeks in France and Switzerland with Brethren Fercken and
Pellet, and then we embarked on the *Argonaut* at Marseilles,
France, for a cruise on the Mediterranean. This took us to
Olympia, in Greece, Constantinople, Smyrna, Samos, Beirut,
and Jaffa. We had a pleasant voyage. At Beirut our company separated, Maijee and I to go on to Jaffa by steamer
and our companions to Jerusalem overland.

When we arrived at Jaffa we felt we could not pass by
without again revisiting the Holy City. It was our sixth and,
in all human probability, last visit to Jerusalem. It seemed
like going to an old home, so warmly did our old friends of
former years welcome us. Among the number was Mr. Bernard Heilpern who accompanied us on our first tour of the
Holy Land in 1884 as dragoman and interpreter. He was

Chevalier Bernard Heilpern.

The Jordan at the End of the Dry Season, when the River is at its Lowest Ebb.

much pleased to see us and insisted on our paying him a visit in his own home. He has retired from active business and is living in a beautiful villa outside the walls of the city, near the "upper pool," where he enjoys a well-earned repose after a long, active and successful career. - Mr. Heilpern is the son of

By the Thousands the Russian Pilgrims Bathe in the, to them, Sacred Waters of the Jordan, where Christ was Baptized.

a Jewish rabbi and was converted to Christianity in early life. He came to Palestine at the age of fifteen and began work on a farm; then in a hotel six months for his board, after which he received a dollar and sixty cents per month. He studied and worked hard and became familiar with a large number of languages. He then began his career as interpreter and dragoman to travelers in Palestine. When the German Emperor visited the Holy Land in 1898, Mr. Heilpern managed all the details of the royal tour with such marked ability that his majesty conferred upon him the degree of Chevalier of

Hohenzollern.   He has been thrice decorated by kings and emperors for his splendid service.   " Seest thou a man diligent in his business, he shall stand before kings."   We enjoyed a delightful visit at the home of our old friend whom we had met so often in Palestine and who had taken such good care

Reservoir at Elisha's Fountain.   The water is used for Irrigation.

of Maijee when we were attacked by the infuriated Arabs at Fejee in 1884.

Our last stay at Jerusalem passed all too quickly.   It included a revisit to the Jordan, Elisha's Fountain and the Dead Sea, where I renewed my youth " by going in swimming." It brought back a flood of memories of boyhood days in Mary-

New German Church in Jerusalem.
Dedicated in 1898 by Emperor of Germany, William II.

land and of the old home, of faces long since vanished and of voices silent for aye. It was a novel experience, walking in the water to the armpits and sinking no deeper, and floating without exertion on the surface. The water is so thoroughly impregnated with salt and other mineral substances that when you wade in breast deep your feet no longer touch the bottom and all you have to do is to move your hands as a rudder to keep you in an upright position and you find yourself walking through the water.

We also enjoyed a boat ride on the Jordan, and although the date was November, 1904, just at the close of the dry season, the early rains were just beginning to fall, and even at this season of the year a great volume of water was flowing through its channel to be lost forever in the Dead Sea. Elisha's Fountain now flows into a reservoir and the waters are used to irrigate the fertile plains around about ancient Jericho, and these are rich in semitropical vegetation. Wonderful changes have taken place at Jericho and Gilgal since we first visited the place in 1884. Four hotels now occupy the site of Gilgal where Joshua's army encamped after crossing the Jordan. The changes that have occurred in the last quarter of a century make the place almost unrecognizable.

At Jerusalem, too, great changes are taking place. Inside the walls the German church, completed and dedicated by the emperor in 1898, marks the center of a good deal of building activity. On the Via Dolorosa, near the pool of Bethesda, a large building is being erected, and outside the Zion gate the German Catholics are erecting a great cathedral on the ground donated to them by the emperor, where they believe the last supper was eaten and where Christ washed his disciples' feet. Outside the walls great activity is noted in building industry. It is said that Jerusalem is having a building boom. The population is variously estimated at from sixty to seventy thousand,

and there are at least forty thousand Jews in old and new Jerusalem.

Our little party began breaking up at the Holy City. Brother Murray decided to remain in Palestine for the winter, and so we left him and continued our journey. Embarking at Jaffa we had an experience something like that of the prophet who sought to flee away from the presence of the Lord. Having knowledge of the storm conditions prevailing at Jaffa, which have not changed since the days of Jonah, we decided to go down from Jerusalem in good time so that we might select our ship and the day of sailing, for there are three or four ships leaving the port each week for Egypt. On the day of our arrival the *Minneh,* an Egyptian steamer, was due, but did not arrive until the next day, and because of this delay our party had an experience never to be forgotten.

All the day that we should have gone aboard, had the ship been on time, the sea was as quiet and peaceful as if storms never ruffled its calm waters. Early the next morning I walked down to the seashore and to the tanneries that have been located here ever since the days of Peter and Simon the tanner, and noticed that the waters were being slightly troubled, with indications of a coming storm. I then told the agent not to purchase tickets for the *Minneh* if the sea was likely to be rough at all. At two P. M. he came to the hotel with our steamer tickets and reported the sea as being moderately smooth. I again said, " If the sea is rough we will not go." He replied: " Never mind, the sea will not be very rough and you will get on board all right."

When the quay was reached I saw the spray flying high in the air where the waves broke over the ledge of rocks a short distance from the shore, and then had it not been for the fact that our fare was paid and all our baggage in the boat we would have returned to the hotel and waited for another ship, as my wife suggested doing. As it was, none of us realized for the moment how rough the sea was, or we would not have undertaken the embarkation under any consideration. The ship was lying at anchor a half mile or more from the shore, and we had to be rowed out in a small boat. As soon as we rounded the point of the rocks and met the full force and sweep of the waves as they rolled toward the shore we knew there was a trying time in store for us. Our little boat met the great waves prow to, and when it seemed as if we should be engulfed, mounted to the crest, at what seemed a decidedly dangerous angle, and then pitched forward into the hollow below only to meet and surmount another monster wave. It was uphill and downhill work, and our boatmen worked with a will. The Arab at the helm called out, " God bless the good boatman," and the half dozen oarsmen responded in calling the blessing of God on all aboard. Of course this was all in Arabic and was used as a song, but their voices had a cheery sound amid the rush of the mighty waters. It was a grand and awful sight. I had often looked out upon the great waves of the sea from the deck of a ship, but never before from a frail rowboat. As the wall of water rose in front of us, with a wicked green color, the top fringed with white spray, it was awe-inspiring, and, had it not been for weak nerves, would have been in a sense enjoyable. I do not now recall that I experienced the slightest sense of fear, but some of us were decidedly nervous.

After reaching the side of the ship our troubles began in good earnest. Another boat, larger than ours, came out to take passengers ashore and it was a question as to which should reach the ship first. Ours came up ahead and the ship's rope was tossed to our boatmen, but unfortunately they missed catching it and it fell into the hands of our rivals, who, seizing the opportunity, pulled alongside the ship, crowding us out and back. The great waves lifted us up and carried our boat under the stern of the ship, which was

rising and falling on the swell of the waves. For a time
it looked as if our frail bark would be crushed by the im-
pact. After having time to think it all over, I am of the
opinion that at no time were our lives endangered, but it
all looked frightful enough at the time to make one wonder
what the result would be. Our sisters were trembling
from the nervous shock, and I felt for the time we were

Jaffa by the Sea, a Rocky and Dangerous Landing.

being tossed on the wild sea in our little boat that I would
not soon try another embarkation or landing at Jaffa.

Finally we pulled alongside the boat that was tossing between us and the ship, already partly filled with passengers and
baggage to be taken ashore, and amidst the yelling of the boatmen and the greatest possible amount of confusion we were
told to come on. The Arab boatmen,—and what fearless, willing seamen they are,—stood ready to assist us across the inter-
vening boat and up the gangway to the deck of the ship.
Brother Trout was across the boat and up the ladder before I

had time to note his movements which were accelerated by the strong arms and willing hands of the Arabs. Then Sister Berkebile was seized and literally carried and dragged up the gangway, being drawn under the rope and chain that served as a kind of guard on the seaside of the ladder. Then came my wife's time for moving. I could do nothing but watch and wait for the outcome. The Arabs carried her safely across the boat and then instead of waiting for it to rise on a wave, they lifted, and pushed and rolled her upward as if she had been a bundle of merchandise. After she was on the ladder with her feet tangled in her skirts, she vigorously protested, but it was all of no use. One of the men who spoke a little English said to her, " No! No!! Madame must go up, not stay here all time afternoon." They set out to place her on deck, and on deck they set her safely, but at the expense of her nerves and a good deal of physical discomfort. I went up, or rather was pulled up without serious mishap. I refused to try to get on the ladder until the boat rose on a wave, then I set my feet firmly on the step. But from that moment I found myself dragged upward and had to go willing or not. In the ascent I came in contact with a Hebrew who was trying to get into the boat below. It was Jew against Gentile, but as I was much the heavier of the two and was being drawn upward by strong arms, the son of Israel had to give way. When I reached the deck he set his feet in the boat below and we were both happy. Brother Berkebile, first looking after the baggage, —and it was well he did or part of it would have been taken ashore in the confusion,—came up the ladder and we were all on deck.

After taking account of stock and feelings we found we were all safe, some of us wet through our clothing, others suffering from severe nervous shock, and not a few bruises, but we were all thankful that it was no worse. I mildly censured the agent for attempting to bring us aboard the ship when the sea was so rough and dangerous, but with Oriental assurance he replied: " I could not help for the rough sea, and we may thank God we are safe on board the ship." And this ended all controversy.

Then came the Arab boatmen to say good-bye, and to receive their expected backsheesh, especially the latter, for the dragging process had been hard on them and they really deserved extra pay for their hard work. The poor fellows had done their best and felt that we would appreciate their efforts to get us safe on board. And we did. Maijee wanted me to give them all the loose change I had in my pocket. We made each of them happy, and with a smile and a God bless you they left us to row ashore in their little boat.

Ours was the last boat allowed to leave the shore for the ship. A policeman determines when the sea is too dangerous to land or embark, and if we had been a few minutes later we should have been spared the experience. Even the mails were not allowed to be taken aboard. Two Chicago ladies who were very anxious to go with us, but were not quite ready to leave the hotel when we did, were unable to embark, and as we learned later had to remain at Joppa four days longer waiting for a ship. They came to Port Said with Brother W. R. Miller, who reported a smooth sea when they embarked.

When it was all over and we were in our cabin alone, if our readers could have looked in they would have seen us on our knees devoutly and earnestly thanking God for bringing us safely through a threatened danger; and so we lay down to rest in peace and quiet under his protecting care.

The day after the storm and our thrilling experience at Jaffa we landed safely at Port Said and proceeded at once to Cairo, where Brother W. R. Miller joined us a few days later. The pyramids were revisited, another look was taken at the body of the Pharaoh of the oppression and a pleasant time generally was enjoyed in the capital city of Egypt. Then we bade Brother Trout farewell, he to return to the loved and longed-for home circle and we to continue our journey to India.

While waiting the arrival of our missionary party at Port Said the Russian fleet steamed into the harbor and entered the

In the Valley of the Jordan, Among the Rich Tropical
Vegetation Produced by the Life-giving
Waters of Elisha's Fountain.

Suez Canal on its way to meet its fate at the hands of the Japanese under Admiral Togo. Thousands of the men who thronged the decks of warship and transport on that November day found watery graves, a few months later, in the Sea of Japan when Russ and Jap met in deadly conflict. This not because these men had a quarrel with each other or aught of resentment, but because the heads of one of the so-called Christian nations was ambitious and grasping. Oh, the cruelty of war, its wastefulness and uselessness! When will the nations of the earth learn wisdom and follow the mandates of the Great Prince of Peace!

After several days of anxious waiting the *Balduino* steamed into the harbor and we met our missionary band bound for India. It was a glad, happy meeting, and there was rejoicing and thanksgiving that the Lord had graciously kept us all and brought us together again. Our enlarged party was made up as follows: Brother W. R. Miller, Sister McCann with Henry and Mary, her children, Brother and Sister Berkebile, Brother and Sister Ross, Brother and Sister Pittenger, Brother and Sister Eby and Sister Gertrude Rowland, now the wife of Brother Jesse Emmert, and Maijee and the writer. We had a pleasant and enjoyable but uneventful voyage from Port Said to Bombay where we landed December 6, 1904. There were happy reunions and a joyous welcome awaiting the Pilgrims upon reaching " Dear Old India " again. Such meetings and such joy may be typical of the meeting when life's voyage is over and we enter the haven of eternal rest.

CHAPTER II.

The Start for the Other Half of the Globe—Discomforts of a
Cargo Steamer—A Burial at Sea—Smallpox on Board the
Ship—The Southern Cross—Seychelles—A Rigid Quarantine—
The Double Cocoanut—Westward Toward the Dark Conti-
nent—The Industrious Ant.

On the nineteenth of April, 1905, we sailed away from
the plague-stricken city of Bombay on our voyage to the other
half of the globe. Plague, cholera and smallpox were claiming victims each day, and we were glad to get away. The
Nuddea, a cargo boat of the British India line, had been selected for the voyage. She stopped at all the most desirable
South African ports long enough to afford ample opportunity
to visit the places *en route.* It was a bright, beautiful summer
sea, a sparkling, welcome sea that greeted us as we began our
voyage. As we glided over its calm, peaceful waters it seemed
as if they could never become ruffled or boisterous from the
effects of storm and gale, for the monsoon had not yet begun
stirring the waters of the Indian Ocean as it does later in
the season when it sweeps across the face of the deep. Much
to our discomfort we learned all this on our return voyage a
few months later.

Brother W. B. Stover, our well-known missionary at
Bulsar, India, and the writer made up the company. The
former is a good traveling companion and did much to make
the tour interesting and profitable. Good companionship is
always to be appreciated either on land or sea, but perhaps
more on sea than land. For the time being you have a little
world of your own, and are constantly thrown together. You
depend upon each other in a great measure for all the social

life you enjoy. The best way to learn to know a man is to take a long sea voyage with him. You see him under many different conditions. You bunk with him, you eat with him, you stand together in sunshine and storm, together you meet danger, and as in our case, you pass by the very gates of death, and the real man opens up to you like as the unfolding bud

A Busy Corner in Bombay, where the Cotton Merchants
do Most Congregate.

and you come to know him as he is. After spending seventy-two days with Brother Stover on board ship I came to know him better than ever before, and the better one knows him the more one loves him.

I cannot say much in favor of the comforts of the *Nuddea*. She was not built especially for the accommodation of passengers. We knew something of this before we went aboard

and found out more afterwards. The steamer lacked most of
the comforts of the modern passenger ship and had in full
measure the unpleasant things usually found on vessels ply-
ing in the torrid zone. Rats, roaches and ants were in evidence
everywhere. The rats visited our cabin at night and once
" when sleep had departed from my eyes and slumber from
my eyelids " I watched with interest three big fellows on a
tour of investigation about our bunks. The roaches,—none
of your diminutive vermin seen in northern climes, but great,
sleek, fat fellows as big as a baby's hand,—were industriously
active during the entire voyage. When you couldn't see them
you could smell them, and neither sight nor smell was a pleasure to eye or nose. But the *Nuddea* suited our purpose, and
one can endure many discomforts to secure the desired end.
She called at a large number of ports and remained long
enough in receiving and discharging cargo to enable us to
see all there was to see at the ports of call and make such in-
vestigations as were desirable. For our purpose this was worth
as much as if we had remained a month at each place.

We had but four cabin passengers for the trip from Bombay to Durban, but our deck was crowded with Moslems and
Hindus, men, women and children bound for South Africa.
They were leaving their homes in India for the land of gold
and diamonds, attracted by the promise of higher wages and
more favorable conditions for making a living. To them the
lower half of the Dark Continent is a veritable land of promise,
and were it not for restricted immigration great crowds of
India's great population would rush into Africa. Our ship
for the time being was a small cosmopolitan world. The
officers were English, the stewards and cooks Goanese, and
the crew lascars from India. There must have been more than
a score of nationalities and religions represented on board the
boat. The mixed multitude afforded large opportunities for
the study of national characteristics, different religions, for

drawing contrasts and noting reflections on the various conditions of humanity in this little world of ours.

Before turning the prow of our ship toward the equator we sailed north along the coast of India to Porebunder, where a day was spent in taking in cargo and embarking passengers. Our deck passenger list was augmented by the addition of eighty-one natives who brought with them on board twenty

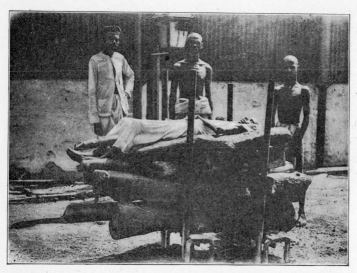

Hindu Cremation. The Fires of the Funeral Pyres are Kept Constantly Burning in Plague-stricken Bombay.

head of cattle and about as many goats and kids. These should be properly classed among the deck passengers, for men, women, children, cows, calves, goats and kids, all live together in intimate relation on the open deck. The Hindu regards the cow and her seven products as particularly sacred, and hence offers no objection to being herded with cattle.

But it is a stench in our nostrils and we got entirely too much of it for our comfort.

Because of these unsanitary conditions, prevailing in the Orient, the traveler is in constant danger from infectious and contagious diseases. When the cholera, plague or smallpox breaks out among these people they die like flies, and it is a most difficult matter to stamp out diseases. For several months all three of these diseases had been more or less prevalent in Bombay, raising the death rate as high as one hundred and twenty to the thousand. In the city of Chicago the death rate is as low as seventeen to the thousand. This gives a striking contrast as to the health of the two cities.

From Bombay our ship's log showed that we traveled a distance of two thousand three hundred and fifty miles to Victoria, the capital of the Seychelles archipelago, lying four degrees south of the equator, and eleven hundred miles east of Mombassa on the southeast coast of the Dark Continent. We were compelled to remain six days in the harbor of Victoria without being allowed to go ashore. The cause of the delay was on this wise:

Two days out from Bombay one of the deck passengers was taken dangerously ill and died the next night. He had a son in South Africa and desired to visit his boy again. But death ended his earthly voyage, and instead of seeing his son he went down to a watery grave. His body was sewed up in a sack made of sailcloth, with heavy iron weights attached. In the early morning the propeller was stayed in its revolutions for a few moments. From the side of the ship I saw an object dart downward, there was a sudden splash as the sea opened to receive the dead, the waters closed over the body and the ship moved on as if nothing had happened. For a brief moment I thought how typical of the shortness of human life is this burial at sea. We are born, we live, we die. For a short time our little world pauses in its onward course, there

is a wound in the earth, an open grave, a downward movement, the earth is closed, the world moves on and we are left
alone to be forgotten.

The day following the burial at sea we were informed by
the ship's doctor that the smallpox had broken out among
the deck passengers and that there was a case of what it was
feared might prove to be the plague. Owing to the crowded
condition of the ship it was almost impossible to segregate
those afflicted with the dread disease. A not very successful
attempt was made in this direction and we settled down to make
the best of an unpleasant situation.

Under ordinary circumstances it is considered a very
serious matter for the smallpox to break out in a community
on shore. The place is at once quarantined and the greatest
possible precautions are taken to prevent the spread of the
disease. But it is quite a different thing to have the disease
appear on board the narrow limits of a crowded ship, among
passengers who by their religious beliefs are fatalists, and
have not the slightest idea of the common sanitary measures
and precautions to stay the malady. Those who are afflicted
are Moslems, and they believe that if it is their fate to die
with the smallpox no power on earth can change the decree.
As a result they are not very careful about avoiding contact
with those who are sick, and so it may easily be carried about
and the danger of its spreading is greatly increased.

And so we go on day by day, and the Lord only knows
what the result will be. A danger bravely met and faced
loses much of its terror, and when it is met with trusting confidence in God instead of fear there come joy and peace in
the consciousness that, although we may be surrounded by
danger and death, yet the Lord doeth all things well. " Thou
wilt keep him in perfect peace, whose mind is stayed on thee:
because he trusteth in thee."

Our voyage thus far, barring the appearance of the small-

pox, has been a most pleasant one. Wilbur, who by the way
is not a very good sailor at best, made frequent offerings to
the sea before he was able to enjoy the voyage, but after a
few days he was all right and equal to the occasion. As for
me I have not felt the slightest symptom of the malady of
the sea.

As we proceeded southward we had a gentle breeze which
greatly modified the heat. I expected, from what I had heard
and read, to find the heat intense under the equator, but in
this was happily disappointed. At no time did either of us
suffer from the heat. Of course the almost constant ocean
breeze modifies the intensity of the heat and makes both day
and night pleasant.

As we near the equator we observe that the days and
nights become more and more nearly equal, and the long twi-
lights, so enjoyable in our northern home, are altogether wanting. Soon after the sun sinks below the water line in the west,
darkness comes down and covers the sea as with a great pall.
For several evenings before crossing the line we have noticed
the North Star approaching nearer and nearer the water line
in the far-away north. One evening we watched it closely as
it appeared just above the horizon and the next we looked
for it in vain, apparently the sea had swallowed it up and we
saw it no more while we tarried in the Southland. But in its
stead we have the far-famed Southern Cross, the noted con-
stellation of the southern heavens, rising higher and higher
each night toward the zenith of the skies. And then there are
numberless new stars brought into view, and our old friend,
the Great Bear, is still with us in the north, and then we also
have Orion showing its beautiful bands evening after evening.
But the southern heavens cannot vie with our northern skies
for brilliancy of decoration at night. The Southern Cross
pales in contrast with Ursus Major and Orion, and many of
our brighter stars are wanting in the southern hemisphere.

April 29, in the early morning, we sighted land, and it was a gladsome view that we had of the group of islands forming the Seychelles archipelago. At three in the afternoon we cast anchor in the harbor of Victoria about two miles from shore. Here we awaited patiently and anxiously the coming of the health officers so that we might learn what was in store for

Victoria and the Harbor, Island of Mahe, Seychelles Archipelago.

us. We had hopes that those who were sick might be allowed to land and be put into the hospital at the quarantine station. Presently the boat came steaming alongside the ship, stopping a hundred yards away. When the officials were informed of conditions on board they said we would be allowed to anchor within a mile of the shore, that no one should attempt to go ashore and that in the morning they would give us their decision as to landing passengers. With this they pulled away and we saw no more of them until ten o'clock the next day. Armed patrol boats came out after we had taken our second anchorage and from that time until we left the harbor, six days later, we were under the closest possible surveillance.

In the evening and during the night refreshing showers of rain fell, but the morning of the Lord's Day came bright and clear. The mountain, covered with forests of rich green, at the foot of which nestled the embowered city of Victoria, presented a beautiful and inviting appearance. It was a quiet, peaceful day. Over the rippling waters of the bay came the sound of the ringing church bells in the quiet town. How gladly we would have answered the call to service, but were hindered. A hundred yards away lay the patrol boats guarding us with Argus eyes, so that no one from the plague ship could go ashore. Presently the health officer's boat again approached us. Stopping a long way off he delivered his decision in a loud voice. To us it meant this: Our sick would not be allowed to land. The passengers for Victoria might be taken in the ship's boat to the quarantine island some miles away, where they would be compelled to remain twenty-one days in strict quarantine. We might discharge such cargo as we had for Victoria, but no help would come from the shore. Potatoes and onions were not to be unloaded. And last but not least, no one on board the ship would be allowed to land.

One is impressed, at first thought, with the idea that there is a good deal of selfishness in humanity when occasion develops it. On our side we felt that the sick might have been taken to the small island, placed in a camp, properly cared for by their own friends who have had the same disease, and no one would have been endangered by the contagion; but this reasonable request was denied. However, after due reflection I felt that the authorities did right. It were better that the few hundred on board the ship should suffer than that the dreadful disease should be spread abroad on their beautiful islands. The many, not the few, are to be first considered in a case of this kind. Were the malady carried

The Vanilla Bean,
As it grows at Victoria in Great Abundance, from which is
Obtained the much used Flavoring Extract.

ashore it might almost depopulate their islands. After we knew what we had to expect we settled down quietly and felt but little more concern about the matter. A supply of lymph was furnished by the medical authorities on shore and the ship's doctor vaccinated all who had not previously taken this precaution.

It really became amusing to those of us on the ship to see how the islanders kept aloof from us. No one would venture near the ship. We established communication with the shore and it was done in this wise: Orders for such things as were wanted were shouted out to the officer in charge of the patrol boat and noted down by him. Then the ship's boat was lowered and fastened astern with a hundred yards of rope. It floated out from the ship to the full length of the rope. Our purchases were placed in the boat, it was drawn alongside the ship, a sailor climbed down a ladder and fastening the articles to a rope, they were drawn on board. In this way we kept up communication with the shore for the six days we remained in the harbor.

We had on board the *Nuddea* six thousand bags of rice for Victoria. The steam tug brought out from the shore large flat boats, or lighters, and cast them adrift near the ship. Afterward these were brought alongside and the rice put into them. After being loaded they were loosened and shoved away and were picked up as they floated about the harbor, and towed ashore by the tug. We received no help from the shore and our crew had to do all the work themselves, hence the long delay. We should have remained here one day instead of six.

After being in port three days permission was granted to land our native passengers. There were thirty-five of them, men, women and children. The ship's boats were lowered and the people with their belongings were placed on board and rowed to the small quarantine island where they will be compelled to remain twenty-one days in strict isolation. After this they and their effects will be thoroughly fumigated and then they will be allowed their liberty. I pitied them. In 1899 we had an experience in quarantine on the desert near Port Said, Egypt, and one experience of that kind is sufficient for a lifetime.

I was deeply impressed with the care taken by the Victorians to keep the smallpox from invading their shores. And how careful they were,—over careful it seemed to us on board the ship. Every point was carefully guarded and closely watched, and they not only watched but kept away from us. They took no chances whatever, and used every possible precaution against the evil. Then I said, " I would to God that every Christian home and community were as carefully guarded and as closely watched to keep impurity and sin from their midst as were these islands of the Indian Ocean to keep contagious disease from their shores." From the very nature of the case greater care should ·be taken, for this disease injures only the body, while sin blackens and destroys the soul. If Christians everywhere should follow the example of the Victorians, what watchfulness and guarding there would be, what care and anxiety, how zealously the home and community would be patrolled day and night to see that no impure book, no picture to induce impure thought, and no person of doubtful character were allowed to enter and carry the deadly sin poison, which is incomparably worse than any contagious disease to which the human body is heir, into the pure life of the Christian home. Were Christians as careful as were these islanders, what an improvement in the moral atmosphere of Christian homes and communities would result.

While we are quietly lying at anchor at Victoria we have ample time to look up the facts concerning the islands. The Seychelles archipelago is a group of small islands, eighty-nine in number, lying four degrees south of the equator and about

eleven hundred geographical miles east of the southeast coast
of Africa. The estimated area of the entire group is only
one hundred and fifty square miles, a little over one-third of
which is found on Mahe, the principal island of the group.
It has an area of fifty-four square miles and a population of
fifteen thousand souls. The population of the entire group is
a trifle less than twenty thousand. Victoria, a beautiful and
healthy little city, is situated on Mahe at the base of a low
range of mountains which bound the coast. Although it is
so close to the equator it enjoys a most delightful climate, and
is noted for its rich growth of tropical vegetation and its enviable reputation as a health resort. The death rate is about
fifteen to the thousand. Were it not so remote from Europe
and America it would be crowded with health and pleasure
seekers. It has a fine harbor and is frequently visited by
the warships of the different nations of the world. Great Britain has made Victoria a coaling station for her navy, thus giving her the advantage of a safe and commodious harbor and
abundant facilities for coaling her fleets in the Indian Ocean.

The islands were discovered by the Portuguese, those
great pioneers in the navigation of the globe, and occupied by
the French in 1742. Fifty years later they were captured by
the captain of a British ship and finally, in 1842, were assigned
by treaty to Great Britain, and since then have remained under
the control of that power. In 1903 the islands were made a
separate colony under the crown of England, the government
being vested in a governor, appointed by the king, and ex-
ecutive and legislative council. The governor resides in Victoria and receives a salary of about five thousand dollars per
year. Religiously the Church of England and the Roman
Catholics are in control and each receives about an equal share
of the government school fund. Good schools are maintained
by both churches, and in addition to these the government

supports a high school of excellent character at which pupils are fitted for Cambridge in England.

The principal exports from Victoria are vanilla beans, cocoanuts, cocoanut oil, cocoa, tortoise shell, soap and guano. On the small islands of Aldabara are found the immense land

Coco-de-Mer, or Double Cocoanut, Grove.

tortoises, it is said the largest in the world, for which the place is especially noted. From here comes an abundant supply of fine tortoise shell, which, being made into combs and ornaments, finds its way into the retail stores of Europe and America. On the island of Mahe is found the coco-de-mer, one of nature's most remarkable productions. It is a double cocoanut. The nuts are strongly and firmly united at the sides, while

the shape of the two is kept quite distinct. Sometimes three
or even four are found thus united, but as a rule nature satisfies herself with the double ones.   These are highly polished *
by the natives of the island and sold to travelers at from three
to ten rupees each, depending on the size and the work required to polish them.

Being unable to go ashore, we addressed a polite letter to
the agent of the steamship company, setting forth our desire

Coco-de-Mer, Double Cocoanut. One of the nuts has been Polished by the Natives, the other has the Natural Shell.

to take with us to America a specimen of the coco-de-mer and
a few of the far-famed vanilla beans grown on the island. We
heard nothing more of the letter until we had sailed away from
Victoria, when the clerk of the ship handed us a package with
the compliments of the agent. It contained what we wanted,
also several fine photographs. We are grateful for the favor
and appreciate it very much indeed.

Now the last bag of rice has been lifted from the hold
of the ship and placed on the lighter and it has been cast loose
and floats away on the waters of the harbor, the great smoke-
stack of the *Nuddea* vomits forth dense clouds of black smoke,

the anchors have been lifted, the ship begins to move and we bid farewell to Victoria. We have been feared and unwelcome guests and I imagine they are right glad to be well rid of us. Especially must this be true of the poor fellows in the patrol boats. For almost a week they watched us day and night and must have grown weary of their thankless task. As the prow of the *Nuddea* turned seaward they shouted a farewell, and the last sight we had of them they were rowing their boats rapidly toward the shore, doubtless heartily rejoicing to be at last relieved of a most disagreeable duty.

We are now sailing directly west on a line four degrees south of the equator. The weather is delightful, the sea smooth and there is just breeze enough to moderate the tropical heat. If all goes well, four days hence we shall cast anchor in the harbor at Mombassa and have our first view of the southeast coast of the Dark Continent.

On board the ship, in addition to passengers, officers, crew, cows and goats, we have myriads of insect life. First and foremost among these is the little red ant. This insect has always been an object of great interest to me. When a lad, my father failed not to call my attention to the words of the Wise Man who holds up the industrious, strenuous little insect as an example of industry and thrift not to be despised by a boy disposed to shirk the heavy duties of farm life. Since those early days I have become better acquainted with her. I have studied her life and habits in Asia and Africa, and especially in the land where the Wise Man lived and wrote so many years ago. The more I study her ways the higher she rises in my estimation.

On board the *Nuddea* her name is legion. If I were to say there are a million ants on the ship I should not miss it unless the estimate were too low. Place a bit of food, uncovered on the deck, and in a few hours you will find two files of the little insects, one hurrying away from the food carrying

bits with them and the other rushing toward it, and there
will be thousands of them intent on business. In the neighborhood of the equator the days and nights are warm. While it
is not oppressively hot, one needs little other than nature's
covering at night. A few nights ago I slept peacefully while
the *Nuddea* made its way across the equator. At about four
o'clock in the morning it grew slightly cooler. I awoke and

Rich Tropical Growth on the Island of Mahe, Vanilla Beans,
Pineapples and Palms.

feeling the need of covering, drew a thin cotton sheet over
me which lay folded at the foot of my bunk. I was only half
awake, but in less time than it takes to write these lines sleep
had departed from my eyes and slumber from my eyelids.
I felt as if a thousand thistles were pricking my flesh, producing
a burning sensation that was far from pleasant. I was out of
the bunk as quickly as possible and turned on the light. I
found my body literally covered with red ants. The sheet,

neatly folded, had become the home of a colony of the insects and they were taking vengeance on me for interfering with their home. Each individual ant was standing on her head kicking her hind legs in the air in order to accelerate the process of getting her mandibles into my flesh. I at once made up my mind that for industry, activity and strenuous effort to get in her work the ant is not to be outdone. A hasty bath relieved the situation and after ridding the bunk of its surplus occupants I lay down again, with the flesh of my body all inflamed and with a deepened respect for the industry of the ant.

CHAPTER III.

The City of Mombassa—Eastern Thought—Dangerous Fishing—
Negro Guides at Mombassa—The Push-man Railway—India's
Merchants in South Africa—Women's Costumes and Hair
Dressing—Buttonholes in the Ears—Ludwig Krapf, the Hero
Missionary of East Central Africa—His One Convert, Mringe
—The Cathedral at Mombassa.

ELEVEN hundred miles due west of Victoria, as the crow
flies, is the comparatively modern city of Mombassa with a
mixed population of twenty thousand souls. It is the eastern
gateway to equatorial Africa and the great lakes of that
region, and is rapidly becoming the chief port on the coast.
When reference is made to miles, the geographical and not
the nautical mile is meant. The latter is the longer by eight
hundred feet and is always used at sea under the name of knot.

The *Nuddea* is a slow boat and it required a little over
four days steady steaming before we sighted the eastern
coast of the second largest continent on the globe, now no
longer a continent, for the great Frenchman, De Lesseps,
cut the narrow neck of land that bound Africa to Asia since
the dawn of creation, and made of her the largest island in
the world. Yes, the *Nuddea* is slow and very slow when
compared with the ocean greyhounds of the Atlantic. Were
the *Deutschland* to do her best she could make the distance
in a day and a half, with possibly a bit of time to spare. But
we are in the East where all things human move slowly.
There is no rush, no hurry. You never do to-day what you
can possibly put off until to-morrow. If not to-morrow,
the next day, next week or next month will do as well.
One must have time for thought, reflection and meditation,

44

and so in the race for supremacy, the East meditates and is easily distanced by her lively invaders from the West.

> "The East bowed low in solemn thought,
>   In silent, deep disdain,
>   She heard the legions thunder past,
>   Then plunged in thought again."

After leaving Victoria we had some good fishing from the stern of the *Nuddea*. The quartermaster put out a line over a hundred yards in length and in thickness like unto an ordinary clothesline. A heavy piece of wire, six feet in length, with a great steel hook fastened to one end, was attached to the line. The hook was baited with strips of white and red cloth and we took in a number of large, fine fish which added variety to our bill of fare. I had the privilege of drawing in two striped beauties, and when another was hooked, not wishing to monopolize the fishing business, I called on our friend, the coffee planter from South America, who took hold of the line gladly and began drawing in the fish. Suddenly, instead of pulling in, the line was drawn out with such rapidity that half a dozen blisters were burned on his hands and fingers. He said, "I couldn't hold it." And little wonder. A great shark had doubtless seized the fish and darted away with its prize. Apparently he caught the hook as well as the fish, for when the line was taken in the great hook was found straightened out. After this incident no more fish were caught. For some reason no one cared to pull them in.

It was not until May 8th, nineteen days out from Bombay, that we cast anchor in the south harbor of Mombassa. The city has two good harbors, one on the north and the other on the south side of the little island on which it is built. Our voyage from the Seychelles had been pleasant. We were favored with a smooth sea and a refreshing breeze

A Member of the "Four Hundred" of South Africa;
Comoro Girl.

all the way. The new moon, rapidly approaching its first quarter, added its glory to the southern heavens, and it was a source of continual pleasure to sit on deck far into the night and look out upon the heavens. Stover Sahib, as he is known in India, brushed up his knowledge of astronomy and we spent many delightful hours together studying the heavens, and felt as the sweet singer of Israel must have felt when he said, " The heavens declare the glory of God; and the firmament showeth his handiwork. Day unto day uttereth speech and night unto night showeth knowledge."

Then, too, we had occasion to rejoice because our small-pox patients were rapidly improving and were pronounced by the ship's doctor to be out of danger, and that there had been no further spread of the disease among the deck passengers who had been most exposed. It seemed almost a miracle that the disease did not spread, for, as already noted, the ship was crowded with steerage passengers. We felt that we had occasion to be thankful to God for his protecting care over us. He had brought us out of our distresses unto our desired haven.

We waited with some degree of anxiety the decision of the medical authorities as to whether we should be allowed to land or not. After our experience at Victoria we knew not what was in store for us. The port doctor came on board, examined the sick, declared them to be convalescing, and as the cabin passengers had been properly isolated we were permitted to go ashore. We heard the decision with gladness of heart and were not long in taking advantage of our liberty. After being imprisoned for nineteen days it is good to get out and feel that you are a free man again.

Sixty years ago, Mombassa was almost entirely unknown to the civilized world. January 3, 1844, a patient German missionary and explorer landed at this place and began work with his companion, Rebmann. From that time dates our knowledge of this part of east and central Africa. When the division of Africa took place between the powers of Europe a few years ago, this part of the country fell to the share of England and the territory is now known as British East Africa. In 1902 a railway was completed by the government from Mombassa to Port Florence, a distance of five hundred miles. The first year it was operated the government suffered a net loss of three hundred thousand dollars. Since then traffic has increased so that for the present year the road promises to pay a dividend. The opening of the railway has largely increased the importance of Mombassa, and it now enjoys a large trade with the rest of the world. Along the line of the road colonies are locating, new towns and cities are springing up, and in a few years this part of Africa will be in a prosperous condition.

The natives on the coast line are not the full type of the negro. Instead of being black they are a dark mahogany brown. Except in color they resemble their darker colored brethren of the Soudan and central Africa. The lips are large, the nose inclined to be flat and the hair short and curly. They are strong and well developed physically and look as if they could do an immense amount of work. They are fond of singing and strike one as being a happy, careless sort of people. They stand in most striking contrast to the Aryan race of India. The latter are meek, and cringing, always making way for the white man. These are self-contained, independent and, without being impudent, have an air of I-am-just-as-good-as-you-are about them. I rather like them on this account.

Our ship cast anchor some distance from the shore and we had recourse to the small rowboats to take us to the wharf. Here we were met by a number of natives wearing long muslin shirts reaching well below the knees, with the usual turban on the head. They were bright fellows and each had picked up a little English. They were anxious to serve us as guides and were most persistent in pressing their service upon us. Finally they all left us but three and one of these, a little fellow with a nut brown skin, regular features and great dreamy eyes, was selected to go with us through the city. When we announced our decision and dismissed the other two they at once began making uncomplimentary remarks about our boy. " He no good proper guide! He know no place, not where to go! He big tief; you look on your pocket, no money; all gone, he steal! He vara much big liar." Our boy proved to be bright and intelligent and made us an excellent guide. Here was another illustration of the fact that human nature is about the same the world over. The successful boy or man must always bear the taunts of those who fail and are too envious to admit merit, unless it be in themselves. When we had gone the round of the city and dismissed our guide we made the mistake of giving him twice the regular fee. It seemed to us it was small enough then, but it aroused his cupidity and he immediately put in a persistent claim for more.

A street railway connects the south port with the city. Its construction and motive power are not equal to our modern trolley lines, but it answers an excellent purpose. The distance across the island is a mile and a half and the fare on the railway is eight cents for the trip one way. The cars are small, being built to accommodate four or five passengers each. These sit back to back, two facing the front and two the rear of the car. A covering is provided to protect the passengers from the heat of the tropical sun. The motive power is furnished by two strong-limbed, long-winded, athletic Mombassites, and they do their work well. These are not Pull-man cars but Push-man cars. Convenient handles are attached for the men to take hold of when they push, and these can easily be transferred from end to end, so there is no necessity of turning the car.

After you have taken your seat the conductor, who by the way furnishes fully one-half the motive power, sells you your ticket and then with his assistant takes hold of the handles and you are off on your journey. And how they do run and push and keep the car moving. I think the greatest surprise to us all was the speed they kept up for the mile and a half. On the way to the city there is a long stretch of down grade. Our men, as they approached the descent, pushed and ran until the car was spinning along at a high rate of speed. When it seemed that it would outrun them they nimbly sprang on the handles and rode with us, and so all together we rushed down the grade at a dizzy speed. Our push-men made much better time than we used to make on our horse cars at home a score of years ago.

First of all we sought out the post office and mailed letters to India and America. Under English rule the entire coast of East Africa enjoys excellent postal facilities. We expected but received no letters, and shall have no word from home until we reach Durban two weeks hence. After walking about the town for several hours we were glad to find a large library and commodious reading room where we found the latest English papers and magazines. Here an hour was spent very pleasantly reading and resting.

A stroll through the bazaars of Mombassa takes one back to Bombay or Bulsar. The shopkeepers are about all natives of India. Here are the Parsis and Hindus in every shop and market place you visit. The native of Africa has not yet developed into the trader. Occasionally you will find a native woman seated on the ground with a little fruit, nuts, or the dried cassava root for sale, but this is about the only attempt one finds among the natives to enter the mercantile lists with the shrewder brown men of India. Practically the retail trade of the city is in the hands of the Aryans. The same is also true of the trades. The masons, bricklayers, plasterers, and carpenters are here from India, and the difference in wages is the attraction. A man receives more than double as much for his work in Mombassa as he gets at home. The natives are the porters, the carriers, and the coolies. They have not had a chance to learn the trades. This will come in time.

The native women wear the sari so common in India, but instead of folding it gracefully over the shoulders as is the custom among the Aryans it is drawn tightly around the body just under the arms, leaving these, the shoulders and the upper part of the bust uncovered. Those who have seen the so-called full evening dress so common in fashionable society in Europe and America will have no difficulty in understanding me when I say if the women of Mombassa should adopt a bit of an armlet for their saris and tie a bow of ribbon on the shoulder they would be in the very height of the latest style so far as the upper part of the body is concerned. It seemed to me that of the two the African woman is the more modest. There is no half exposing, half concealing any part of the body.

The head is uncovered, unless the woman has something to carry, and everything in the shape of a burden is carried on the head, on which a pad is fixed and on this the burden is placed. Whether it be a five-gallon tin pail of water, a loaf of bread, a cup of milk, an orange or an anna's worth of sugar, it is placed on the head and safely carried away. The women also pay a good deal of attention to the dressing of their hair. It is parted in narrow seams from the neck to the forehead and firmly plaited and twisted into rows. The head looks as if miniature furrows had been drawn across it. It makes a seamy looking head and to us is far from being pretty. But our tastes are largely a matter of cultivation and it is presumed this method of dressing the hair is the latest

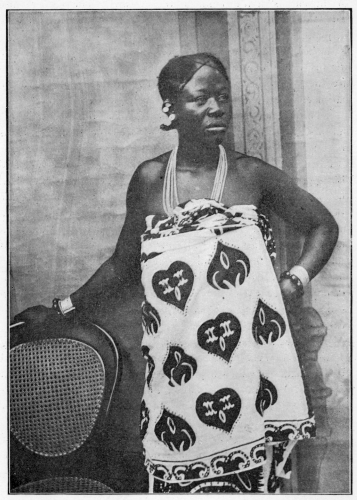

A Swahili Woman of South Africa; a Common Coast Type.

thing out among the leaders of fashion on the coast of Africa, and because of this it must be in good taste.

The ears are not pierced, but four button-hole-like cuts

"I have just had my hair dressed."

are made around the rim, and into these are forced large, double buttons, made after the fashion of sleeve or collar buttons. The ear being filled with these large wooden buttons painted in variegated colors, the organ of hearing is given a peculiar appearance. Rings are worn in the nose, both in the sides and through the cartilage in the center, and

The Hair Dresser at Work on the Street.   A Common Scene in the Coast Towns.

also in the upper lip. I saw but one illustration of this kind. A woman had a hole pierced through her upper lip through which you might pass an ordinary lead pencil. I saw but one example of a protruding lower lip. Among some of the tribes it is quite the style to have the lower lip drawn out and down and fastened in that position until it becomes fixed and grows in that shape, giving a peculiarly hideous expression to the face. They are decidedly of the opinion that it adds to their beauty. How our ideas of beauty differ in this world!

While there are many things in and about Mombassa to interest the traveler, he can never fail to be intensely interested in the story of Ludwig Krapf, the patient German missionary whose name is inseparably connected with the gateway of eastern Africa. He had spent seven years in Abyssinia, making a vain effort to penetrate central Africa from the north. Frustrated in his plans and disappointed and hindered in his work, he was finally driven out of the country. Then, accompanied by his faithful wife, Rosina Krapf, the sharer of all his joys and sorrows and his constant companion, he embarked on an Arab boat and after a long and perilous voyage landed at Mombassa on the third day of January, 1844. Krapf was in Africa several years before David Livingstone turned his face toward the Dark Continent. On a hilltop not far distant from the present site of Mombassa a mud hut was built, known as the mission house of Rabai, and here the Krapfs made their home and began their work.

The labors of the patient missionary were begun under the most trying circumstances. Within a few months after their arrival he stood by the open grave of his beloved wife and child. He was heartbroken, and there is perhaps nothing so sad as the thought of this man standing alone amid the crushed hopes of his life. He has left on record in his diary something of his feelings. He tells how his heart and body wept and that he could not mention his wife's name, or speak of her death for a long time without tears. The death of a loved one is hard enough to be borne when we are upheld by the sympathy of friends, but here was this man alone in a strange pagan land bearing alone the great sorrow of his soul.

But all this wrought no change in his purpose. He wrote home in these words: " Tell our friends at home there is now on the east African coast a lonely missionary grave. This is a sign that you have commenced a struggle with this part of the world, and as the victories of the church are gained by stepping over the graves of her members, you may be the more convinced that the hour is at hand when you are summoned to the conversion of Africa from its eastern shore." *

Krapf spent six years at Mombassa translating the New Testament into the Swahili language and working when able to do so. Soon after the death of his wife he was stricken down with fever and his life was despaired of. At this time he says he prayed most fervently that his life might be spared to see at least one soul converted in Africa. His prayer was answered, and he had when he left Africa one convert to the Christian faith.

Looked at from a human standpoint, Krapf's life would seem to have had the word failure written around it. Thirteen years in Africa, years of privation and suffering, and those at Mombassa of the deepest sorrow, and what was there to show for the sacrifice? A broken-down body and a shattered constitution, two lonely graves on the hillside at Mombassa and one African convert. But God has ordered it that no effort for good in this world is ever lost. Krapf builded better than he knew and he lived to see some of his strongest hopes more than realized.†

His one convert was a cripple, named Mringe, and he was a great comfort to the lonely and bereaved missionary. He writes of his crippled companion thus: " Mringe was with

* " The Price of Africa," p. 199.
† " Missionary Annals."

me during the night. We discoursed toward midnight about the world to come and the city of God. My poor cripple devoured the words as they fell from my lips, and I saw that an impression was made on him, and felt happy indeed, for it is in moments like these that one feels the importance of the missionary's calling. A missionary who feels the workings of the Spirit within him, and is upheld in its manifestation to others, is the happiest man on earth. In his sight what are royal or imperial honors compared with the office of a preacher in a bush or a lonely hut?"*

Although broken in health, with but small hope of recovery, Krapf remained at his post and continued his labors until two new missionaries were sent to take up the work. He remained with them until they were established in the mission and then returned to Europe. The other day, in looking over some volumes in a bookstore, at Zanzibar, I noticed one with this title: "Krapf's Dictionary of Swahili and English."

Rebmann and Erhardt were the men selected to take Krapf's place at Mombassa, and to these two missionaries in connection with Krapf is due, in part, the credit of the discovery of the snow-clad mountains, the great lakes of Victoria and Alberta, the source of the Nile and the fertile plains of central Africa. They made and sent to Europe a map of the region, since known as the "Slug map" because the drawing of the lakes resembled a slug, which excited great interest and resulted in sending out exploring expeditions, and these verified the conclusions of the missionaries.

Interesting as it would be to follow the labors of these self-sacrificing men, we must forbear. We shall, however, beg the reader's indulgence while we take a brief review of the results. Rebmann remained at Mombassa twenty-nine years, refusing even to take a furlough. The mission board had

---

* "The Price of Africa." p. 199.

dropped Mombassa as being an unfruitful field. But "Old John Rebmann," as he was familiarly called, never lost faith in his work and refused to leave his post. Finally, with much reluctance, reënforcements were sent. "He was but fifty-five years of age when Mr. Price found him, but fevers and the suffering of Africa had made him prematurely old and feeble. When reënforcements came, at last, though very reluctantly, the blind old veteran consented to turn the care of his little band of believers over to the younger missionaries. In his lifelong battle with heathendom he had been able to keep together a little company of Christians whose number equalled the twelve of his Master, and John Rebmann was content. Mr. Price began his work at Mombassa by purchasing a tract of land for his school. *The site was near the grave of Rosina Krapf, the first Christian grave in East Africa.*"*

Sixty years have fled since Ludwig Krapf, with broken heart, mourned the loss of his beloved wife and child and wept in loneliness in his mud hut at Mombassa. To-day there are in the Mombassa district, under the mission which Krapf founded, ten mission stations, eighteen schools, twelve hundred pupils, and about two thousand communicants of the church. There are forty-four European missionaries, men and women, and they have twenty-six native helpers. A large cathedral is nearing completion at Mombassa and is being built in memory of the men who gave their lives to the work of opening up east Africa for the introduction of the religion of Christ. Rosina Krapf's grave did not long remain the only one in that territory, and now the graves of the missionaries may be counted by the score. A number of them were murdered by the natives, and others succumbed to the deadly fever.

---

* "The Price of Africa," pp. 210, 211.

But one must look beyond Mombassa to follow the results of Krapf's labors. Take the railway train at Mombassa
and travel to Port Florence, five hundred and eighty-five miles
inland, and there you will find a steamer on which you take
passage for Entebbe and Kamala, the principal towns of
Uganda. Here you will find yourself in the midst of one of
the most remarkable missionary enterprises in the world.
With this work the name of Mackay is inseparably associated. Stanley visited him when on his way to relieve Emin
Pasha and pays a high tribute to this indefatigable worker.
" For ten years he labored in Uganda (1878-87), as builder,
carpenter, smith, wheelwright, sanitary engineer, farmer,
gardener, printer, surgeon and physician. He also vigorously
prosecuted his linguistic work, and set a high standard for
all future translations. There he lived until King Mtesa's
death in 1884, through Mwanga's persecution of the converts, much of the time alone, for he was not allowed to
leave Uganda until in 1887, when he left for Usambiro on
the southern shores of the lake, full of plans for the future of
the work. Here he labored on, refusing to return to England
till other men came out to take his place." In 1890 Mackay
died and he rests in an African grave. Writing about Mackay, Stanley says next to David Livingstone he was the greatest
missionary that Africa has known.

And now after all these years the labors of Krapf and his
successors have borne abundant fruit. In Uganda there are
eleven hundred native churches, with Sunday and weekday
schools where the children, born in paganism, are taught to
read and write and at the same time are made acquainted with
the Gospel. There are not far from fifty thousand native
Christians, and, most remarkable of all, they are self-supporting and contribute annually to the Christianization of Africa.
They have built of their own means a large cathedral at the
capital of Uganda and are becoming rapidly civilized. When

the humble part taken in this great work by the Krapfs is considered, who will say that they labored in vain? Rosina gave her life and her devoted husband his health and strength to opening up East Africa to the civilizing influence of the Gospel of Jesus Christ. And behold and study carefully the results.

CHAPTER IV.

Alexander Mackay—A Wise Father and a Dutiful Son—Determines
to be a Missionary—Uganda Chosen as the Field—Hardships
and Death Among the Missionaries—Printing the Gospel of
Matthew—Slave Traders and Persecution—Death of Hunting-
ton—Torture of Native Christians—End of a Noble Life.

ONE who became first among the missionaries of modern
times was a layman, Alexander Mackay. He was the son of a
minister of the Free Church of Scotland, in whose quiet home,
bookcases stood well filled with books, and maps of the un-
evangelized countries of the world hung upon the walls. The
father became the willing playmate and the careful instructor
of his son, thus holding his confidence from the very first. The
mother taught the daily Bible lessons. And in the evening
after a lesson had been well recited, by way of reward she
would tell the little listener a missionary story. Such stories
are capital food for the coming missionary to go to sleep on.

Among other things she told him that she herself in earlier
years had been very much drawn toward the mission work,
and had longed to be used in this capacity, but when she found
she could not go to any heathen land with the Gospel story,
she had determined to do all she could to help others who
might be able to go. Missionaries, she said, were needed in all
parts of the world,—she would be a missionary at home.

Often after the story, the child mind would put the question, as any thoughtful child would, " What field is the most important, mother?" And she would answer that all were important, that the Gospel must be preached in all the world;
not once but over and over again; before God all were alike
valuable. Then another question: " Mother, would you like

61

for me to be a missionary? Would you like for me to go to Africa?" With the mother answer, "Yes, my child, if God prepares you for it. Not otherwise." How precious to every child are the stories mother tells! Who can sow in wider fields than the devoted Christian mother!

At the age of fourteen he was sent to Edinburg. He entered college there, and after completing the regular course, he returned home eager to obtain his father's consent that he might go to Berlin to learn engineering, for he had acquired a great liking for mechanics.

This turn in young Mackay's mind was rather disappointing to his father, who had always indulged the hope that his son would succeed him in the ministry. But he gave his consent to the Berlin proposition, hoping that in some way it would all work out to the glory of God.

In Berlin, Mackay applied himself with his usual diligence, he mastered the German language, and was so successful in his other studies that after a few years he became the chief instructor in a large engineering establishment.

At Berlin, also, he had his religious principles put to the test, for he was naturally thrust into the society of the most clever unbelievers. So, to make sure of his faith, he early associated himself with such persons as he knew were altogether free from skepticism, and determined that all the while he would be there his Christianity should be very real and practical.

In 1873 his sister wrote him that she had heard an impressive sermon on the needs of Madagascar as a mission field, and that the speaker had urged young men with qualifications for the work of missions to go out and spend their lives for the uplift of the people in that great field. She sent him carefully prepared and complete notes on the address, so that he might grasp the situation for himself. And with what result? He volunteered for Madagascar. In due time, however, he received the reply that men of his kind, with special qualifications in mechanics, were not in demand just at the time in that field, but would be before long. So from that day forth, Mackay did all he knew to prepare for the time when he would be sent somewhere as a missionary to the foreign field.

In 1875 there was a call by the C. M. S. (the Church Missionary Society, Church of England) for young men to go to Mombassa, east coast of Africa, to take charge of some settlements of liberated slaves, and he offered his services for that work.

About the same time Stanley's lengthy letter from Africa appeared in the *Daily Telegraph* calling for strong Christian effort in a part of the country he had seen. His words ran as follows: "Now where is there in all the pagan world a more promising field for a mission than Uganda? . . . Here, gentlemen, is your opportunity; embrace it! The people on the shores of the Nyanza call upon you."

And Mackay wrote to the mission secretary, "My heart burns for the deliverance of Africa, and if you can send me to any of those regions which Livingstone and Stanley have found to be groaning under the curse of the slave-hunter, I shall be very glad."

Stanley's letter made a sensation. Three days after its publication one person gave $25,000 to the C. M. S. to set the work a-going. Another soon gave a similar amount. In a very short time over a hundred thousand dollars was in hand for the project.

Who should go? The first response to the committee's appeal was from Lieut. Shergold Smith, who had been some time before invalided home from the east coast of Africa. He was valuable, having been on the east coast. Next came Mackay. He was valuable, knowing mechanics. Others followed, Wilson a preacher, Smith a doctor, Clark an engineer, O'Neill and Robertson. One James Robertson also joined the party on his own responsibility, having been refused by the physicians on account of ill-health.

Meanwhile, until the time for the missionaries to sail, Mackay set to work to build a boat that could be taken apart and put together again, so that in parts it might be carried by coolies to the interior and put together again for use on Lake Victoria. He took his toy printing press with him, and all such tools as he thought might come handy where none at all were to be had.

After having volunteered for Madagascar, and then for Mombassa, to be sent to Uganda seemed like being unstable. But he reflected that Duff had first desired Africa, and became a missionary to India; Livingstone had first thought of China, and afterward turned his attention to the great dark Continent; so Mackay rejoiced in the thought that the hand of the Lord was with him, and that he was getting into the largest possible sphere of opportunity open to him.

At the farewell meeting, Shergold Smith said he was willing to take the lowest place, and Mackay said that he wished to remind the committee that in less than six months some one of the party, perhaps he himself, would be dead; but " in case of such news coming to you," he said, " do not be cast down, but send some one else immediately to take the vacant place."

They sailed to Zanzibar. The original design was to work their way in from this point, and establish a line of mission stations from there to Victoria Nyanza, thus establishing a kind of a highway from the coast to the extreme interior, where the principal work was to be carried on.

Again and again they renewed their efforts to penetrate into the interior, but made slow progress indeed. Robertson died, the first of a long list of lives sacrificed for Uganda. Before they got half way, Mackay was prostrate with the fever, but recovered. The other Robertson went home sick. Those were days of exceeding patience and perseverance, as with a long

line of native followers who bore upon their heads all that the
missionaries had, they bored and wormed and dug their way
through the dense and untried jungle country. Some of the
coolies deserted, and many died. The natives of the interior
were often excessive in their demand for bribes. At times
there was no water to be had. There was never shelter, while

Kamala, Capital of Uganda.

the heat and the damp and the snakes and the wild beasts, to
say nothing of the fever, were ever showing the dark side of
the question.

Next Clark was invalided home. It was seven hundred
miles of jungle to the point of their destination! Dr. Smith
died of dysentery! After nearly a year Lieut. Smith and Rev.
Wilson first set foot on Uganda soil. They nearly lost their
lives at the hands of a few hostile natives while crossing the

lake, but when they visited the king they were made welcome. And after the formalities were over, he called them aside and asked them if they had brought the book,—*the Bible.* What a joyous *yes* their answer must have been.

How could they converse with the king, without either knowing the language of the other? These things often come to pass in mission work. There was a lad called Dallington Scopion, who had been raised in a mission school at Zanzibar, and learned English there, who had accompanied Stanley into the interior as far as the Uganda country, and had remained there. It was he who translated for the missionaries now, and it was he who wrote for the king, to the missionaries, letters before they reached the place, addressing them, " My dear friend white men," and telling them to hurry and come!

After some months the king of Ukerewe escaped from the hands of some Arab traders, and fled to the missionaries for refuge. The traders were angry and demanded his surrender, but the missionaries, knowing the probable result, naturally declined to give him into their hands. That same night the traders came upon the house by stealth and slew the whole party, both Lieut. Smith and Mr. O'Neill, together with all the natives who were with them, except two who made their escape!

Soon after this Mackay reached Uganda. Only he and Wilson remained, of the eight who had set out for the work two and a half years before. Two had died, two had been killed, and two sent home as invalids! Uganda, that land of promise, with nearly two million population, situated right on the equator, surrounded by dense jungle, a territory of seventy thousand square miles, and seven hundred miles distant from the sea, seemed never more hopeless!

Mackay became intimate with Mtesa the king, who was much interested in what he showed him of ordinary tools. He rigged up a magic lantern, and gave talks on astronomy and the circulation of the blood. When he built himself a house with a thatched roof and a wide veranda to it, Mtesa was again surprised, for hitherto all the dwellings in Uganda were mere huts. Type was made of wood,—afterwards of lead,—and the men working with him were meanwhile learning to read. The Gospel of Matthew was the first to be translated.

Native Boat on Lake Victoria Nyanza.

Then came renewed troubles. The slave traders were at their miserable work, exerting all their influence against the missionaries, because they opposed slavery. Next came some Roman Catholic priests, who chose to settle themselves in the midst of Protestant mission work rather than occupy any part of the whole dark Africa where Protestants were not! These told the king a different story from what the other missionaries had been telling him, so that he became somewhat confused and perplexed. Mackay had been conducting services in the king's court. In this the priests not only refused to participate, but they secretly persuaded the king that Mackay could not be trusted,—that he had some ulterior motive! At this the Mohammedans urged the king the more that he should adopt the religion of the Koran. And once when the king was sick, the heathen priests seized their opportunity, and persuaded him that the influence of the foreigners was bad, so that an order was issued to kill all who might be found on the roads round about the capital! Frequently during this trying period the missionaries heard the cry of pain from the victims caught

Entebbe, Seat of Protectorate, Victoria, Nyanza.

along the road, followed by the loud laugh of the Arabs after the dread deed was done.

A short time after this, his companion in the work was invalided home, having seen much illness, and Mackay was left alone with his native assistants. A party who had been sent out to join them fell upon evil, and only two of them reached Uganda. Of these Hannington, afterwards the bishop, returned home sick. Thus men came and went, but the one who stayed from the very first was Mackay.

In 1882 the first converts were baptized. There were five

of them. And the missionaries were filled with hopes for the future. When the queen died Mackay was asked to make a coffin like unto those that European royalty are buried in, and it took a month to finish it. The funeral was a royal one. It was an opportunity well used by the missionary. Afterward when the king died Mackay was called to make the coffin. He did it, knowing, however, that he might lose his life at any moment at the hands of the new king, for when a new king ascends the throne of an unstable government, no one knows what will happen next! Especially is this true among the African chieftains.

When Mwanga, the young king, had the government well in hand, he inaugurated a reign of terror, torturing and burning to death two of Mackay's brightest Christian lads. They went to their death singing, and witnessing to their faith in God! Not knowing who would be called to lay down his life next, all haste was made to organize what Christians there were into a native church-council, and to prepare them for self-government. This is an incident showing how the greatest persecutions serve only to strengthen the hands of the church. These things have been repeated from the beginning of Christianity. At this time, in the midst of death, they printed sheets of prayers and parts of Gospels, and circulated them more freely and more rapidly than ever before, each day dawning with the probability of its being the last one to them! And so the number of inquirers, and those who were willing to walk in the narrow way, increased in spite of all.

Bishop Hannington was on his way with a party of missionaries to join the forces on the field. He had chosen a more northerly route than that by which the others had come, thinking to shorten the distance. It was Krapf who had long before suggested this course as being both nearer and healthier.

When the king heard of the bishop's coming, the Arabs persuaded him that he was coming in "by the back door," with none other intent than to "eat up the land." The king whose hands were red with blood, and whose heart was filled with suspicion, became a ready listener to this story, and fearing

Wakikuyu.   Native of Equatorial Africa Showing
Ear Ornaments.

that it might be true, that some foreign power might come in and take his throne because of his wickedness, hired a band of assassins and sent them out to meet the bishop on the way. One morning the bishop had pressed ahead of his company, eager to catch the first glimpse of the great lake. At that moment, being alone, he was seized by the men who had shadowed him, and taken prisoner. Word was sent to the king that they had captured their man. The reply came to make short work of it, and the poor man was speared to death. He spent the last hours in prayer and reading his Bible, as the reply of the king was expected. All but four of those with him were murdered, the four contriving to escape. And the king, when he wanted to show himself insolent and arrogant after that, arrayed himself in the bishop's robes!

Meanwhile, Mwanga was assuming the air of innocence before Mackay, and pretending that these crimes were done without his knowing it, that he was very sorry for the accidents, that he really did not desire such things to happen in his kingdom, and that he could not help it, while Mackay, with childlike spirit, answered, sometimes carefully reproving the king, and sometimes earnestly entreating him. It was a dangerous hour, and the missionaries thought to go to the south end of the lake for a time, but Mwanga insisted that Mackay remain, either because he thought his skill would be of service to him, or in the hope of some gift. He showed favor to Mackay, but continued mercilessly to torture the native Christians. On one occasion thirty-two were slowly burnt alive by the direct orders of the king. The manner these died only added luster to the faith, for even the executioner said that he had never killed such brave people before, people of his own color and kind!

The heroic deaths of these simple children of the soil, of these childlike martyrs of the cross, filled the land with the desire to learn the religion. It is the story of the early centuries told over again. The Mohammedans continued to do all in their power to incite the king to kill Mackay and drive out the Christians, so that more than once the council to settle upon his death was summoned, and as often it was dissolved again without action. He had been of too much service to the king. He had been of too great good in the past. And the chief magistrate did not forget the service rendered when royalty demanded a coffin to be buried in.

The tempest continued to grow, and Mackay felt that the best thing to be done was to go to the south end of the lake and rest awhile, and wait till the storm blew over. He had been invited home, but always said he could not go till other workers were on the field and were ready to take his place.

At the south end of Victoria Nyanza, dwelling at Usambiro, when Bishop Parker arrived in company with four others, he welcomed them to the field. After so many years, he was especially rejoiced in the companionship thus afforded him. But Parker got the fever and died there. Blackburn also fell under the hand of the fever about the same time.

At this place Mackay met Stanley, who was then in Darkest Africa on the Emin Pasha business. Stanley was so impressed with Mackay that he said of him afterwards that he was the best missionary since Livingstone.* Stanley urged him to go with him and his party to Europe, but he preferred to remain by his post.

Another observation made by the great explorer and traveler was that he thoroughly sympathized with Mackay in his love of books. The Zanzibari servant of Mackay's had expressed himself to Stanley in these remarkable words: "Alla ho Akbar. Books! Mackay has thousands of books, in the dining room, bed room, the church, everywhere. Books! Ah, loads upon loads of them!"

He was preparing material for a boat to use on the lake, and repairing an engine, and fixing up some pumps that had gotten out of order, when he was taken ill again. He had been down with the fever often before,—who that has lived in the

---

*"In Darkest Africa," Vol. II, page 393.

tropics has not?—but this time it was too much for his weakened frame and he fell asleep Feb. 8, 1890, in the same bed where Bishop Parker had died. And his coffin was made from boat material that he himself had gathered.

From the standpoint of one who does not love the Bible, such a life would be counted a failure. But to Faith it is the full measure of success. The field was raw and the tribes were naked. Up to the time of Mackay's death no woman had come to the field,—the men preferring to do the rough foundation work first. Beginnings are made, and the builders go on with the work. God buries the worker, but he carries on the work. Mwanga himself was exiled, and in exile became a Christian shortly before he died. A new king, Daudi, was set upon the throne, and Daudi is a Christian. Tens of thousands in Uganda who now daily call upon the name of the Lord, bear living testimony to work well done. The man who can believe in the hidden things of God can understand the spirit of missions.

Always surrounded with a good number of books, always planning for a great deal more of work, always doing something for the general good, always having an inexplainable passion for souls, often forgetting your own good in seeking the good of others; no time for regrets, nothing to brood over, always rejoicing, always doing all possible for the glory of God,—this is the missionary spirit. This was the spirit of Mackay.

CHAPTER V.

FOUR days we lay at anchor in the harbor at Mombassa. We had six thousand bags of rice on board for the place. The first, a bright, clear day, we had opportunity to see the place and made the best possible use of our time. And then we had two days of rain, and how it does rain in the tropics! We see nothing like it in our northern homes. The water comes down in sheets and torrents as if the fountains of the great deep were broken up. I feel confident that twelve inches of rain fell in twenty-four hours. To have opened the hold of the ship would have been seriously to injure the cargo with the floods that came down from the clouds. The thing to do was to wait in patience, and we waited. The fourth day the sky was clear, the cargo was discharged, and at five in the evening we were off for Zanzibar, a hundred and fifty-five miles away.

In the evening I had a conversation with three of our passengers who came from the vicinity of Nineveh, on the Tigris river, a father, his son and a friend. They are Chaldean Christians, and the father told me they belonged to the country of Father Abraham. His name is George Bar-Asa, literally George, the son of Asa; his son is called Greory Bar-George and the friend Steven Bar-Isaac. Thus they retain the ancient method of giving names. Always as we pass by them they salute us with these words, " The peace of our God be with you." The father speaks English brokenly, and he invited us to visit his country. He said: "You come my home, no hotel. Hotel no good. You live in my house. I make you home and welcome." We thanked him for his proffered hospitality, and said we had in mind a visit to his country if the Lord spared our lives. They go to South Africa to visit some friends and then return again to their own country, the home of " Father Abraham," as the father proudly called his native land.

It was high noon the next day when we entered the port of the city of Zanzibar, distinguished as the largest city on the east coast of Africa, and the greatest clove market in the world. Four-fifths of the world's supply of this aromatic spice comes from this place. Heber's line, about the spicy breezes of Ceylon's isle, would be true of Zanzibar, for here you have the smell of the cloves all the day.

Two islands, Zanzibar and Pemba, with an area of one thousand and twenty square miles, and a population of two hundred thousand, form the British Protectorate of Zanzibar. In 1896 some trouble arose as to the successor to the sultan. A pretender took the throne and possession of the palace and defied the recognized authority of Great Britain. An English warship was conveniently near at hand. A few well-directed shots from a twelve-inch gun sent the only gunboat the sultan had to the bottom of the harbor, and a few shells directed at the palace, and the affair was settled. The war lasted half an hour, and, that there should be no more trouble, the British took the islands under protection. Now the succession is orderly and the government good. The masts of the sultan's gunboat stand ten feet above the water as a warning of the fate of bad sultans.

The city of Zanzibar has a hundred thousand people, a splendid harbor, and is a coaling station for the British navy. Its population is made up largely of native Africans, with a sprinkling of whites and a shower of Aryans. The "Aryan

The Sultan's Palace, Zanzibar; Front View, Facing the Sea.

brown " is in evidence everywhere. Wherever shops are kept
and merchants do most congregate, he is to be found. As at
Mombassa, so here the trade of the town is practically in the
hands of the Parsis, Hindus and Moslems of India. They are
shrewd, quick-witted, sharp business men, and they succeed
in their calling.

Stover Sahib asked a merchant the price of the double
cocoanuts displayed for sale in his shop, and the answer was,
" Twenty rupees, Sir." " But," replied the Sahib, " I can
buy them at Seychelles for three rupees." " Yes, yes," said
the dealer, " I pay only one rupee for them at wholesale, but
I must have a little profit." The Sahib gave assent and we left
the shop wondering what the merchant's idea of a big profit
could possibly be.

At another shop, canes of dried rhinoceros skins were
being manufactured and offered for sale. The skin is sawed
into strips of the proper size, and then rounded with a plane
and polished with sandpaper. Upon inquiry we found they
were selling at four and a half rupees each; and the next day
they were purchased at two, and this about double the price
a native pays for the same article. One of two things you are
compelled to do, in making purchases here, either pay three
or four prices for what you buy, or bargain and bargain. It's
the rule of the East.

In 1864 the Universities' Mission to Central Africa was
established at Zanzibar. We enjoyed a very pleasant visit
with those in charge of the work at the present time. When
Livingstone, the greatest of African missionaries and explorers, returned to England in 1857, he aroused the country
against the evils of the African slave trade. The appeals he
made for help to rid the world of this crying evil at Oxford
and Cambridge resulted in their united efforts in forming a
mission under the auspices of the Church of England, under
the foregoing title. Its avowed purpose was the suppression

of the slave trade and slavery, and it took an active part in this great work.

The "master builder" of the mission was Bishop Steere, an able, scholarly and most energetic worker. He spent about twenty years in translating parts of the Old and all of the New Testament into the Swahili language. He also made a dictionary, and translated "Pilgrim's Progress," a primer, stories and other books of a religious character into the ver-

Native Quarter, Zanzibar.

nacular of the natives. And while on his deathbed he was at work on the translation of Isaiah.

It was Steere's ambition to purchase the great slave market at Zanzibar, and on the ground erect a church, school and residence buildings, and this he accomplished in 1873. Now the East African Cathedral marks the site of the old slave market, where so many of Africa's dark children were sold into bondage. The church has a coral roof and the clock in the tower, the gift of the sultan, strikes eastern time. At six in the evening we heard the deep-toned bell strike twelve.

A singular fatality occurred to the bishops of the Universities' Mission. Bishop Smythes died at sea and was buried in the Indian Ocean, on a summer evening in 1894; and two years later Bishop Maples was drowned in Lake Nyassa. Since the founding of the mission, sixty-six missionaries have died in the work. They have five mission stations on the island of Zanzibar, and their work also extends to the mainland, where they have schools for the education of the natives. The lady workers of the mission are actively engaged in laboring among the native girls in Zanzibar, Likoma and Nyassa. They also have a large number of schools in charge of native teachers, whom they have educated, and who, in every case, are members of the Church of England.

The object for which the mission was founded has been accomplished. The African slave trade has been abolished. The story of this unrighteous traffic has been told over and over again, but few realize the gigantic proportions of this once putrid, festering " open sore " of the world. I am reminded of it as I wander about the great slave market of Zanzibar, and meditate upon the great evils which resulted from the sin of the inhuman traffic of which this was an important center. I thought of my own country which only a few years ago was torn and bleeding by the war of the rebellion, which resulted directly because of the introduction of slavery into the Colonies. I set it down again here: This and other great wrongs practiced by the white race on the colored makes me almost ashamed of the race to which I belong.

The beginning of the slave trade which Henry Drummond characterized as the " heart disease of Africa," dates as far back as 1441, when the first slaves were carried into Europe and given as an offering to the pope. It received the sanction of the Christian (?) nations of the world and was not only the heart disease of Africa, but of all white nations. Its cause is to be found in the changed condition in Europe, brought about by the breaking up of the Roman Empire and the discovery of the New World, which brought about an increased demand for labor. The African field had an abundance of laborers; these were easily obtained, and the trade increased so rapidly that in a few years after the first negroes were brought into Europe, the number annually imported amounted to seven hundred. To this was almost immediately added the great demand for laborers in the New World. In the West Indies and on the coasts of North America the colonists must have laborers to work in their fields, and these were found and stolen from among the black sons of Africa. It was the spoliation of the weak by the strong. After the introduction of sugar making into the West Indies the cane plantations absorbed a large number of slaves.

The trade grew so rapidly that as early as the opening of the seventeenth century the British slave trade was an accomplished fact. Chartered companies were formed for the importation of slaves, and in the next one hundred years over two millions were imported into the British colonies. Over six hundred thousand were brought into Jamaica alone, which at that time was a great center of the trade. A careful estimate places the number of negroes deported from Africa to the New World, during the eighteenth century, at no less than six million. This shows to what extent the traffic was carried on. In 1830, twenty-three years after the abolition of the slave trade, according to Buxton's estimate, over one hundred and fifty thousand slaves were being imported into the New World every year. It seems a strange thing to say, and a sad confession to make, that when the writer was a child, sixty years ago, the population of Africa was being depleted at the rate of over two hundred and fifty thousand of its strongest men and women each year to furnish slaves for Christian states.

Slave catching was an easy thing in Africa. The traders were well armed and their thunder-and-lightning producing sticks, as their guns were regarded by the superstitious natives, terrorized them and they were taken captive and led away. Some were purchased from chieftains, who had taken them as prisoners of war, or criminals of a tribe; some would sell themselves in time of famine in order to be fed, and later on chieftains who were strong in the number of their followers, would capture slaves for sale.

The price paid for slaves was nominal and amounted to but a few dollars in real value. Money was not used. Four yards of bright-colored calico, a few strings of glass beads, a bit of brass wire, an old worn-out flintlock musket, a few pounds of gunpowder or a gallon or two of rum, were the mediums of exchange. Women were bought at one-fourth the price of men, and children were either killed or thrown in without pay.

It is stated on the best of authority that at least one-third of the slaves died either on the march to the coast, in the slave pens awaiting the arrival of the ships, or on the voyage to the ports where they were finally sold. The six million slaves imported into the New World, in the eighteenth century, meant that ten million negroes had been taken from their homes in South Africa. Men and women, stark naked, were stowed away in the holds of the slave ships, from six hundred to a thousand in a single vessel, fed twice a day and treated far worse than the humane farmer treats his cattle when shipping them to market. When the trade was prohibited and the penalty of death attached, slavers, when chased by armed vessels, would throw the negroes to the sharks, or in the last extremity batten down the hold, the officers and crew take to the boats and then blow up the ship, thus destroying the evidence of their nefarious business.

Professing Christians who stood in defense of this traffic

in human beings were not wanting. They said many of these negroes would be killed if they remained in Africa, and they were being rescued from death. It was a necessity of the time; it increased trade and commerce; the lands of the New World could not be cultivated without the African; it found employment for many people and added to the wealth of those engaged in it; the condition of the negro was better in slavery than in his native state; he would be Christianized and made better, and last, but not least, it was argued that the slaves liked it, too. Strange indeed that people professing to be followers of Christ could find arguments so specious to satisfy their conclusions in allowing so great a sin.

But there were other men who saw the sin of the evil in all its horrors. Livingstone, in his last journal, tells of the horrors of capture and march, the dreadful cruelty of the slave stick, and the barbarous treatment of women and children, while whole districts were being devastated and depopulated by the murderous slave hunters. Others besides Livingstone have spoken of the horrors of the traffic in humanity. Stanley says: "My eyes catch the sight of that continual lifting of the hand to ease the neck in the iron collar. Many months have they been fettered together; their bones stand out in bold relief in the skin, which is wrinkled and drawn up." Another adds: "It was wearisome to see the skulls and bones scattered about everywhere; one would fain not notice them, but they are so striking as one trudges along the sultry paths that it cannot be avoided." It is said that the slayer's path to the sea could easily be followed by the bleaching skulls and human bones.

We had an ocular illustration in Zanzibar of what Stanley meant in his reference to "easing the neck in the collar." The iron collars and chains are no longer used for slave gangs, but nowadays are used for chaining criminals together. I saw a half dozen prisoners carrying burdens along the street, chained together with the old slave fetters. Heavy iron collars are locked about the neck and these are fastened together with chains about three feet in length, and so the men are chained together. They make " the way of the transgressor " very hard in Zanzibar.

When Richard Baxter begain raising his voice against the slave trade, he stood alone; but in 1750 the Quakers, and ten years later the Wesleyans joined in the crusade. From its organization in 1723, the Brethren church was also firmly opposed to slavery and the slave trade. To " Little Denmark " belongs the honor of being the first nation to declare against the traffic, to be quickly followed by the United States in 1794, forbidding the importation of slaves into its territory. England passed an act to abolish the slave trade in 1807. It was decided that these two nations would jointly maintain a naval force of not less than eighty guns on the African coast, for the suppression of the slave trade. Then came the abolition of slavery in the United States in 1863, and so much of the " open sore of the world " was healed. Among Christian states the traffic ceased.

In 1879 slavery was abolished in Zanzibar, and the slave collars are now put to a better, if not a more humane, use. As I reflected upon what had been done here, where, in all its hideousness, the " black sore " festered to the disgrace of the name of Christianity, I thanked God that the dreadful nightmare had been dispelled and that the cruel slave trade of Africa is now but a sad memory.

Zanzibar is the center of a large ivory trade, and about seventy per cent of the entire product is handled by an American firm. I need scarcely refer to the fact that the elephant tusks furnish most of the ivory. These are carried in from the interior on the heads of the natives. Each man is supposed to carry sixty pounds and receives for his services about ten cents a day and a supply of food. As the tusks are carried

Ivory Market, Zanzibar.

many hundreds of miles the cost of transportation is considerable. Ivory is collected by traders in the interior and these are mostly Arabs of the Moslem faith. They are cruel, rapacious, and do not hesitate to commit murder, burn villages and devastate districts in order to rob the natives of the ivory they have found.

Stanley, writing on this subject in "Darkest Africa," has this to say: "Every tusk, piece and scrap of ivory in the hands of an African trader has been steeped and dyed in blood. Every pound weight has cost the life of a man or child, for every five pounds a hut has been burned, for every two tusks a whole village has been destroyed and every twenty tusks have been obtained at the price of a district with all its people, villages and plantations. It is simply incredible that, because ivory is required for ornaments or billiard games, the rich heart of Africa should be laid waste at this late year of the nineteenth century (1889), signalled as it has been by so much advance, that populations, tribes and nations should be utterly destroyed. Whom, after all, does this bloody seizure of ivory enrich? Only a few half caste Arabs and negroes, who, if due justice were dealt to them, should be made to sweat the remainder of their piratical lives in the severest penal servitude."

A visit to the ivory market is interesting, and, were it not for Stanley's terrible pictures of the cruelties practiced in obtaining it, would be enjoyable. Tusks there are of all sizes, varying in weight, say, from twenty pounds to as high as two hundred pounds. The latter, however, are exceedingly rare. The illustration shows some of the largest tusks ever brought to Zanzibar. The smaller tusks are the best, being of finer grain. These are used entirely for making billiard balls and ornaments, and sell in the market here in a large way at four dollars per pound. The larger tusks are cut up mostly for piano keys and sell for three dollars a pound.

CHAPTER VI.

The Clove Industry—Old Glory and the American Consul—The
Home of the African—Wages—Tippu-Tib—Dangerous Navi-
gation—Winter is Coming—Southward to Cape Good Hope—
Mozambique.

ZANZIBAR is the one great clove market of the world, and
you may find the place where clove merchants do most congregate by following the " spicy breeze " that comes to you
when you reach the market place by the sea where the spice
is bought and sold. The island of Pemba, adjoining Zanzibar,
is the greatest clove-producing territory in the world. Its soil
is peculiarly and wonderfully adapted to the production of
the spice.

The seed of the clove must be planted fresh from the trees
or it will not grow. The drying process kills the germ of life
and renders the seed valueless. The only way it can be transported is to put it in fresh water, and even this method is
not always successful. Because of the difficulty of transportation it has not been cultivated in other countries. The plants
are of slow growth and not ready to transplant until they are
two years old, and then they must be shaded from the sun
until they are firmly and thoroughly rooted. The Arab planter
prefers five-year-old trees for transplanting. He allows the
young trees to spring up around the old ones from self-sown
seed. When these are of the proper size he " sets " them out
and thus saves the labor of planting the seed and caring for
the young stock.

After planting from seven to ten years elapse before the
tree begins to yield a profit, and at first this is very small.

Picking Cloves on the Island of Pemba, near Zanzibar.

The yield is from five to fifty pounds of dried spice to the tree, depending upon the age and size of the trees, also upon the season, cultivation, fertilizing, and pruning or topping. It is said that by proper care the crop might easily be doubled. The trees are set from eighteen to thirty feet apart, depending upon the character of the soil. In Pemba the clove tree may be said to grow wild and is very hard to kill. When once firmly rooted, drought does not injure it. In times of protracted drought the leaves and buds dry up and drop off, the bark looks dry and dead and the tree seems past recovery; but when the rains come again it puts forth leaf and bud and produces a crop. Sometimes the Arabs burn the grass and weeds that spring up in the grove and the trees are often badly scorched, but soon recover from this setback. The tree grows to the height of from forty to sixty feet.

The buds appear in January and February of each year, corresponding to our summer months in the North, and the picking begins at any time in July to November. The clove of commerce is the unopened bud of the flower. Just before it opens it turns a reddish brown and is then ready for picking. If allowed to remain on the tree until the flower opens it loses its strength and is of very inferior quality.

Women are the best pickers. They climb the trees and strip off the cloves by the handful, placing them in blue cotton sacks suspended from the neck. Others stand on the ground and by means of a hooked stick pull down the limbs and gather the spice. In this way many of the limbs are broken. When their sacks are full they carry them to the overseer who measures them, using for the purpose a wooden bowl holding about five pounds, called a fishi. The pickers receive two cents per bowl and average about twelve cents a day for their work. Some of the very best pickers make as high as twenty cents a day.

After picking, the cloves are spread on mats to dry, and in five or six days are thoroughly dry and have taken on the familiar brown or black color. The little stem which adheres to the clove when picked is now very brittle and is easily rubbed off. After the rubbing process the mass is thrown on a heap where it goes through the sweating process and then the cloves are sifted and the stems taken out. These are also sold at about one-seventh the price of the spice. You will often notice some of these stems among the cloves you buy. These are bought and mixed in so as to increase the dealer's profit. After the drying, rubbing, sweating and sifting process the cloves are put into sacks, one hundred and forty pounds each, and are taken to Zanzibar, where they are sold to exporters. The local government receives a tax of twenty-five per cent on all the cloves exported. The price at wholesale is about ten cents per pound. Seven-eighths of all the cloves produced in the world come from Zanzibar market. Last year's crop was a very large one and is estimated at twenty-four million pounds. It is a matter of some interest to note that nearly the entire world's supply of cloves should be grown on a small island containing three hundred and eighty square miles, with a population of but fifty thousand souls.

Walking along one of the streets of the city to-day near the seaside we caught sight of the stars and stripes floating in the breeze. It was a heartsome sight, good for the wanderers far from home and native land. We raised our hats and after saluting " Old Glory " decided to call on the American consul, for it was over the United States consulate that the dear old flag spread out its stars and stripes to the breeze on "Africa's coral strand."

We had a short but very pleasant and enjoyable visit with the consul, Mr. Mitchell, of New York. He looks after American interests in this part of the world in an able and satisfactory manner. In proof of his ability and energy he has just been promoted to a consulate in China, where both pay and responsibility are greater. Mr. Mitchell is like unto Nimrod, a "mighty hunter before the Lord." The consulate rooms look like a museum. All the trophies are the result of the skill of the consul in hunting big game. His collection is as unique as it is valuable, and to him it has the added value that he made it himself. There are lion and lioness skins, leopard skins, and the skins of about every variety of deer and hart beast in Africa, some of them very rare. On the wall are the heads and horns of a great variety of animals. There are elephant feet, looking like great stumps, hollowed out for umbrella stands. Mr. Mitchell shot and killed an elephant larger than Barnum's noted Jumbo. He very kindly showed us through his collection, gave us information as to the trade of the city and treated us most cordially and kindly.

The natives of this part of Africa are a light-hearted, happy sort of people. They are fond of music, and one often hears them singing at their work. They are respectful to strangers, and you will find but few idlers among them. There is not half the lounging and loitering on the streets of Zanzibar that is to be seen in some European and even in some American towns. Walking about the streets we heard many times these words of greeting from native lips: "Jam-ba San-na Bop-pa." The literal meaning of which is, "A very good morning to you, father." They are pleasant and polite. They have an air of independence about them in striking contrast with the lower caste people in India. The latter are cringing and always make way for the whites. The Zanzibarians have an air about them which, while not impudent, seems to indicate that they feel they are as good as you are. I like this spirit of independence.

Stover Sahib finds his Gujerati very useful in our walks about Zanzibar. In the shops and on the streets he uses it without stint, there in bargaining and here in inquiring the

way to places we wish to find. Yesterday as we were walking we met a man who seemed much pleased to hear himself
addressed in his native tongue. He smiled and inquired from
whence we came, and when the facts were learned we found
that he lived not far from Bulsar himself and had often been
there. He was here on business with two of his brothers, and

Africa Hotel, Zanzibar.

he insisted upon our going with him to his place of business
and meeting his brothers. We went and they all seemed as
much pleased as if they were meeting old friends. There is
a touch about one's native tongue, when away from home in a
foreign land, hearing only a strange language, that warms
up the heart and establishes a feeling of fellowship and friend-
ship at once. Our new-found friends were glad to see and
hear the Sahib, and we were also glad to see them, and especially since their seeing us made them so very happy.

In some places the African house, or rather hut, very

much resembles a giant beehive. It is from ten to fifteen feet in diameter. A heavy pole is set up in the center, which forms and supports the center of the roof. A circle of the required diameter is drawn about the center. Poles four feet high and about a foot apart are set in the ground around the circumference. The rafters are tied with bark thongs, or the fiber of the cocoanut palm, to the center pole and to the upright poles. This is the framework or skeleton of the building.

A Zanzibari's Home. Homely, but Home After All.

The walls are completed by entwining grass about the poles and this is plastered over inside and out with mud. A thatch roof made of grass is put on, a door three feet high is made at the desired place, and the hut is completed. Among the tribes where polygamy is practiced,—and this is common, especially among those who have become Mohammedans,— when a man brings home a new wife, a new hut is built for her.

In Zanzibar, in the native quarter of the city, the houses are somewhat more pretentious than those here described. I was interested in the primitve methods of construction and watched their building operations. The houses are either square or oblong. The outer walls are from eight to ten feet in height, and these are made by setting up poles of the required height, firmly planted in the ground. At the ends the poles are longer so as to form the gable. Smaller poles are now tied transversely to the upright posts about six inches apart. A center post of proper height is fixed so as to give the roof the necessary pitch, and hold the ridge pole on which the upper ends of the rafters rest. The structure is now ready for roof and the mud to finish the walls. In its present stage of construction the building very much resembles a large cage. Not a single nail or wooden pin has been used in putting the skeleton together. Every stick and pole has been firmly and securely tied in, and the frame structure looks as if it had been nailed and bolted together. The interstices in the walls are now closed with mud. The material is made stiff enough to be moulded into balls, and is then forced between the poles and pressed firmly in its place. When completed, the walls have the appearance of having been constructed of mud balls. The roof is of thatch made of grass, laid on in many thicknesses. Doors are made where desired, and the house is ready for occupancy. The houses are substantially built and afford some degree of comfort to those who dwell in them.

Wages here range from ten to twenty cents per day for common work, skilled labor being correspondingly higher. It is about double what is paid in the interior of India. This brings the Indian coolie to South Africa. The cost of living is also somewhat higher. It costs about the same to live here as in a city of corresponding size at home. Hotel charges are from one to three dollars per day, and I am told that the hotels are fairly good. In the interior living is cheap for those who

Negambo Street, Zanzibar.

can satisfy themselves with the native bill of fare. This means corn bread, eggs, poultry, goats' milk, and such few vegetables as are grown. Any fruit in the shape of canned fruits or vegetables is very expensive in the interior. Everything of the kind must be carried on the heads of porters, and if the distance is great the cost of transportation is very high.

We find quantities of food in the market places and in the bazaars. Just now is the time of oranges,—great, fine, juicy, sweet, thin-skinned oranges, which may be had at from twenty to forty cents a hundred. In flavor they are fully equal to California's best fruit. If they were seedless and had the same rich color of the navel orange they could not be excelled. Mangoes are hardly ripe enough to be at their best, but the pineapple, rich and juicy, is abundant. Of course the cocoanut is found in great abundance. This species of the palm is partial to the sea coast and is not found inland.

At Zanzibar most of our deck passengers disembarked, taking with them their cows, calves, goats and kids. After the disembarkation the temporary cow stable was flooded with sea water, and the deck thoroughtly scrubbed and disinfected. This treatment was vigorously repeated a number of times, and now the foul smell of the stable has disappeared. The smallpox has also abated. The tent amidship, where the patients were kept, and everything in the shape of clothing which they had used, were tumbled into the sea and disinfectants vigorously applied. We are now well rid of the disease and are thankful to the Lord that we escaped as well as we did.

The four days at anchor were made good use of by the ship's crew, aided by a lot of muscular Zanzibarians, in discharging twenty-six thousand bags of rice and a thousand packages of various articles of merchandise. The *Nuddea,* lightened of this immense burden, has risen several feet out of the water, not a very desirable thing in time of storm and rolling seas. But we are not likely to meet with storms at this season of the year.

The house of Tippu-Tib was pointed out to us, and the name brought to memory the interest taken in Stanley's preparation for his last journey across Africa. The expedition was fitted out at Zanzibar early in 1887, the object being the search for, and relief of Emin Pasha. Tippu-Tib, known as African king, slave trader and collector of ivory, made a contract with the great explorer to furnish men and assist him in his journey across the Dark Continent. Stanley expressly stipulated in his contract with the Arab that there was to be neither trading in slaves nor slave catching; there was to be no pillaging or oppression of the natives. In consideration of a considerable sum of money, Tippu-Tib undertook to furnish Stanley with six hundred native carriers and to assist him in his work.

How the wily old Arab deceived him is told by Stanley in his book, "Darkest Africa." Tippu-Tib proved a master in the art of delay, prevarication and double dealing. His failure to carry out the contract entered into resulted in a great loss to the expedition, much anxiety and many weary miles of travel in the jungles of central Africa. At one time no man had greater influence in that part of the country, and he made a fortune in the slave and ivory trade. He is now an old man, living quietly in his own house at Zanzibar.

It was here also that Stanley reappeared after his marvelous journey across the great continent. It was three years and over after he plunged into the unknown regions at Stanley Falls, on the west side, until he reappeared on this side, and the cables flashed the news around the world that the expedition had succeeded in its object. All civilized nations rejoiced and did honor to the man who had risked so much and accomplished so much and endured so many hardships to relieve a fellow-man in distress.

Native and Residence Quarter, Zanzibar.

At four o'clock in the evening of our fourth day's stay at Zanzibar, the order was given to heave anchor, and in half an hour we were slowly passing out of the harbor. The masts of the sultan's sunken warship soon disappeared in the distance, as well as the hulk of a great steamer partly submerged on a reef, illustrating the danger of navigation on this coast. As the sun sank behind the rippling waters of the Indian ocean, we lost sight of the American consulate, where the old flag was still floating in the breeze, and were soon out at sea on our way to Mozambique, six hundred and fifty-three miles distant.

Now, as we go south, we find it steadily growing cooler. It ought, according to our northern notion of things, to be getting warmer, but it is not. A blanket at night and heavier clothing for the day are coming into active demand. I have unpacked my heavy overcoat in anticipation of the wintry breeze that will meet us as we go farther south. And then these are the last days of May, and I think of lawn mowing, gardening, sowing and planting, the opening flowers and blossoming trees at home. Who of us in the northland would think for a moment of associating the pitiless ice and snow of December with the springing grass, opening buds and the flowers of May? But that is the way it is down here. Winter has set in and one must radically change his notions of the times and the seasons, and this is hard to do after having had it the other way for three score years. The early spring poet is not in evidence here now, and the editor has peace. He comes out of his winter fastness in November and December.

Yes, things are sadly changed around in these parts. At noon time you look for your shadow where you have been accustomed all your life to see it, but it is not there. It has changed to the other side of you. Something strange has happened. Either the sun has gone wrong, or we have gone to the other side of the sun, but it is better to take the latter conclu-

Tippu-Tib, Slave Trader.

sion. At noon, these days, if you face the west, the sun shines on your right hand and your shadow falls to the south. It is just the other way at home. 'Tis strange! Yes, passing strange, and yet 'tis true. Not very long ago I met a good Christian brother who entertained strong convictions as to the shape of the world. To him it was flat before and still flat after our talk. I am of the opinion if he were with me on this cruise I could convince him that after all the earth is a globe.

When Vasco da Gama, the great Portuguese navigator, sailed down to Cape Good Hope, and up this side of Africa, he and his hardy sailors observed the conditions referred to in the foregoing paragraph. When they returned to their homes, they told about the sun shining on the other side of them and their shadows falling to the south at noon, and were promptly disbelieved and branded as untruthful men by their friends. We now know, as a matter of fact, that they were giving to their unbelieving associates the strongest possible evidence that they had reached the southern hemisphere.

What wonderful navigators those old Portuguese were. Before Columbus discovered America they had been searching for an ocean highway to India. In 1486 Diaz sailed south along the west coast of Africa until he sighted a bold headland jutting into the sea. He called it the Cape of Storms, because of the rough weather he encountered there; but on his return to Lisbon, his king changed the name to Cape Good Hope, " for now," said he, " I have good hopes that by this route we shall reach India." And his hopes were fully realized. July, 1497, Vasco da Gama sailed from Portugal, and ten months later landed at Calcutta, and the ocean route to India became an assured fact. The Portuguese made many discoveries and planted their king's flag on many lands. To their descendants little is left but the memory of their renowned ancestors. A narrow, ribbon-like strip, extending from Cape

Delgado on the north to Delagoa bay on the south, is the measure of their attenuated influence in Africa. They did the sowing, others the reaping and gathering in the harvest.

We were just called out by one of the officers to see a waterspout, the first one either of us had ever seen. It could be traced plainly from the clouds to the sea, where the water rose in an irregular, column-like shape. We were too far away to get a good view of this strange phenomenon of the sea.

At Mozambique, a small Portuguese town, we lay at anchor from four in the afternoon until six the next morning. A visit to the shore revealed nothing of interest. We asked an official for information as to population, trade, etc., and he said the census of the place had never been taken. He seemed much surprised to be asked a question of that kind. What difference does it make how many people live here? Judging from the number of houses we saw in our tramp ashore we concluded that there might be three or four thousand people in the place. It is a clean, well-ordered, quiet little place under Portuguese and Catholic rule.

Here we took on board a hundred sacks of cowrie shells, each sack holding about three bushels. They are for the Bombay market. They are found in great quantities at Mozambique, and are used in central India as a medium of exchange. In some places it is the only money the poor people have. They are also used very extensively in decorating harness and trappings for horses, bullocks, camels and elephants in all parts of the Orient. The demand is large and the supply is inexhaustible. The sea continually washes them ashore, and they are gathered and shipped to different parts of the East.

Five hundred and seventy miles south of Mozambique is the port of Beira. It was scarcely ever visited by vessels until the outbreak of the last Boer war, when it suddenly grew into a place of considerable importance. It became the port of entry for the supplies of the British army. Here the mules, shipped from New Orleans in such great numbers while the war lasted, were landed and taken inland. The place is now connected by rail with Capetown, fifteen hundred miles away. But it has lost much of its importance since the close of the war. While it is on Portuguese territory, and nominally under the same rule, British influence predominates and it is only a question of time when the zone of British influence will include this little that is left to Portugal.

For several days we have been cruising along the coast of that part of Africa where one of the world's greatest missionary explorers did a part of his work; for in the annals of missionary endeavor no name shines brighter than that of David Livingstone. He was first of all a man of peace, and if his counsels had been listened to and his methods of dealing with the black race followed, the bloodshed and cruelty which stain the record of this part of the southern hemisphere would have been avoided.

One who knew Livingstone well, and who plunged into the wilds of Africa to search for the supposedly lost missionary, Stanley, has these words, full of force and meaning, for the man who did so much for Africa: "If you look at illustration of his route, you will see that it is the rude figure of a cross. And now you may be able to draw the moral point I have to tell you. You ask me what has been the cause of missionaries being imperiled. Wherever the good man went, he was received. A few rejected him; but the majority listened to him calmly and kindly, and some of them felt quite ready to be of his profession and belief. But the words he dropped were similar to those of the angels over Bethlehem, ' Peace on earth, good will to men.' On the other hand, in northern Africa, it was an attempt to invade by violence; but it failed, and there was not one that had the courage to step out of the ranks and press on. But this lone missionary pressed on until

he had drawn the rude figure of the cross on the southern
continent of Africa, and then with his dying words: 'All I
can add in my loneliness is, May heaven's richest blessing come
down on every one—American, English, Turk—who will help
to heal this open sore of the world.' The open sore will be
healed. Africa will be redeemed." Perhaps here, better than
any other place in this book, it will be fitting to give Brother
Stover's chapter on Livingstone.

CHAPTER VII.

Livingstone—His Wholeheartedness—His Devotion to Mission Work—Resolves to Give His Life to China, but goes to Africa —Exploration and Mission Work—Death of His Wife—Fever Stricken—Meetings of Stanley and Livingstone—Death Comes to the Kneeling Missionary.

IT was in the month of March, 1813, that Livingstone was born in a Scottish home. His parents were in moderate circumstances, and at ten he began earning wages on his own account. From the very first he saved money from his little wages, that he might secure for himself what so many others had help in obtaining, a good education. In the evening at home, and at spare moments in the factory, he studied Latin, and whenever there was a day off, it was spent in collecting various specimens to illustrate and verify his studies in the natural sciences. In time he was able to study medicine, and continued until he took his medical degree.

Going at everything he undertook, with a whole-heartedness that was characteristic of him, when he was converted he early united with a missionary society in the village, that his religion might be as practical to him as his study of the sciences had been. In the missionary society he became familiar with the great missionaries of the church of the past, he learned to know the fields that were foremost in the minds of Christians as the mission fields to be occupied, and came to know Robert Moffat, missionary to Africa. Moffat presented Africa to the consideration of Livingstone as a field for him to work in, but after reading the appeal of Gutzlaff for China, he resolved to give his life for the people of that country. But the opium war closed China for the time, and

David Livingstone

he turned his whole heart toward Africa. And his was not a feverish rush to the field, but a continually fuller preparation patiently carried on till the time came for his going. Then there was nothing to keep him back.

The last night at his home was spent in conversation with his parents about the great work of missions, and they agreed together there that the time would come when men of wealth would prefer to support whole families of missionaries, and esteem it an honor to do so rather than spend their money foolishly for horses and for games and personal extravagances. David wanted to talk the whole night, but the good counsel of mother prevailed, and they slept awhile. In the early morning he led the little company in the family prayers, and the gray-haired father walked with his son from Blantyre to Glasgow, where the latter was to take the Liverpool steamer, bound for the great Dark Continent. What joy a consecrated parent feels in giving a robust son or daughter to the greatest work of the Lord, only such a parent can tell!

He went under the auspices of the London Missionary Society, sailing by way of Brazil, and reaching Capetown in 1841. He was then twenty-eight years old. He was instructed to join Moffat, and remain at his place until he should return from a trip to England. Getting an insight of things, he soon observed that the native peoples were gradually going further north, and the mission station where they were then located would not be the place for any considerable work. His deductions proved true. It is wise in a mission society to create a center of operations only where the most people are to be found. This point with them would not be Kuruman.

With another missionary and two native Christians he went seven hundred miles on a prospecting tour, and finally decided that the place for the center of their work ought to be Mabotsa. He purchased land there and put up a hut. Then he wrote to the society what he had done, and told them he did it on his own responsibility, hoping they would approve, but he was subject to them, and willing, as he said, " to go anywhere, provided it be forward." He married Mary, the daughter of Robert Moffat, and they spent their first year together at the new mission station.

His observations of the mission and the missionaries during his first year show his keen insight into a bad state of things. He saw they were divided into little parties, and heard with sorrow their evil reports of one another. This is what he wrote home at the time: " The missionaries on this side the river are in a sad state. Every man's hand is against his neighbor. Whatever may have been the original cause of dispute, the present state of feeling amongst our brethren is disgraceful. These are not on speaking terms with those, and those hate these in return, and amongst the whole there exists a pretty considerable amount of floating scandal; all uniting on this side to scandal a certain brother, and on the other side generally favorable to him and unfavorable to those on this side. The devil is in it, but they cannot see him, or rather won't. I am determined to stand aloof from both parties."

His solution of the difficulty would lie in organization, not having a bunch of leaders, but one. His preference went out for a delegated leader, a missionary superintendent, one who would know his business and do it. But what if that leader should become something of a despot? Livingstone says: " I should greatly prefer the despotism of *one* than of many." And as to the committee system of working things, wherein each one had to get his own experience and then would work accordingly, he says: " The present system is a real liberty-committeeocracy. It would take a day's talk to explain the whole subject."

During this first year, while at Kuruman, as ever afterward, he made it a point to come into as close contact with

Masai Man with Beads and Ear Ornaments.

the native peoples as possible, so as to feel as they felt, and to know their thoughts and desires.

His work as a missionary from the first was clearly to do the greatest good to the greatest number of people. Though never a brilliant preacher, he was ever simple and practical in giving instruction, realizing that what the people need most of all can be understood by them if sufficient care is taken to make the explanations explain. And when converts were added, he seems never to have been anxious to make a glowing report home, knowing that while such a report might be desirable at home, it would be bad in the long run for the church on the field.

A native chief invited Livingstone to come over into his country, and he made a tour to the land, visiting Mokhatla, the chief. Finding a very dense population there, it was decided that he open up a school, and locate in the town of Chonuane. Serious drought visiting this place, they were compelled to move to another point, and chose Kolobeng, forty miles westward, and situated on the side of a river. But in this point there was difficulty, as the Boers were suspicious of the intention of the Englishmen.

Some tribes away to the north, close to Lake Ngami, whither no explorer had yet penetrated, were sending word by their chief that they would like to hear the gospel story, and Livingstone determined upon the long journey. After two months he reached the lake, having crossed the South African Desert to do so. Another chief lived yet farther north, who was also eager to see him, but after repeated attempts to go, being broken down with the fever in every attempt, he gave it up for the time, and returned to Kolobeng. On this journey, seeing that the work was hindered, on the east by the Boers, on the north by fevers, on the south by scanty population, the idea became a fixed purpose with him, that a route to the western sea must be established, and a more healthful

Mesai Girl, Showing Arm Rings and Beads.

station to the north determined upon. When he came home, he found his little child had died of an epidemic then raging.

Again, this the third time, he set out for the country beyond Lake Ngami, taking his wife and children with him. Sebituane had specially insisted upon it, and Livingstone felt that it was a call from God. Going into the land, he was warmly welcomed, and Livingstone felt that he was the best native chief he had yet met. This chief promised to select for them a healthy place for location, but before it was done, he sickened and died. Under these circumstances it became painfully evident that the best thing to do was to go back for the time to the old station at Kolobeng.

In journeyings oft, and in perils betimes, it was evident that to take his wife and children with him was not wise. Moreover, the little ones were getting of such an age that they ought to be in school. So he journeyed with his Mary and their children to the Cape, whence they went to England, and he returned, once again alone, to the depths of the Dark Continent.

Now, the new mission stations must have a way to the coast. This would insure access on the part of the mission workers, and better facilities for the work, as it was too far to try the experiment from the Cape, away to the south. Moreover, if such a highway were once opened, commerce would spring up and the inhumane slave trade be hindered, which was such a block to missions, and a blot to Christianity and Christian civilization.

He went up to Lake Ngami, taking men with him, promising that he would return with them to their homes if they came, and after months of boring through the impenetrable forest wormed his way to Loanda on the west coast.

There was an English ship ready to sail. Seven months of unspeakable hardships, privations and incessant labors had

African Mother and Child.

so weakened him, together with the many attacks of fever in a fever-stricken land, that he was well worn out. But he refused to go home, because he had promised the natives to return with them to their homes! And in this he won the native heart completely. This was his manner of dealing with mankind white or black! His word was as good as his note!

Recovering his health on the sea coast, again he set out for the interior, and continued his explorations, ever eastward, till he came out at the east seaport town of Quilimane! In this journey he had traveled through marsh and desert, through jungle and plain, over mountains and ravines, for two thousand miles! He had discovered Victoria Falls, and had accomplished what hitherto no European had done,—he had crossed the continent! On the way he surveyed the land and definitely located with map and chart the points he visited! Meanwhile, he preached the Gospel as he went.

And now at the end of sixteen years, he consented to return for a furlough home! Need we be surprised that he found himself almost the most famous person in London? Need we be surprised that he was given a gold medal by the Royal Geographical Society, that he was given the freedom of cities, that he was introduced to the royal family? Humble soldier of the cross, with his heart in the mission field, need we be surprised to learn that he made it a rule *not* to *read* his praises blazed abroad in all the daily papers now?

Livingstone's life divides itself into three parts, though the missionary part extends throughout the whole. The first, when he went out under the London Missionary Society. The second time he went out, it was under appointment of Government, as consul to Quilimane, a town in Portuguese territory, and commander of an expedition for the exploration of the central and eastern portions of Africa.

Before sailing on this second voyage, in an address to the

A Swazi Warrior.

students of Cambridge, he said: "I beg to direct your attention to Africa. I know that in a few years I shall be cut off in that country, which is now open; do not let it be shut again! I go back to Africa to make an open path for commerce and Christianity; do you carry out the work which I have begun. I leave it with you."

Going by way of Capetown, he was heartily received there. After reaching his destination, his first efforts were directed to exploring the Zambesi river and its tributaries, which the slave hunting Portuguese had been keeping concealed, saying there was only one mouth to the river, that at Quilimane. He now wore a blue cap with a gold band, by which he was ever afterwards known throughout the land, as a mark of distinction, representing the government of the queen. When coming up the Zambesi he met Makololo people, who were so glad that they wanted to embrace him. Wiser ones among them insisted that it were not best to do so now, lest they spoil his new clothes!

The Shire river, flowing directly south into the Zambesi, was explored to its source, the beautiful Lake Nyassa, in a very fertile country. On this journey was Livingstone specially horror-stricken by the outrages of the slave trade. Wherever they went they saw skulls or skeletons lying strewn about where the unfortunate victims had breathed their last. Whole villages had been burned, and a veritable desert made of this once flourishing valley.

He had helped the Universities Mission to select a suitable place for their work along the river, and he was about to go again to the Nyassa Lake, when his wife took the fever, and after a week's illness died. As she lay lifeless on a rude bed, a number of boxes covered over with mattresses, he stood before the body and wept like a child. She had been a mis-

A Zulu Medicine Man.

sionary equal only to himself, and now he was left without her. Most touching are his letters at this time.

He was going again into the interior, when the government recalled the expedition. He went by his little steamer from Zanzibar to Bombay, where he sold the steamer and returned to England. This was a trying period of his life, extending from 1854 to 1864.

The last expedition covers a period of eight years, 1865 to 1873. This time he went under the auspices of the Royal Geographical Society. Going by way of Bombay, he took with him thirteen sepoys and nine liberated slave boys from the mission school at Nasik. He also added ten men from the Johanna islands. Going again from Zanzibar, when they came into the real difficulties of the jungle and desert, the Johanna island men revolted, and so Livingstone sent them back, giving them supplies for the journey to the coast. Arrived there, they told all kinds of stories of the murder of Livingstone, to screen their own weak-heartedness!

His one object this time was to explore central Africa and find the head-waters of the Nile. At the end of the year he wrote in his journal: " We now end 1866. It has not been so fruitful or useful. Will try to do better in 1867, and be better, more gentle, and loving."

Pressing northward he passed through a series of the most trying experiences. The country had been so impoverished by the slave raids that nothing could be found to eat. His goats that he kept for milk were stolen. His medicine chest was also stolen, and he was nigh unto death of fevers. Twice he had barely escaped being struck with the spears of malicious natives. He had discovered Lake Bangweolo, and would go on to the north, but he could not. He had discovered Lake Moero, and had traveled south to Bangweolo. With hunger and sickness, with weakness, and with ulcers on

his feet, he decided that he must stop for the time, and go down
to Ujiji,where he had arranged to have supplies sent, in the
care of a certain Arab. But when he reached Ujiji after
much exertion and greater exhaustion, he found that the Arab
had disposed of all his stores that had been entrusted to him,
the rumor that he was dead having been confirmed by divina-
tion!

Meanwhile Livingstone's friends, aroused by his long continued silence, and the frequent reports of his death, were not
wanting in their efforts for his relief. An expedition had been
sent out, which went from Zanzibar inland to Lake Nyassa,
where they had assurance that Livingstone was yet alive.
They returned to England with the glad report. Another expedition was sent out, but before it accomplished anything,
the New York *Herald* arranged with Henry M. Stanley to go
on a search for him, with instructions, "Do what you think
best; but *find Livingstone.*"

A Welsh orphan boy named John Rowlands, brought up
in a poorhouse, shipped as a cabin boy at fourteen, adopted
by a New Orleans merchant whose name he later chose, prisoner of war on the Confederate side, a volunteer in the United
States navy, a newspaper correspondent, African explorer,
member of the English parliament;—this is the short story of
the life of Henry M. Stanley.

In January, 1871, Stanley arrived at Zanzibar. After
months of pressing on into the African interior, in November
of the same year he reached Ujiji, on Lake Tanjanyika.
Quickly they ran up their flags, and prepared to fire off their
guns, so that the whole country would ring with the sound,
and if Livingstone were near, or anyone that knew of him was
near, they would be attracted, and give the news. There was
soon an interesting crowd. And suddenly a youth, one Susi,

A Group of Mashangaan Warriors.

the Nasik mission boy, came up, and, in good English, said to Stanley, " Good morning, sir."

Stanley, surprised, replied, " Who are you? "

" I am Susi, Dr. Livingstone's servant! "

" What! is Dr. Livingstone here! "

" Sure, sure, sir! Why, I left him just now! "

" Run, Susi, and tell the doctor I am coming! " and Susi ran.

Soon Livingstone appeared, worn, wearied, and in much faded clothes. Stanley took off his hat before him and said: " Dr. Livingstone, I presume."

" Yes," was the reply, as they shook hands heartily.

" I thank God, doctor, I have been permitted to see you," said Stanley.

" I am thankful that I am here to welcome you," was the reply.

Stanley had brought abundant supplies. A few months they dwelt together. They went round the end of the lake in a canoe, and Stanley became extremely ill. Livingstone nursed him with the affection of a father, to his recovery. Stanley pressed him to return to England, but he replied that his task was now so nearly completed that he could not think of going yet. But six or seven months more was all that was needed. Livingstone returned part way with Stanley, when he fell ill again, and was nursed well as before. And when they separated, the one for the jungle where he was to find his death, the other to England, where he was to be welcomed on all sides and greeted, Stanley was a different man, influenced for good by the heroic character of a humble Christian man.

It is interesting to compare what these two said of each other:

Stanley said: "We had a sad breakfast together. I could not eat. My heart was too full. Neither did my companion seem to have an appetite. We found something to do which kept us longer together. At 8 A. M., I was not gone, and had thought to be off at five.

"We walked side by side. I took long looks at Livingstone, to impress his features thoroughly on my memory.

"You have come far enough. Let me beg of you turn back. Farewell."

Livingstone said: "He laid all he had at my service, divided his clothes into two heaps, and pressed the better heap upon me; then his medicine chest, his goods, and everything he had, and to coax my appetite he often cooked dainty dishes with his own hands.

"You have done what few men could do. I am grateful to you for what you have done. God guide you safe home, and bless you, my friend. Farewell."

After Stanley had gone, Livingstone had to wait a long time till the supplies he had ordered should come from Zanzibar. When they came, he again set out to find the sources of the Nile. The thought that he was near the land of Moses was very dear to him, and he read his Bible through and through a number of times.

It was his last journey now. The way was wet and trying to his weakened body, but he kept ever on. It was cold and rainy, and not only he, but his men, felt the exposure very much. Once setting out he tried to ride, but had to give it up, and permit himself to be carried back to the village they had started from, on a litter.

His tent was gone, and his men built a hut for him. This was on the banks of the Molilano. Again they carried him forward a few days, and they halted on the shores of the Lake Bangweolo. Here they built a better hut, but their leader was in great pain.

On the first of May, 1873, early in the morning, the servant was alarmed by the deep quiet that reigned in the hut,

and called the boy Susi to look what was the matter. Together they went in, and found Livingstone kneeling by his
bedside, with his face buried in his hands on the pillow. They
touched him. The body was yet warm. His great soul had
gone to be with its Maker while he was on his knees, in his
chosen attitude for prayer. Livingstone was dead.

Faithful Christian servants buried the heart and other
parts, then rudely embalmed the body and tied it to a pole
so that two could carry it on the shoulders, and thus bore the
remains of their beloved master a long and tedious journey
to the sea,—to Zanzibar!

The corpse was taken to England, and the humble mis-
sionary-explorer, missionary-traveler, who had grown weary
in voluntary exile among the slaves and down-trodden of the
earth, was mourned by thousands, borne on the shoulders of
the great, and laid to rest with kings in Westminster Abbey.

CHAPTER VIII.

A Tiresome Voyage—Durban, South Africa—Natal, the Land of
Fruit and Flowers—The Horned Jinrikisha Men—Rough Rid-
ing—"Go to the Ant, Thou Sluggard."—The Aard-Vark.—
Devastation of an Island by the Ants.

AFTER spending forty days and forty nights on board ship,
be that ship ever so good and seaworthy, one is glad to escape
from the routine of sea life and rest again on the lap of old
mother earth. There is a sameness about ship life that becomes indescribably monotonous if kept up for a lengthened
period. This is especially true of the food provided. There
is an abundance of it, too much in fact, but then it is the same
thing over again and again; it becomes like the manna and the
quails in the wilderness, a thing not so much to be desired
after the long using of it. But all things have an end, and
so our voyage to the Southland ended and we landed at Durban, the finest harbor on the southern coast of Africa.

If one lands at Durban with the notion in his head that he
is now in a pagan country it will soon be dissipated. Durban
is the principal city of Natal, with a population of some sixty
thousand. It was a surprise to me to find in South Africa a
good deal of the push and enterprise so common at home.
Durban has fine public buildings, a large library and well-
furnished reading room, a splendid system of electric tramways,
fare four cents, electric lights, well-paved streets, kept scrupu-
lously clean, a splendid supply of pure water, fine mercantile
buildings, beautiful residences, and in fact all the modern,
up-to-date improvements found in European or American cities
of the first class. It reminds one of a southern city at home,

124

Harbor of Durban.

the presence of the blacks adding to the similarity. These make some pretense of dressing in European costume, except that they are rarely to be seen wearing boots or shoes. Were it not for the occasional group of native Kaffirs, men and women, in scanty attire, from the interior, one would never realize from his surroundings that he was in a heathen land.

Durban is the chief city of Natal and one of the most beautiful towns in South Africa. It enjoys a semitropical climate, the heat and cold both being moderated by the waters of the great southern sea. Natal and Zululand, inclusive, have an area of 29,200 square miles with a white population of a hundred thousand and a million blacks. These are Zulus and Kaffirs and are rapidly becoming less savage and more civilized. The capital, Pietermaritzburg, is located fifty-four miles inland from Durban and has a population of thirty-one thousand. It contains the government buildings and is a flourishing place.

Natal is a fruitful land, and it is not to be wondered at that the Boers left this beautiful and fruitful territory with many regrets for the barren veldt beyond the Vaal river. Many of the tropical fruits grow in the greatest profusion and are of the very finest quality and flavor. The pineapples are by far the best, as to sweetness and juiciness, I ever tasted. Heretofore the pineapples of Ceylon stood first, but these must in the future give place to the luscious fruit of Natal.

The fruit and vegetable market at Durban well repays one for a visit. The city is surrounded with orchards and vegetable gardens, and in season fruit is very cheap. The finest pineapples may be bought for twenty-five cents a dozen. The fruit trade is in the hands of the Indians. It is a very rare thing indeed to see a native of Africa engaged in trading. I found two in all the city of Durban who were engaged in the sale of South African relics. These were the isolated cases met with on our visit to the Dark Continent.

Durban Fruit Market.

Durban is noted for her jinrikisha men with their picturesque costumes, their swiftness of foot and their strength and
endurance.   The jinrikisha, as found at Durban, with rubber
tires and ball-bearing spindles, is a most comfortable, convenient and cheap mode of transportation.   Fares are estimated by
distance and in the city are from six to twenty-five cents,
depending upon the length of the journey.   The rate will average about ten cents a mile.   The men are great, athletic fel-

Riding in a Jinrikisha in Durban.

lows and it is surprising how rapidly and with how little fa-
tigue they get over the ground.   Their costumes are a striking
feature of their make-up; this is especially true of the head-
dress.   A pair of large, finely-polished horns forms the principal part of the decoration.   To these are added plumes, made
of pampas grass or ostrich feathers .The coat is usually one of
many colors and comes half way between hips and knees.
Otherwise the lower limbs are bare except for a coat of white-
wash applied in a very good imitation of tight-fitting white

Jinrikisha Men with Horns and Decorated Heads.

lace stockings with black feet. There are a large number of these men in Durban. They are all Zulus and Kaffirs and are attentive to business, respectful and honest. If you engage one to call for you at a certain time and place you may depend on his being there on time.

President Roosevelt has made the name "Rough Riders" a household word at home and abroad, but it is the candid opinion of the writer that if he and his gallant followers, who won fame in the Spanish-American war, were to ride from Johannesburg to Ladysmith on the Central South African Railway they would have an experience in rough riding not afforded in the late Boer war nor in the cowboy days of the Wild West. Up to the time of making the trip I could not have been induced to believe that there was even a possibility of a train of cars remaining on the track and at the same time being thrown so violently from side to side by compound curves and uneven roadbed as I found was the case on board the fast express train from the Rand to Natal. You engage your seats several days ahead of the time of starting, and they are reserved for you as are berths on sleeping cars at home. When the train pulls into the station you will find your name and the number of your seat posted on the side of the compartment you are to occupy. Four persons are accommodated in each compartment, and when arrangements are made for the night there are four comfortable sleeping berths. The two seats afford two of these and by lowering two nicely-cushioned shelves which are securely folded into and against the sides of the compartment two more equally comfortable beds are provided. If you wish special bedding, pillows, sheets and blanket you pay fifty cents and it is provided at one of the stations reached after nightfall and is removed from the compartment in the morning.

Immediately after leaving Johannesburg the trouble began. The curving in and out, simple and compound, the jolting of the car over the rough roadbed, the sudden jerking

Railway from Durban to Johannesburg.

of the engine as the speed increased, and beyond all previous experiences, accentuated a dozen times over, I had the roughest railroading of my life. The ox-cart trip to the Dangs was a pleasure-jaunt compared with what the Central South African Railway can do when it works itself aright. I have had transportation on construction trains, passed over the English Channel in the great storm of 1891 and crossed the Atlantic Ocean in severe gales, but have never been tossed and pitched and thrown from side to side as on this railway. It was really a frightful experience and I pitied the nervous people who were going down with us on that long night. Sleep was entirely out of the question. A sudden lurch would send you to the opposite end of the seat and then another would drive you back again. And so the long, weary night passed and at last we reached the fertile plains of Natal and were done with the curves. If I had a desire to inflict punishment for wrongdoing I would sentence the culprit to make a score of trips from Johannesburg to Pietermaritzburg on the South African Railway.

The fertile fields, the vegetable gardens, the fruit orchards and the fine plantations of Natal are enjoyed all the more when approaching them from the Rand, for you have the barren, treeless veldt in contrast with them. And we enjoy things in this world by contrast. After eight months of continual sunshine how gratefully are the clouds welcomed that presage the coming of the life-giving rain in India. After the barren plains how beautiful are the gardens and orange groves of Natal.

Traveling inland from Durban, after crossing the Vaal River and entering the Transvaal, I noticed thousands of little mound-shaped hillocks, at places almost covering the plain. At first sight one concludes that these are so many partly buried boulders strewn over the veldt. But if the traveler approaches one of them he soon finds his mistake. They are the home of the ant, and each dome is an ant hill, and there are millions of them, not ants, but ant hills. As each hill contains a multitudinous family of the little people, no one has even ventured to guess at the number of their innumerable hosts. The mounds are alive with the little hurrying insects, and these make it exceedingly uncomfortable for the individual who invades their precincts. They are armed with a pair of strong, sharp mandibles, which they easily bury in the flesh. They also possess an interior chemical laboratory in which formic acid is manufactured and kept in a small sack in the abdomen for use. When the mandibles are buried in the flesh a small syringe, part of the insect's anatomy, is brought into service and a very small portion of the acid is injected into the wound, causing a burning sensation.

In the aard-vark, or ant-eater, the insects find their greatest enemy. I noticed that many of the ant hills had holes broken into one side. It was the work of the ant-bear. With his sharp snout and strong claws he easily tunnels to the center of the mound, and then thrusting into the principal thoroughfare of the industrious insects his long, slender, slimy tongue, which is coated with a glue-like substance, he waits until it is thickly coated with a mass of struggling victims. It is then quickly drawn into the mouth, the toothsome morsel disposed of and the tongue again thrust in among the ants. This is repeated until the entire colony has gone to serve the aard-vark as an appetizer for his meal. Other ant hills are attacked in the same way until the animal has feasted to repletion, when he rests from his labors for the time being.

Were it not for the fact that the ants multiply so rapidly their enemy would soon annihilate them. But the destruction of a few hundred thousand million only incites the survivors to greater activity in their efforts to renew their thinned ranks. Like the honey bee, there are workers, neuters, drones, and females, but while the bees have but a single queen the ants have a large number in each colony. These are constantly dropping tiny eggs scarcely visible to the naked eye, which are gathered up by the workers and placed together where there is proper heat for their growth. In an incredibly short time the ravages of the ant-eater are repaired and a lively colony awaits another visit from the enemy.

A friend who joined us from the Zambesi near Victoria Falls told us of the ants marching across the country in great armies and driving away or destroying everything on their line of march. It brought to mind the descent of the ants made upon the island of Grenada. " They descended from the hills like torrents, the face of the earth was covered with them. Rats, mice and reptiles became an easy prey to them; and even the birds, which they attacked whenever they alighted on the ground in search of food, were so harassed as to be unable to resist them. Streams of water were crossed and every obstacle was overcome by them. Fire was tried, but failed to remove the plague. Finally a hurricane tore up the roots of the sugar cane where they made their nests, and a heavy rain rid the people of a plague which the government vainly offered a hundred thousand dollars to have accomplished; but this only after great damage had been inflicted."

The story of Khama, the converted African chieftain, is of such intense interest that I must not pass it by. It is presented in a very abridged form from the *Review of Reviews*, published in London. It is among the most interesting stories to be found in the missionary annals of Africa.

Khama was the son of Sekhome, the chief of the tribe, a heathen among heathens, full of the superstitions of his people. His son attended a mission school and as he came to study the Bible he was led to accept the teachings of Christ as the rule of his life. He married a Christian wife, and his life was a happy one. Presently his father determined that Khama should take another wife, according to the native custom, and without consulting his son he arranged for a marriage with the daughter of his chief sorcerer. He had even paid over the cattle to the sorcerer for his daughter's hand. It was contrary to all rule and precedent for a bridegroom to cast off one who had been betrothed to him.

The local native sentiment was all on the side of Sekhome in his attempt to compel his boy to live up to the time-honored custom and order of his tribe. It had always been the custom for the son of the chief to marry into as many families as possible. By this means he established relations with the various headmen of his tribe who were always proud to boast that they were related to the chief by marriage. Then, too, a chief's rank was gauged by the number of wives he had. "Many wives very great chief," was the way it looked to leaders of society in Khama's tribe, and great was the consternation when it became known that the son of the chief, under the influence of the missionaries, was determined to be the husband of only one wife.

Now, Khama said that Mabessi, whom he had married according to the Word of God, was a good, faithful, loving wife to him and he would have no other. God's Word said one wife and that was his rule. He had not yet heard of the convenience of divorce as it is practiced among some Christians (?), where a man may have three of four wives and a woman the same number of husbands, and let us hope Khama may never hear of this dark stain on the name of Christianity. He said to his father, " I refuse on account of the Word of God to take a second wife. You know I was always averse to this woman, having refused to take her to be my wife before I became a Christian. Lay the heaviest tasks upon me with reference to hunting elephants for ivory, or any task you like as a proof of my obedience, but I cannot take this woman as my wife."

Great was the wrath in the camp when Khama made this determined declaration. Old Sekhome determined to crush the spirit of his son by blood, but when he called upon his tribe to help him he was met with refusal. He now fled terror-stricken to a place of refuge, for according to the ancient custom Khama would have taken him and killed him, but instead of cutting his father's throat as he was entitled to do, he forgave him, and allowed him to come back to his throne again, on the one condition that he should no longer endeavor to enforce bigamy on his offspring. But the old man, unmindful of the favors shown him, kept on scheming how to destroy Khama until finally he was banished from his tribe and remained in exile for many years.

In 1872 Khama was elected chief of the tribe. He at once recalled his exiled father, but he was compelled to exile him again. Now came twenty years of wise, patient, tolerant, civilizing rule. Khama, although a Christian who had risked his life and chiefship for his faith, adopted no intolerant policy when he attained supreme power. At the beginning of his reign he assembled his people and emphatically announced his own adherence to the Word of God. He said he would not prohibit heathen ceremonies, but they must not be performed on his grounds, and as their chief he would contribute nothing to them. He was about, by public prayer to Almighty God, to ask a blessing on their seed-sowing, and afterwards would set to work. Whoever wished to have his seed charmed could do so at his own expense, but he himself had no such custom now, any more than in former years.

On one point he was merciless. When but a boy he had been saddened by the ravages made by strong drink among his people. When he became chief, he used to say when he was a boy, he would like to rule over a nice town where there was no drunkenness. When at last he became supreme ruler of the Shoshong he determined to make short work of the liquor traffic. Up to that time the white men in his territory seemed to have open license to do as they pleased about importing brandy and selling and drinking it as suited their pleasure. The result of debauchery, delirium tremens and violent deaths was apparent enough to all. The black man was a ready learner from the white man's example. To the extent of his ability he secured and drank all he could get. Khama determined to put a stop to all this debauchery.

First of all, he summoned the white traders and told them they must sell no more strong drink. They pleaded for the importation of brandy for their own use. "Very well," said Khama, "only, if you are allowed to import it there must be no more drunkenness." Within a week several of the traders were drunk. Calling them together again he said to them, "Take everything you have and go! You ought to be ashamed of yourselves. I am trying to lead my people to act according to the Word of God, which we have received from you white people, and you show them an example of wickedness such as we never knew. I will not have you and your brandy among my people." Thus this African ruler forbade the importation of strong drink into his country, and he also forbade the manufacture and sale of the native beer.

How would it do to import a dozen Khamas to the United States, give them supreme power and make them mayors in New York, Boston, Philadelphia, Baltimore, Washington, Pittsburg, Chicago, St. Louis, Kansas City, San Francisco and other large cities? What a pleading there would be for just a little wine, beer, whisky, brandy and rum for our own consumption. How many Christians (?) would plead for a little strong drink for the stomach's sake. How crime would be lessened, the police forces diminished by two-thirds and the prisons and jails emptied. Really I should be delighted to see the experiment tried. Who would pretend to foretell the happy results?

Under the wise rule of this converted African, no white blood in him, and he fresh from heathendom, his people prospered and were happy. Palapye, his capital, covers twenty square miles, and has a population of forty thousand souls. It is pleasantly shaded by large trees and the houses are comfortable cottages, much better than the average to be found in the country.

Khama is a diligent and industrious ruler. It is said he rises early in the morning and, first of all, calls his people together for prayer and worship. Afterwards he sits deciding cases of dispute, trying offenders, and hearing the grievances or requests of any of his subjects. He is a father, a patriarch and a ruler among his people. The rest of the day is spent in the management of his numerous gardens, farms and cattle. In 1895, in company with two of his principal headmen, Khama visited England, where he made a strong and successful protest against having his country placed under the government of British South Africa. He made a very favorable impression in England and his very reasonable request was granted

CHAPTER IX.

Crossing the Transvaal—The Kraals and the Homes of the Natives
—Palace of the Zulu Chief Cetewayo—The Black Man's Burden—The .Mother and Child—Pounding Corn—Diamond
Mines—The Largest Diamond in the World—The Great Falls
on the Zambesi—The Cape to Cairo Railway.

IN crossing the Transvaal by rail it occurred more than
once to the writer that the natives when they first began house-
building and home-making, must have gone to the ant for a
model of their huts. The veldt is covered with dome-shaped
ant-hills, and all the native huts are likewise dome-shaped.
They are for the most part well proportioned and their shapely
domes present a pleasing appearance to the eye. The skeleton,
or frame-work, is made of poles bent and securely fastened
in the required shape. This is covered with a coarse grass
common to the country, which is impervious to water. It
is braided and plaited so that it forms a strong and durable
outside covering, as well as an excellent roofing for the dome.
When finished, the houses turn the rain readily and exclude
both heat and cold.

A native kraal or village, viewed from a distance, has the
appearance of a group of great ant-hills. The huts are built
around an open space, in the center of which is placed the cor-
ral in which the few sheep or cattle belonging to the natives
are gathered for the night to save them from the prowlers of
the darkness. Lions are still to be found, and these are very
destructive to cattle and sheep. Around about the village the
ground is farmed, corn is planted and attended when the

Native Kraal.

native is not working in the fields of the white man. Vegetables are also grown, and as the needs of the black man are not many, he manages to get on in a poor way from year to year.

The finest specimen of native South African house-building is found in the accompanying photogravure, and is really a handsome structure according to architectural taste in this country. It is the home of the noted Zulu Chief Chingwayo, or Cetewayo, who is seated in the center, with four of his principal headmen standing. The outer covering of the dome-shaped building is carefully and skillfully plaited and interwoven so that it presents a pleasing appearance to the eye. The door opens into a square court closed on four sides, except a narrow opening at one side of the house, where entrance is gained to the court. The door of the structure opens into the inclosed square so that the inmates of the house are entirely hidden from outer view when the door is open, and privacy is thus secured. The headmen form a kind of cabinet to the chief and are his principal advisers in matters of state. Each one is armed with a stout club with a ball on one end and a shield made of rawhide, which becomes so hard when thoroughly dried that it cannot be penetrated with spear or arrow-head unless these are driven with tremendous force.

The old-time slavery does not exist in British South Africa as it once did among the Boers. But a system of servitude that is not many removes from it has taken the place of slavery. The natives are compelled to work for the whites a certain number of months, when called upon, and the pay received for their labor is the privilege of living on the owner's land, farming a small patch of corn or vegetables and raising a few cattle or sheep and a flock of chickens. The work is done on their patches at such times as they are not needed by the white boss. The system is unfair and places a great hardship on the black man. It would seem that wherever the white comes

The Palace of Cetewayo, Zulu Chief. He is Seated with Several of His Warriors About Him.

into contact with the black the latter is looked upon as an inferior being, having no rights that the white man is bound to regard. Kipling should revise his " White Man's Burden " and tell us of the burden-bearers of South Africa.

A volume might be written on the care of children by the different races of the world, without exhausting the subject, and one of the most interesting topics would be the different methods of carrying children. Among our people the little ones are carried in the arms, a most inconvenient method when the mother has household duties to perform. The Hindus carry the youngsters astride the hip, while the Egyptian mother places her child astride her shoulder. In South Africa the mother has a comfortable fold in her blanket where the pickaninny rests and is carried about with ease by the mother and with comfort to the little one. It enjoys its snug quarters, and the hands of the mother are free to do such work as falls to her lot to perform. Her cooking, corn grinding, water carrying, hoeing in the field and her laundry work can all be carried on to good advantage with her babe at her back. Then, too, she always knows where to find little ebony. This plan has some advantages not to be despised by more civilized people. At least it so occurred to me when I recalled a mother carrying a heavy child on one arm and doing her cooking and kitchen work with the other.

Instead of two women grinding at a mill, a sight so common in Palestine a score of years ago as to excite no comment, in Africa we have two women pounding grain in a mortar. In both cases the object is the same, to reduce the grain to meal. A wooden mortar,—the one used in the illustration is a type for all that are made,—is provided, also two heavy pounding sticks four feet in length and two and a half inches in diameter, with ends slightly ovaled. The corn is thrown into the mortar, a little water is poured on it to loosen the outer hull, and then

Mother and Child.

the pounding sticks are brought into active use. The work of pounding is the work of the women, and as a rule the supply for the day is all that is prepared at one time. Sufficient unto the day is the meal pounding thereof. Occasionally men take a turn at the pounding, but this is the exception to the general rule. A trial with the heavy pounding sticks satisfied the writer that pounding corn is hard, wearisome labor, for it requires a good deal of physical exertion to reduce the hard, flinty Kaffir corn to such a degree of fineness that it will pass for meal.

Another method of reducing the corn to meal, much slower and more laborious than the mortar and pestle process, is also very common among the poorer people. This method is so well shown in the illustration that it scarcely needs explanation. A large stone properly hollowed out is provided for the grinding. In the hollow the grain is placed and sprinkled with water, and then the woman, often with her little one resting quietly and comfortably on her back, kneels down, seizes with a tight grip an oblong flint stone and begins her slow, but exceedingly tiresome, process of meal making. It takes time and muscle before a sufficient quantity of corn has been ground for the meals of the day for her hungry family, especially if she has many mouths to feed.

As the rubbing proceeds the meal is pushed off the stone onto a palm leaf mat made for the purpose. After the rubbing and pounding is finished, the meal is allowed to dry and then by a skillful manipulation of the mat it is tossed into the air and in this way the hulls of the corn are removed and the coarse corn flour is made ready for the cooking. It is then thrown into a vessel containing boiling water and stirred and cooked into a stiff mush. If the native be the fortunate possessor of salt, a little of this condiment is added and the meal is ready for the eating. The family now gather around the cooking vessel, each armed with a short stick, flattened at one end and

Pounding Corn.

given a slight spoon shape, with which the food is conveyed from the pot to the mouth. This forms a very large part of the native food in some parts of the country. Beans, cabbage, turnips and other vegetables are also grown and are at times placed on the bill of fare. The writer had opportunity to taste of the cooked corn meal and vegetables and found the food well cooked and palatable. The group of men gathered about the large dinner vessel are laborers and are shown as they go about their daily vocations. In some parts of the interior the breech clout is not worn and the workmen labor in a nude state.

In many parts of Central and South Africa the question of clothing does not enter into the native's life problem. Both Livingstone and Stanley report numerous tribes who were entirely destitute of clothing. And this condition still obtains in some parts of the country. Where the people have come in touch with the missionaries and with higher civilization clothing to a moderate extent is worn. Usually a blanket for the cold days of winter and a thin cotton covering for summer wear is the rule. The breech clout is also worn and when work is to be done the blanket, whether it be of wool or cotton, is laid aside. It has been found that the style of dress worn by the whites is not conducive to the health of the natives. When the men work they perspire freely and are often in the rain. Without change of garments they allow their damp and wet clothing to dry on the body, and severe colds, rheumatism and pneumonia result. From the present condition of the people it would appear that the blanket, to be laid aside when laboring, is best for them. To say the very least, it is unwise to force our style of dress upon them. In fact, they could be led to adopt European forms of dress without compulsion, for whenever a native can do so he puts on trousers, vest and coat and apes the fashions of the whites.

It is a strange sight to see a group of natives strutting along the road after some European " boss " has made a liberal

Woman Grinding Corn.

distribution of his old clothing, for which he has no further use. They are a sight to behold. The garments are unselfishly distributed, and each dresses in his first tailor-made suit according to what has been allotted to him. One satisfies himself with a vest many sizes too large for him, another is content with a single undergarment, while others select coats, battered hats, traveling caps, and other articles that may happen to strike their fancy at the time distribution is made. Dressed in this way, their nakedness is made all the more conspicuous.

Hand-shaking among the Zulu-Kaffir people is peculiar in that the hands are laid palm to palm with extended thumbs. This instead of grasping hands, as is our custom. The gentle pressure of the hands, so fraught with meaning among peoples where the hand-shaking custom prevails, is entirely lost to the Zulu. The highest and most respectful form of greeting is the " inkosi," and is only given to a superior. The hand is raised above the head, the thumb laid flat on the hand and the fingers are bent slightly forward, while the words, " inkosi, inkosi," are several times repeated. The first time I witnessed this form of greeting was in a congregation of native Christians. I was compelled to inquire the meaning of the peculiar gesture, and was informed that no higher sign of respect can be given than the " inkosi " greeting.

At Pretoria I was reminded of the diamond mine only a short distance from the capital of the one-time Boer Republic. The diamond mines in South Africa are the richest in the world, and here many an Englishman has become a millionaire. Mr. Rhodes was the most notable example of this kind. And no wonder men become rich in diamond mining when a single stone has a value reaching into millions. Only a short time ago a diamond was discovered in the Pretoria mines which easily bears the distinction of being by far the largest stone of the kind in the world. It was discovered sticking in the side

Inkosi.

of the excavation and is known as the "Cullinan" diamond, in honor of the fortunate finder.

Weighed in carats, the stone turns the scale at 3,022, or nearly two pounds, Troy weight. It measures four inches in length, two and a half inches in height and one and a half inches in thickness. It is said to be entirely free from defect and a

The Great "Cullinan Diamond," the Largest Stone of the kind in the World. Worth $5,000,000.

stone of the first water. Various estimates of its commercial value have been made. Conservatively it is said to be worth as diamonds sell in the market the enormous sum of five million dollars. Compared with the great Kohinoor diamond, now in the possession of the king of Great Britain, it weighs nearly four times as much as that famous stone, which is rated at 790 carats. It is preserved in its rough state up to the present time. In cutting and shaping, it would lose about one-half its weight.

It has long been the boast of Americans that the Niagara Falls are the largest in the world. But after the discovery of the Zambesi and its great falls, named in honor of Great Britain's best and noblest ruler, our American falls are relegated to a second place in the world's great aquatic displays. A comparison will show how the Victoria Falls outrank the Niagara. The latter are one hundred and fifty feet high, while in the former the water falls four hundred and ten feet. The Victoria are a mile and a quarter wide and when the Zambesi is swollen to high-water mark by the rains, the water rushing over the falls is double that which falls over the Niagara. Height and volume taken into consideration, the Victoria would furnish a score of times the power to be set in motion by the American falls.

The natives have very appropriately named the Victoria Falls the Mosi-oa-Tanga, the literal meaning of which is, " The smoke that sounds." The terrific roar of the falls is to be heard for many miles. The water falling from such a great height, much of it is changed into a mist, which, smokelike, can be seen far away as it rises above the great chasm. The sounds seem to come from the smoke or mist, hence the poetical native name. The mist rises to a great height and then comes down in the form of rain.

The falls are a thousand miles up the Zambesi from Beira, and the railroad fare is $100, second class. The railway crosses the river just below the falls over the highest bridge in the world. When the site was selected for the steel truss work that was to span the great gorge, a light cord was attached to a rocket and thus thrown from one rocky embankment to the other. To this was attached a thin wire, which was then drawn across the chasm, and this process was continued until a great steel cable with an electric carriage, with a single wheel suspended, was stretched across the dashing and foaming

Victoria Falls S. Africa.

rapids of the river more than four hundred feet below. To the electric carriage was attached a large rail-inclosed platform and by this means the engineers were carried across the river. It was capable of sustaining a weight of eight tons and on this aerial tramway several thousand tons of bridge material were carried across the deep chasm. The bridge has been completed, and thus another link has been added to the great Cape-to-Cairo railway, which a few years ago was a dream in the fertile brain of Cecil Rhodes, but which is now one of the possibilities of the near future. From Cairo the railway is already completed to Khartoum and is being pushed toward the equator from the north, while in the south the Zambesi has been bridged and the road is to be carried still farther north. Not many years hence one may take a train at Cairo, Egypt, and without change of cars reach Capetown. With this great trunk line all the principal seaport towns will be connected by rail. Already Mombassa is connected with Ugandi and Lake Victoria in this way. Thus the Dark Continent is being opened up by the harbinger of civilization.

The possibilities of parts of the country are said to be very great and especially is this true of British East Africa and the Ugandi protectorate. Parts of this territory are yet but little known and in the interior the race of dwarfs is still to be found in their primitive condition. Johnson, who visited among these strange people, says they are exceedingly agile at tree-climbing and are also quite willing to make friends with the stranger who comes peaceably among them. " One of the striking effects of a visit to dwarfland is the way in which a seemingly uninhabited forest suddenly becomes alive with these little people when they are sure of the friendliness of the intruder. It has reminded me of an effect in pantomime. I have gone into the dense vegetation with one or two native guides in friendly relations with the pygmies, or possibly with pygmies who had already become friends of mine.

They have uttered cries and signals, and suddenly from under the leaves of the great plants on the ground, and from amongst the branches and leaves of the trees overhead, have appeared little pygmy men; the women were not so courageous and were probably hidden away in the huts."

These little people, the men four feet six inches to five feet in height and the women correspondingly smaller, wear no clothing and live in beehive-like huts. But where vegetation is luxuriant they find all the shelter they need without the trouble of building. Unlike most heathen tribes, the pygmies are not given to ornamenting the body. Very often holes are to be seen bored through the upper lip, in which are placed quills or flowers.

The following estimate of parts of British East Africa is made by Lord Delmare, who has purchased immense tracts of land at Nairobi on the Mombassa and Lake Victoria railway and holds it for actual settlers. He says:

" There are enormous timber trees, evergreens, grasses, and clovers; perennial streams abound; the climate is temperate—it will grow anything; and this is a chance in a thousand for men with little money. Each person of age in a household may have free six hundred and forty acres.

" Such land in Australia and New Zealand is worth ten to twenty pounds per acre. English vegetables, wheat, oats, barley, roots, fruit, etc., grow splendidly without irrigation. Potatoes are the staple crop, and command a good price in South Africa. Coffee, in which I am sure there is a future, simply grows like a weed. For sheep grazing, land can be leased up to ten thousand acres at one cent an acre."

Recently Mr. Curtis wrote concerning the railway and the central part of Africa, saying that the " Cape-to-Cairo Railway," the entire length of the continent, will sometime be built, and it is now moving on at the rate of several miles a day.*

*Chicago Record-Herald, June 11, 1906.

Group of Zulu Warriors.

The direct distance from the Cape of Good Hope to the Mediterranean, roughly speaking, is 5,300 miles. The railway, when finished, will probably be about 6,500 to 7,000 miles. The exact distance will depend upon choice of routes. If you will take a map of Africa you will see that there is already quite a gridiron of railways in the southern part of the continent, a total mileage of something more than 7,000, and trains are now running to the town of Kolomo, which, you will notice, is in the Province of Rhodesia, about 100 miles north of Victoria Falls. And during the present year the line will be completed to Matongo. Next year it is planned to extend the track as far north as Lake Tanjanyika, 2,200 miles from Capetown, which will be crossed by steamer, thus saving about 400 miles of construction.

The next gap between Lake Tanjanyka and Albert Nyanza is about 500 miles, and that will be the most difficult of all the construction, because nearly the entire area is covered with an almost impassable jungle, abounding in wild beasts, reptiles and insects, whose stings are filled with poison, to say nothing of the miasmatic swamps. Albert Nyanza Lake, which is one of the sources of the Nile, will also be crossed by boat, and that will be the end of the southern part of the system and the halfway station of the line, about 3,600 miles from Capetown. From the northern shore of Albert Nyanza northward the construction is being done by the Egyptians, and the line follows the Nile to Fashoda and Khartoum. The grade will be easy, but many bridges will be needed. Construction will be comparatively cheap and the material can be handled on the Nile. There are already steamers upon both lakes, and a telegraph line about 10,000 kilometers in length has already been constructed and is in operation.

The telegraph people report a great deal of trouble with monkeys, which swing on the wires and break them with their weight. In some places the linemen have had to substitute bars of copper and heavy cables instead of the ordinary copper wires. The track layers have also been frequently interrupted by lions and other wild beasts. Mr. Williams says that in several places buffalo, lions, zebras, giraffes, rhinoceroses, etc., are so bold that they have come down to see the cars go by and people shoot at them from the train windows. Hippopotami also abound in the rivers. They upset a boat at Victoria Falls last winter.

In one of the English papers not long ago I read the story of a station agent, who was imprisoned in his station by a couple of innocent and unsophisticated lions, who took possession of the platform as coolly as if they owned it. They wandered up and down all the morning, and then lay down to sleep in front of the station door. The agent telegraphed the chief dispatcher, who ordered the next train to run through without stopping. The king of the forest and his companion woke up and yawned as the locomotive shrieked defiance at them and rushed by, but did not appear at all alarmed at the demonstrations of the iron horse. The station agent had no gun, and begged the dispatcher over the wire to send down a professional hunter by the next train to relieve the blockade, which was done. Both lions were shot from the car windows. Since then the trainmen have gone armed.

CHAPTER X.

A Hardy, Strenuous Race, the Dutch Farmers of South Africa—
Where they Came from—A Struggle with Savage Men and
Wild Beasts—Their Religious Belief—A Spartan Mother.—
The Huguenots—The Slavery Question—The Line of Cleavage
between Britain and Boer—The Great Boer Trek.

NOT the least interesting people of South Africa are the
Boers, a mere handful as populations are reckoned, who gave
Great Britain a harder blow than did the American colonists
in their successful fight for independence, or Napoleon the
Great and his veteran soldiers of France in the twenty years'
war. Prophetically true were Paul Kruger's words when he
said to the British Commissioner: "You may defeat us in the
end, but it will be at a cost that will surprise and stagger the
world."

While in South Africa we journeyed across hills, valleys
and veldt to the city of Pretoria, the one-time prosperous capital of the Transvaal Republic. Visiting the battle fields and
the homes of the Dutch farmers, passing by the silent resting
places of the Boer and Britisher, "who sleep their last sleep
and have fought their last battle," standing by the grave of one
of the most heroic personalities of modern times, Paul Stephanus Kruger, noting the location of the concentration camps,
where, declares W. T. Stead, the great English writer, the
lives of twenty thousand helpless women and children were
cruelly sacrificed to the exigencies of an uncalled-for war,
there came to mind with the fullness of detail the great tragedy
enacted on kop and veldt with all its horror, its bloodshed
and frightful destruction and desolation of the homes and

Chief Cetewayo and His Wives.

country of the Boers. Kruger's armies were defeated, but at a cost that surprised and staggered the world.

A very brief historical sketch of these remarkable people must be given if we are to have even a superficial knowledge of the forces that have made them the heroes of modern times. We cannot appreciate the Boer without a knowledge of his past history. And that we may start with an impartial view of his characteristics an Englishman, an American and an Australian are allowed to speak a foreword.

Take a community of Dutchmen of the type of those who defended themselves for fifty years against all the power of Spain at a time when Spain was the greatest power of the world. Intermix with them a strain of those inflexible French Huguenots who gave up home and fortune and left their country forever at the time of the revocation of the edict of Nantes. The product must obviously be one of the most rugged, virile, unconquerable races ever seen upon earth. Take this formidable people and train them for seven generations in constant warfare against savage men and ferocious beasts, in circumstances under which no weakling could survive, place them so they acquire exceptional skill with weapons and in horsemanship, give them a country which is eminently suited to the tactics of the huntsman, the marksman, and the rider. Then, finally, put a finer temper upon their military qualities by a dour fatalistic Old Testament religion and an ardent and consuming patriotism. Combine all these qualities and all these impulses in one individual, and you have the modern Boer— the most formidable antagonist who ever crossed the path of Imperial Britain. Our military history has largely consisted in our conflicts with France, but Napoleon and all his veterans have never treated us so roughly as these hard-bitten farmers with their ancient theology and their inconveniently modern rifles.*

---

* Conan Doyle in " Great Boer War."

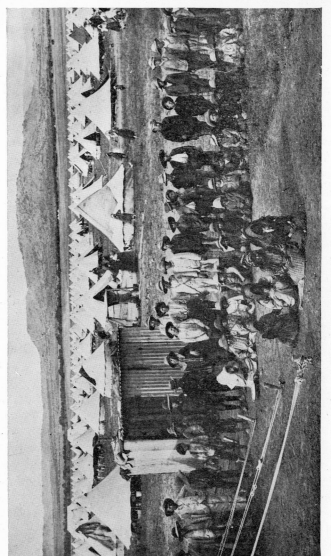

Detention Camp.

The Boer was a splendid type of the human animal. It took all the power of the greatest empire on the earth to crush a handful of Boers; and even then Great Britain was able to subdue them only at enormous cost of men and money and irreparable impairment of prestige. They were glorious fighting men, these Boers. The blood that flowed in their veins was unadulterated Dutch—the only unconquered blood in history. For you will remember that Cæsar could not overcome them, and with the genius of the statesman-soldier that he was, he made terms with them, and the Batavian legions of the Roman army were Dutchmen. These Boers were a great deal more than fighting animals. They were perhaps the most religious people on earth. If they were mighty creatures physically they were exalted beings spiritually. They knew how to pray as well as to fight. They made their living, too, and asked no favors. Also they builded a state.*

Hales, in his "Campaign Pictures of the Boer War," has this to say of these strenuous fighters among whom he lived for some time as a prisoner of war: "Our men, when wounded, are treated by the Boers with manly gentleness and kind consideration. When we left the laager in an open trolley, we, some half dozen Australians, and about as many Boers, all wounded, were driven for some hours to a small hospital, the name of which I do not know. It was simply a farmhouse turned into a place for the wounded. On the road thither we called at many farms, and at every one men, women and children came out to see us. Not one taunting word was uttered in our hearing, not one braggart sentence passed their lips. Men brought us cooling drinks, or moved us into more comfortable positions on the trolley. Women, with gentle fingers, shifted bandages, or washed wounds, or gave us little dainties

---

*Senator Albert J. Beveridge in "Young Men in New Home."

that come so pleasant at such a time: whilst the little children crowded round us with tears running down their cheeks as they looked upon the blood-stained khaki clothing of the wounded British. Let no man or woman in all the British Empire whose son or husband lies wounded in the hands of the Boers fear for his welfare, for it is a foul slander to say that the Boers do not treat their wounded well. England does not treat her own men better than the Boers treat the wounded British, and I am writing of that which I have seen and know beyond the shadow of a doubt."

And now for a few cold facts concerning the way the Boers came to be in South Africa. First of all, the discovery of the country. The earliest reference is found in the annals of the great Portuguese navigator, Diaz, who sailed to Cape of Good Hope in 1486, six years before Columbus won imperishable fame by the discovery of the New World. Eleven years later, Vasco da Gama, a fellow-countryman, rounded the cape, sailed north and finding a small bay entered it and landed on Christmas day, 1497. He named the place Natal in honor of the birthday of Christ. For a century and a half the records are silent as to events in connection with the newly-discovered territory. It is known that small colonies settled at Natal and Capetown and these became ports of call for sailing vessels in those early days. To-day Natal, now called Durban, and Capetown, are large cities and are the principal ports of the country.

The Portuguese, although the greatest navigators of the fifteenth century, made no permanent settlements at the Cape. The climate was much colder than that of their native land. Like the Spaniards, they were lured on by their thirst for gold and searched all the western coast for hidden treasure. At the Cape there were savage men and ferocious beasts, the swamps reeked with malaria and the winters were rough and cold. Against these difficulties the new settlers put up a half-hearted fight and lost in the end. At last in 1542 the country fell into the hands of the Dutch East India Company, where it remained until the beginning of the last century. When the general peace of 1814 was declared, after the titanic struggle between France and England, lasting twenty years, Cape Colony was ceded to Great Britain. A sum equal to thirty million dollars was paid to the stadholder for the newly-acquired possessions, and the imperial government was established over Cape Colony. On three sides the ocean marked the boundaries of the colony, and it would have been well if the fourth had been as well defined. Then there had been no Boer war. The "Hinterland," the vast regions lying to the north of Cape Colony, was not thought of in those days of treaty making. Had Great Britain bought the vast territory, an empire in extent, lying north of Capetown? She answered, unhesitatingly, "Yes!" The Boers, with equal spirit, said, "No!" And so the trouble began.

With the coming of the Dutch, Hollanders and not Germans, as is sometimes thought, the country began to grow and prosper. They were a sturdier race than the Portuguese whom they supplanted. They had done battle with the elements in their native land and had in them the qualities which go to make strong men and women. Of these there was no lack. The rudeness of the climate, the savagery of the natives, and the ferocity of the wild beasts brought to the fore the sterling qualities which count most for success in a new country. And they succeeded. They had the spirit of our own Pilgrim Fathers and were as successful in overcoming difficulties. "Cold, poverty and storm are the nurses of the qualities which make for empire. It is the men of the bleak, barren lands who master the children of light and heat. And so the Dutchman at the Cape prospered and grew in that robust climate."

They were few in numbers and their needs were reduced to a minimum. Self-denial and self-reliance were dominant. They found at the first near the coast all and more than they needed to supply their wants. They built houses, founded homes and after the manner of the fathers worshiped God. They held tenaciously to the religion of the reformers and added to it a good deal of the Old Testament doctrines. They believed that they were in close affinity with the Israelites. They believed in human slavery and were absolutely certain that the negro bore the curse of Cain and that it was their inalienable right to subdue him and make of him a servant of servants unto themselves. They held war to be right because the Israelites fought against and drove out the inhabitants of Palestine. They sought for a Canaan where they might maintain their own notions about religion. To these strenuous men and women modern religion was full of corruption and worldlyism, and they sought to isolate themselves as far as possible from these influences and to preserve, in an uncorrupted form, the good old religion of their fathers.

The following incident is so strongly illustrative of these characteristics of the Boers that a digression is made in order to tell it. On our return voyage from South Africa we had as fellow-passengers one hundred and eighty Boers on their way to the German possessions in Africa. They were making a trek and had with them all their earthly belongings. Among the number were two families of the well-known Joubert name. They held religious services every day when possible and also attended our English service. The Jouberts spoke English fluently and were intelligent people. The men had been in the war, were made prisoners and had been transported to India. One evening we sat together on deck and spent an hour in singing. Among other hymns was the one in which this line occurs, concerning the old-time religion:

"It was good for our fathers and it's good enough for me."

After the singing closed Mrs. Joubert asked with a good deal of feeling the following question, " Do you think we shall be able to maintain the old-time religion when there is so much worldliness crowding into the church? Will the old-time religion be good enough for our children? "

Then she spoke tenderly and feelingly of her family and said: " My boys and girls are all with me except my firstborn. He was but a lad of eighteen when he went into the war to fight the English and he was the best boy I had. In a battle he was shot and instantly killed. He was a fine-looking lad, the best of all my boys, a true Christian, *and then he was such a good shot."* The tears rolled down the cheeks of this Spartan mother as she told of her sorrow, and we went to our cabin, leaving her alone with her grief and the memory of her dead boy.

With passing years the Boers gradually worked their way inland and up the slope toward the great central plateau which reaches out to the great valley of the Zambesi River, fifteen hundred miles away. In the meantime they received an important reinforcement. The Edict of Nantes had been revoked by the tyrant of France and four hundred thousand Huguenots, in whose veins ran the best blood of that country, were driven away from their homes by a merciless and cruel persecution. Three hundred of these godly people found their way to South Africa, settled among the Dutch and were assimilated by them. It was a strong addition to an already strong and virile people. And so the blood of the Huguenots enriched that of the Boers as it has done that of many other nations of the earth. In all South Africa no names are more honored than those of the Jouberts, Rouxs, Dupleix, Villiers, Dutoits and a score of others brought to the Boers by the Huguenots. The veteran General Joubert who so often and so success-

fully met the British in deadly conflict was a direct descendant
of an old French family of that name.

For another century or more the Boers pursued their conflict with the unfavorable conditions in their chosen country,
but always gaining ground and gaining skill as horsemen and
as marksmen. They were cattle raisers, shepherds, and herds-
men, as were the sons of Jacob, and in order to secure pasture
for their flocks and herds were scattered over a vast expanse
of territory. It required six acres of land to support a sheep
and three times as much for a cow, hence large farms became
a necessity. Six thousand acres was the usual size, while
some of the larger stock owners had twice and three times as
much. An annual rental or tax of twenty-five dollars was
paid the government on each six thousand acres. The large
amount of land necessary for stock raising and their fixed
aversion to British rule, for the Boers never took kindly to it,
led them to push northward and to secure more land and
freedom from unnecessary restraint.

At the time Cape Colony came under British rule the
Boers numbered about twenty-five thousand souls. They also
owned at that time a slave for every Boer. These were treated
about as the Americans treated the negroes held in bondage
by them. Their condition was neither better nor worse than
that of their brethren who had been taken captives to the New
World. In 1820 about five thousand British emigrants landed
in Cape Colony and this number augmented with the passing
years. It is the opinion of Mr. Conan Doyle that had it not
been for the faults of the British rule the farmers and cattle-
men might have been led to accept and in the end become
faithful subjects of the government. On the whole the government was mild, clean, honest, tactless and inconsistent.
It might have done well had it been content to leave things
as it found them. But to change the habits of the most con-

servative of Teutonic races was a dangerous venture, and led to the most serious difficulties.

The first and most serious point of difference between Boer and British was the question of slavery. The latter looked upon human slavery as a great evil to be corrected. Their consciences had been educated to look upon compulsory servitude, and rightly too, as a wrong to be righted, and naturally the government took the part of the servant against his taskmaster whose strenuous nature often made him anything but a gentle master. The Boers, on the other hand, regarded the negro as an inferior race, bearing the mark of the curse of God and claimed that his proper place was in slavery. He was their black property, just as the sheep and cattle on the veldt were their property. They being the chosen people of God held that the heathen were given unto them for an inheritance, and like unto the Jews of old the divine rod of vengeance against the heathen was placed in their hands. Between these two views so widely different there could be no reconciliation. There was no middle ground for either party. The same conditions brought civil war to our own country and troublous times to South Africa.

It was upon this very difference that the first conflict between Boer and British took place. A farmer had been arrested and committed to jail for ill treating his slaves. This was an infringement of their rights not to be endured. The Boers rose in rebellion, blood was shed, the rising suppressed and five of the participants were hanged. An English writer says this punishment was unduly severe and exceedingly injudicious. A brave race can forget the victims of the battle, but never those of the scaffold. The making of political martyrs is the last insanity of statesmanship. However, the thing was done and the most bitter resentment left behind. This was shown when, after the Jameson raid, which preceded the last Boer war, the leaders of that ill-fated venture were sentenced to be hanged, and it seemed that they were to be executed, the very beam upon which the Dutchmen had been hanged having been brought from a farmhouse to Pretoria that the Englishmen might die as the Boers died in 1816. This was the line of cleavage between Great Britain and the Afrikanders.

In 1834 came the abolition of slavery in all the domains of Great Britain, a noble action redounding to the lasting credit of the government. But this action only exasperated the Boers. The slave owners were to be paid for their " property," but payment was to be made in London and this was a hardship, for the farmers could not go to London for their money. The middleman got in his work and bought up the Boer claims at half their value. Indignation meetings were held, resolutions were passed, and the spirit that cut the dykes of Holland to destroy the Spaniards burned in the hearts of men, women, and children. Rebellion was useless, the vast plains of the north stretched out before them. Here they would go and find new homes far away from the hated Britishers who interfered with their liberty and their religious views. They yoked their oxen to their great wagons, loaded on them all their earthly belongings, with women and little ones seated inside, the men, each armed with a trusty rifle, walking alongside, and the Great Boer Trek began. They drove their flocks and herds with them and among the ten-year-old boys who helped round up the cattle at nightfall was one who became a thorn in the flesh of Great Britain in after years. His name was Paul S. Kruger.

It was a strange exodus, and it was easy for the Boers to find its counterpart in that of the children of Israel from Egypt. Like the Jews, they claimed they had been oppressed in Cape Colony, their property had been taken from them, and now they had set out to find a land of Canaan where they might be free. As they made their weary way through dense

Treking in South Africa.

forests and across veldt and river they sang psalms and gave praise to God for what they regarded as his leading. They surmounted every obstacle and overcame every difficulty and with dogged determination pushed onward and still onward until some fifteen hundred miles lay between them and their old homes. They crossed the Orange river and founded the Orange River Free State. Here was fine grazing land for their herds and rich soil for the farmers. Here they met twelve thousand spearmen of a branch of the Zulu tribe and killed a third of them without loss to themselves. Others of the trekkers passed on to Natal, where they found a veritable milk and honey land. Its fertile fields produced bounteous harvests, its valleys abundance of pasture, and the flowers of the plain rich stores of honey. After their long and weary journey it must have seemed a real paradise to the hardy Boers of Cape Colony.

CHAPTER XI.

In the Land of the Savage Zulus—Kruger the Lion Killer—A
Fight with England—The Wrongs Inflicted on the Boers—
Majuba Hill—The Discovery of Gold the Undoing of the
Dutch Republics—Conan Doyle's Statement—The Great Boer
War—The Transvaal a Desolate Plain—Seeking for New
Homes.

It is estimated that about ten thousand took part in this
first great trek of 1837. These were the " Voortrekkers," the
advance guard, and were soon followed by others ; and so gradually the Boers emigrated to the new colonies. The Zulus
were as savage and unrelenting as the North American Indian, and the fierce wild animals were not to be despised.
Paul Kruger killed a lion single-handed before he was fifteen
years old and, it is said, he slew some fifty lions while he lived
in the Transvaal. But Zulus and lions gave the Boers less
concern than did the British. In Natal they had met and
overcome the Zulu chief, Dingaan, thus wresting that fruitful
land from the savages. Here they settled, built houses and
established their homes. They had risked much and suffered
more that they might have a free government of their own,
rid of their old-time enemies. But after the Boers had defeated
the Zulus and had settled down quietly in their new possessions
the British made claim to Natal. In order to establish their
claim by might three companies of soldiers were sent into the
colony. These were promptly met by the Boers and badly
cut up in a bloody battle. The survivors fortified themselves
and later large reinforcements came to their aid. It was the
old story over again. Might makes right. The farmers were
finally dispersed and driven out, and again they trekked and

carried with them bitter hearts and the story of their wrongs, inflicted upon them by Great Britain, to their brethren of Orange River and the Transvaal.

At this time the dominant government asserted the doctrine that a British subject could not throw off allegiance by going into unoccupied territory. No matter to what part of South Africa the Boer trekked in search of a refuge from his enemies he was still a subject and a pioneer in establishing new British colonies.

Let an English author tell of the wrongs suffered by these patient farmers who sought only to be left to themselves and for freedom to worship God according to their own notions and consciences:

" Had they wrongs at all? It is difficult to reach that height of philosophic detachment which enables the historian to deal absolutely impartially where his own country is a party to the quarrel. At the end of their great journey, after overcoming the difficulties of distance, and of nature, and of savage enemies, the Boers saw at the end of their travels the very thing which they desired least—that which they had come so far to avoid—the flag of Great Britain. The Boers had occupied Natal from within, but England had previously done so by sea, and a small colony of Englishmen had settled at Durban. The home government, however, acted in a vacillating way, and it was only the conquest of Natal by the Boers which caused them to claim it as a British colony. . . . We may at least allow that there is a case for our adversary. Our annexation of Natal had been by no means definite, and it was they and not we who first broke that bloodthirsty Zulu power which threw its shadow across the country. It was hard after such trials and such exploits to turn their back upon the fertile land which they had conquered, and to return to the bare pastures of the upland veldt. They carried out of Natal a sense of injury, which has helped to poison our re-

lations with them ever since. It was, in a way, a momentous
episode, this little skirmish of soldiers and emigrants, for it
was the heading off of the Boer from the sea and the confine-
ment of his ambition to the land. Had he gone the other way,
a new and formidable flag would have been added to the mari-
time nations."*

The Boers were now settled in the vast territory bounded
by the Orange river in the south and the Limpopo in the
north. Large numbers of their brethren had come to them
from Cape Colony and these recruits swelled their number to
between fifteen and twenty thousand. They were scattered
over a territory as large as Ohio, Indiana, Illinois and all the
New England States. They established a democratic form of
government under which the individual had the greatest possible liberty. They had internal troubles, but settled them in
accordance with their own laws. Their wars with the Zulu
and Kaffir savages, their fear and hatred of the English and
their religion were the ties which held them together. Again
the British appear on the scene of action. In 1848 the Imperial Government placed a garrison at Bloemfontein and in-
corporated the district between the Orange and Vaal rivers in
the British Empire. The Boers protested and fought, but
were defeated and settled down to the new order of things
with increased bitterness against the British who seemed to
follow them wherever they went.

The most of the Boers were now located in Transvaal,
across the Vaal, and petitioned Great Britain for a formal
declaration of their independence. The authorities had little
disposition to lay claim to the barren plains of the Transvaal
and determined to grant the request. "The great barren
country, which produced little save marksmen, had no attraction for the Colonial Office, which was bent upon the limita-

*Conan Doyle, "Great Boer War," pp. 7, 8.

tion of its liabilities. A convention was concluded between the two parties, known as the Sand River Convention, which is one of the fixed points in South African history. By it the British government guaranteed to the Boer farmers the right to manage their own affairs and govern themselves by their own laws without any interference on the part of the British. It stipulated that there should be no slavery, and with that single reservation washed its hands finally, as it imagined, of the whole question. So the South African Republic came into existence."

This all occurred in 1852 and two years later the Orange Free State came into existence as an independent power, followed by the deliberate withdrawal of Great Britain from the territory. These were troublous times for Great Britain. The Crimean war was on and she gladly relinquished her claims to territory of a very doubtful value and a people who could and would shoot as well as pray. She had her hands full nearer home, and so gave her consent to the forming of the two sturdy republics in South Africa which were destined fifty years later to strike her a staggering blow and to hold the united forces of the empire at bay.

For a quarter of a century after the organization of the South African republics the Boers pursued their strenuous lives. They had constant warfare with the natives, using and becoming proficient in the tactics they were to use so effectively against their old-time enemy in the years to come. It cannot be said that the new republics succeeded well financially. Taxes were not easy to collect and the state officials were compelled to serve on uncertain salary. And now for the British again. In 1877 the entire territory was annexed to the empire. What led up to this result is a long story, the telling of which would take more space than is available. A protest signed by the Boers was sent to London and disregarded. It is believed by many Englishmen that if the gov-

Majuba Hill.

ernment had at this time promptly carried out its promises to the Boers, war would have been avoided. But irritating delays came and in 1880 the Boers took up arms and in a few short, sharp actions showed the English and the world that it is the rifle in the hands of marksmen, and not military drill, that makes soldiers. The disastrous defeat of the British at Majuba Hill ended the war. Mr. Gladstone, then premier of Great Britain, magnanimously restored the Boer republics. The treaties which followed were not clearly defined and gave rise to many quibbles and much negotiation later.

In 1886 came the discovery of the rich gold mines in the Rand, a district of territory located in the Transvaal Republic, and this led to the speedy undoing of the republic. President Kruger said: " It is certain that had no gold been found in the Transvaal there would have been no war." To a large gathering of his countrymen who were rejoicing over the discovery of the precious metal the old veteran, General Joubert, said: " Instead of rejoicing you would do better to weep, for this gold will cause our country to be soaked with blood." At this time the population of the country was placed at fifty thousand by an English authority, but now came an influx of population which soon outnumbered the Boers. From all parts of the world came treasure seekers and a rich treasure they found. It is estimated that five billion dollars' worth of gold may be taken from the mines without exhausting them. The metal is evenly distributed in the great bed of ore in the reef which crops out in a ridge some seventy miles in length. Mines have been carried to an enormous depth and gold found distributed as at the surface. In the Rand there is no risk in mining. Given the capital, machinery and workmen, a regular income is assured.

The Boers showed that they had as keen an eye for business as for wild animals and savage blacks. The mines were in their territory and while they did not profit by mining

Native Miners and the Old-fashioned Mush Pot; Noonday Meal.

they did get gold from the miners. The mines were taxed, a dynamite monopoly was formed and the revenue of the government rose from seven to twenty million dollars in a very few years.

The " Uitlander," as the Dutch called the foreigner, was allowed to take no part in the government affairs. The right of franchise was denied him. The shrewd Boer saw that if the franchise was given the Uitlander, he being in the majority, the days of Boer domination would be at an end. This led to an endless dispute and was taken as a pretext by Great Britain to enter again into the politics of the Transvaal. It is the fixed conviction of many of the best writers and thinkers of England that the British government deliberately sought the overthrow of the Dutch republics, that the Jameson raid was a part of a general plan, of which the home government was cognizant, and that from the first opening of the negotiations which immediately preceded the war it was the fixed determination of the English to overthrow the republics and annex the territory to the empire. It is not our purpose to enter into a detailed discussion of these various questions which occupied the attention of the two rival governments for several years before the outbreak of the last war. Conan Doyle has summed up the Boer side of the question, and no one will charge him with partiality for the Afrikanders:

" But it is a poor cause which cannot bear to fairly state and honestly consider the case of its opponents. The Boers had made, as has been briefly shown, great efforts to establish a country of their own. They had traveled far, worked hard and fought bravely. After all their efforts they were fated to see an influx of strangers into their country, some of them men of questionable character, who outnumbered the original inhabitants. If the franchise were granted to these, there could be no doubt that though at first the Boers might control a majority of the votes, it was only a question of time before the newcomers would dominate the legislature and elect their own president, who might adopt a policy abhorrent to the original owners of the land. Were the Boers to lose by the ballot-box the victory which they had won by their rifles? Was it fair to expect it? These newcomers came for gold. They got their gold. Their companies paid a hundred per cent. Was not that enough to satisfy them? If they did not like the country why did they not leave it? No one compelled them to stay there. But if they stayed, let them be thankful that they were tolerated at all, and not presume to interfere with the laws of those by whose courtesy they were allowed to enter the country.

"These people were as near akin to us as any race not our own. They were of the same Frisian stock which peopled our own shores. In habit of mind, in religion, in respect for law, they were as ourselves. Brave, too, they were, and hospitable, with those sporting instincts which are dear to the Anglo-Celtic race. There was no people in the world who had more qualities which we might admire, and not the least of them was that love of independence which is our proudest boast that we have encouraged in others as well as exercised ourselves. And yet we have come to this pass, that there was no room in all South Africa for both of us. We cannot hold ourselves blameless in the matter. 'The evil that men do lives after them,' and we have erred in the past in South Africa. On our hands, too, is the Jameson raid, carried out by Englishmen and led by officers who held the Queen's commission; to us, also, the blame of the shuffling, half-hearted inquiry into that most unjustifiable business. These are the matches which helped to set the great blaze alight, and it is we who held them."

On the eleventh of October, 1899, war was declared against Great Britain by the Transvaal Republic, and the Orange River Free State united her fortunes with her northern brethren. The history of the war, which surprised the world, gave the English a staggering blow from which it will take years for them to recover, and determined the fate of the South African republics, has been written over again and again. Books by the score, and magazine and newspaper articles by the thousands have made the story familiar to the world. I have neither the heart nor the disposition to trace the bloody and cruel tragedy in its sickening details. Oh, the cruelty of war, the wickedness and sin of it, and yet Christian(?) nations, in direct violation of the teachings of Christ, loose this "hell" on earth for gain and prestige. While Great Britain lost more men in killed, wounded and from disease than the entire number of Boers engaged in the war, while she heaped up a great war debt under which her overburdened taxpayers are struggling to-day, and while she suffered an irreparable loss of prestige, the Boers lost more. They staked their all,—homes, country and earthly possessions,—on the fortunes of war,— and lost.

Only a few years prior to the Boer war the indignation of the civilized world, and especially of England and America, was aroused because of the cruelty of the Spaniards in Cuba. Weiler gathered the women and children into detention camps after destroying their homes, and thousands died from disease and starvation. Before the British were able to overcome the Boers they adopted the Weiler policy. The homes of the Boers were burned, their horses and cattle taken and their farms made so many desolate wastes, and the women, children and noncombatants were placed in concentration camps. While the English did all they could to save the lives of their helpless prisoners, the inevitable resulted. Without knowledge of sanitary conditions they died by the hundreds and thousands. The only excuse made for this crime against humanity was that it was a necessary war measure.

At the conclusion of the war the Transvaal was a great

Spion Kop, Scene of a Terrible Struggle and Defeat of the British.

desolate plain. The words of Paul Kruger had become a ful-
filled prophecy. The world was startled at the cost of the
war. It required two hundred and fifty thousand British to
overcome forty thousand armed Boers and to work the complete desolation of their homes and country. The winners in
the struggle have appropriated large sums of money to assist
the Boers in rebuilding their homes and restocking their
farms. But the rehabilitation of a country desolated by war
is a slow process. The Boers overcome by mere brute force,
disarmed and disfranchised, brooding over their defeat and
their wrongs and hating the British flag as the symbol of
foreign conquest, are restless and uneasy. The last chapter of
their history in South Africa is yet to be written. God pun-
ishes nations for their wrongdoings in this world. Russia
has just received at the hands of a heathen nation a foretaste
of what is in store for her, and when the day of reckoning
comes Great Britain will receive in full measure for the wrong
she has done to the brave Dutchmen in the Dark Continent.

Will the Boers remain in South Africa? Mr. Stead says:
"Returning from my first visit to South Africa, where I had
been engaged in the somewhat romantic adventure of endeav-
oring to reconcile my brother Boers to their new status as
British subjects, I have been engaged in the forlorn attempt
to lay my finger upon some point in the map of South Africa
where I could honestly and in good faith assert, 'Here the
British government has done good.' The net result of my re-
searches has, I must ruefully confess, been the reverse of en-
couraging. So far as I can see, looking back over the history
of the last sixty years, it would have been better for South
Africa if, as Mr. Rhodes once suggested, the imperial factor
had been eliminated from the problem, and the South Africans had been left to work out their own salvation without
the blessing or the curse of the providential oversight intermit-
tently exercised by the home government."

Paul Kruger.

Mr. Stead stands among the very first English writers and his opinions carry with them the greatest possible weight. The future must determine what is to come to the Boers. A friend writing to me asks the question, " Will the Boers remain in the Transvaal? " The answer is, Some of them are leaving now and others are likely to follow. If those who are going out as " Vortrekkers " make favorable reports of the new countries, large numbers are sure to follow them.

Under the leadership of the Jouberts a number have already gone into German East Africa. One hundred and eighty of this advance guard took passage with us on the German steamer *Somali* on the return voyage from Durban. We had them for fellow-passengers as far north as Taoga and Mombassa.

In answer to a question whether the Boers were leaving the Transvaal in large numbers, Mr. Joubert said: " No, but if we find German East Africa a country suitable for our purposes a great many will follow us. Those who have preceded us, among them my brother, have sent back very favorable reports. We are to settle down and give the country a fair trial, and if found as represented a large Boer colony will be formed."

Continuing, Mr. Joubert said that the German government offered them every possible facility to induce them to settle in its territory. Large tracts of land were given free of charge, custom duties remitted, and every possible consideration shown new settlers.

When asked if they were leaving South Africa because of British rule the answer was guarded. They were in search of new homes and better land than they had left behind. They did not like the way England had treated them, but they had no resentful feelings. At Dar-es-Salaam, where the *Somali* stopped for some time, the Boer emigrants laid in a large stock of the very best modern rifles and a heavy store of ammunition. They were now in German territory and were allowed to carry rifles, and felt like men again.

At Tonga the most of the Boers disembarked. Their great, lumbering wagons, packed with household goods, were lifted out of the hold of the ship, placed upon lighters and so taken ashore. Horses and cattle, men, women and children followed in small boats, and we soon lost sight of these peculiar people. The Jouberts continued with us to Mombassa, where they left us, after hearty farewells, to travel by rail to a point where they would join those who landed at Tonga. We were deeply impressed with the piety, the religious fervor and the honesty of purpose of the Boers with whom we had been quite accidentally thrown into company. Wishing them Godspeed in their new homes we parted, to see no more of them in this world.

At the Grave of one of the most Heroic Figures in Modern History, Paul Stephanus Kruger, Pretoria, South Africa.

CHAPTER XII.

Africa—The Great Sahara Desert—Will it be Irrigated and Made
Fruitful?—The Early Home of Christianity—Its Schools and
Scholarly Defenders of the Christian Religion—The Persecu-
tion of the Church—The Abyssinian Church—Missions and
Missionaries—Opportunities for Work—Polygamy—"Lobolo"
a Gift for a Wife—Superstitions—Witchcraft and the Witch
Doctor—Independent Character of the Negro—Back to India
—Dental Curiosities—A Narrow Escape from Shipwreck.

AFRICA, the second largest continent on the globe, was
cut loose from Asia, to which it was bound by a narrow strip
of land, the great Frenchman, De Lesseps, accomplishing the
feat by which the waters of the Red and Mediterranean seas
were united, thus making it the largest island in the world.
Speaking in round numbers, as being most likely to be remembered, the distance north and south is five thousand miles, and
from Cape Verde on the west to Cape Guardifui on the east,
as the crow flies, four thousand eight hundred miles. It has
an area of twelve million square miles and a variously estimated population. There may be one hundred and sixty million people living in the Dark Continent.

In northern Africa the great Sahara desert occupies a
territory twice as large as India. Recently it has been discovered that for the most part it is underlaid, at no great depth,
with fresh water. Recent experiments in well digging for
irrigation have proved successful, and now it is proposed to
form a chain of wells across the desert and a railway is also
talked of. Much of the land is productive if water is applied.
The desert may yet be turned into a garden, and the question
answered, "Why did God make the great Sahara desert?"

If the plans be carried out the Sahara will be broken, one of the world's greatest waste places redeemed from death and millions of people may find happy homes and prosper on what is now a sandy waste. Central and southern Africa have immense quantities of rich lands which can easily be brought to a high state of cultivation.

Africa had the honor of furnishing a refuge for the infant Jesus when his life was sought by Herod. When his life work was finished and his disciples were filled with the power of the Holy Ghost on Pentecost it is certain that there were "dwellers in Egypt" present who heard Peter's wonderful sermon. These would carry the new religion down into their own country. We have become so accustomed to regard Egypt as a country quite separate and distinct from the great continent of which it is but a very small part that we fail to associate it with Africa.

The teachings of Christ found ready acceptance in the dark continent and it very soon became a stronghold of the new faith. At an early date Alexandria rivalled Antioch as a great center of Christianity. It was just at the close of the second century, one hundred and sixty-six years after the death of Christ, that Tertullian wrote that in the cities there were fully as many Christians as there were pagans. So rapidly did Christianity spread, and so many were the churches organized that in the year 235 A. D. a great council of all the churches in Africa was held and attended by thirty-five bishops.

Tradition informs us that the writer of the second Gospel established a Christian school at Alexandria, and it is a matter of history that at a very early date after the crucifixion a church school was flourishing in that city, and it had a marked influence on those who came in touch with it. The missionary spirit was developed, and from the school at Alexandria, when in charge of Pantænus, were sent forth missionaries into eastern Africa, Arabia, India, Ceylon and as far south and east as the Malay Archipelago. It was the golden missionary age of the church.

The good Bishop Athanasius, and his helpers, laid hands on Frumentius and sent him to carry the Gospel to Abyssinia, about A. D. 330. The Abyssinians, known also as Ethiopians at that time, readily and joyfully accepted the teachings of Christianity. Frumentius, afterward known as the bishop of Ethiopia, was noted for moderation, great wisdom, marked piety and his remarkable influence over the emperor of this part of Africa. There can be but little doubt that the way for the introduction of the doctrines of Christ was made the easier for him because of the baptism of the Ethiopian by Philip. He would carry with him to the court the religion taught him by the evangelist, so that the name of Christ was known in Abyssinia when the missionary arrived. Be this as it may, Frumentius succeeded in establishing Christianity on so firm a foundation that it was the only primitive church in all Africa that withstood the Mohammedan invasion and its unsuccessful attempt to crush out the church which was in Abyssinia.

Kurtz, in his church history, tells of the enviable place Africa occupied in the intellectual leadership of the early Christian church. It is to Africa that we are indebted for such great writers and leaders as Tertullian, the father of primitive church history; Origen, selected by the church, because of his scholarship and faithfulness, to defend Christianity against its most formidable foe at that time, Celsus, the intellectual giant of pagan Rome; Clement, the man of love, the teacher and scholar who was at the head of the school at Alexandria; Augustine, the defender of the faith; Cyprian and many others now regarded as the early church fathers who made Africa the very center of religious thought and missionary enterprise. Of all the great names revered by the church

now, after the apostles, for the first four centuries, more than
half of them came from Africa.

But not only in missionary effort, in scholarship, in intellectual development and in leadership did the church in
Africa reach a high eminence. She also furnished many of
the noble band of martyrs who sealed their faith with their
blood. So rapid was the spreading of Christianity in northern
Africa that pagan Rome became alarmed. And well she
might when more than half the population of all the cities
had already accepted Christ. At this rate of conversion and
increase it would be but a few years until the whole lump
would be leavened, and all the cities of this favored region
would become not only almost but altogether Christianized.
Rome itself was threatened with overthrow by the new religion, and by the very sect which was everywhere spoken
against.

Think a moment of what all this meant. Rome, rich,
proud, profligate, seeking only pleasure and steeped in debauchery,—to this city came the teachers of Christianity with
their message. "They called themselves apostles of a Son of
God; but their Son of God was a village carpenter, who had
lived in sorrow and had died on the cross, and their message
was a message never heard before on earth. It was to invite
their fellow-men to lead new lives, separate themselves from
the abominations of the world, to care nothing for wealth and
to be content with poverty, to aim only at overcoming, each
one for himself, his own sensuality and selfishness, to welcome
pain, want, distress, everything which the world most shrank
from, if it would assist him in self-conquest, and to expect no
reward, at least in this life, save the peace which would arise
from the consciousness that he was doing what God had commanded."*

*Froude's "Great Subjects."

This was the message carried into Rome and into Africa, by men who believed their message and lived their beliefs, that was rapidly undermining the gods of the pagans and threatening to overthrow them in the citadel of their strength. The only remedy left in the hands of the enemies of the cross was persecution, and to this they now had full recourse.

The persecution of the Christians having been determined upon, the Emperor Serverus promulgated a decree, A. D. 202, forbidding, under penalty of death, the conversion of a pagan to Christianity. This meant death to the teacher as well as to the convert, but teaching and conversion went on. All the great centers of the Roman Empire ran red with the blood of Christians, and of all these none suffered more than Africa, unless it were Rome itself. She furnished men and women by the hundreds who were willing to suffer and die for their faith in Christ. Had he not died a cruel death for them? They counted it all joy that they were found worthy to suffer for his sake.

And so the bloody and cruel work went on. History has recorded but few of the names of those who suffered death under the persecutions of Serverus. Leonidas, the aged father of Origen, was beheaded at Alexandria; Felicitas, a slave girl who had accepted Christ and chose rather to be torn to death by wild beasts in the stadium than to deny her Lord; Potamiæma, also a slave, a maiden of great personal beauty, who, for defending her honor and her moral purity, was accused by her master of being a Christian and was with her mother tortured to death in boiling pitch. " Perpetua, a young mother of high birth, twenty-two years of age, was accused of being a Christian. In spite of imprisonment and torture, the pleading of her father and the love for the infant in her arms, she was true to her faith, and was thrown into the arena to be torn by the horns of a wild cow, only to be relieved from her anguish by a stroke from the dagger of a gladiator."

The persecution of the church, not only in Africa, but in Rome as well, became a great element of strength to her. The better thinking class of people turned against the perpetrators of the horrible cruelties. They saw the composure and the willingness with which the Christians met death, the thing they most feared. They were not slow to reach the conclusion that these people had found something which the cold, dead teaching of the Roman philosophers could not give. They were led to investigate and finally to accept the faith themselves. Even the executioners themselves, in some cases, noting the triumphant death of the Christians, accepted Christ and were in turn martyred. It strengthened the tie that bound the Christians together and cleansed and purified the church. Those who were faithful could not be moved by threatened death and torture, and those who were not true were weeded out. Every martyr who fell for Christ brought scores of converts to the faith, and again the blood of the martyrs became the seed of the church.

The church in Africa continued to grow and prosper until there were more than nine hundred Christian churches in that country alone. It now seemed as if the entire continent would be gloriously redeemed unto the Lord. But the church had reached the height of its prosperity and glory in Africa. One writer says: "In the height of Christianity's glory in northern Africa there were nine hundred churches of Christ in that region. O, that they had understood their calling! If, instead of spending their chief strength in the theological and ecclesiastical arena, they had turned their magnificent powers to the evangelization of Africa, instead of being still the 'Dark Continent,' it might have become the most luminous portion of the whole planet a thousand years ago."

It would be a matter of interest to trace the causes which led to the decline of Christianity in Africa, but space forbids more than a mere reference to it. Intellectual pride, resulting from the education of the head to the neglect of the heart, is the death of all spirituality. After the death of the fathers the heart side of the school work at Alexandria may have been neglected, or at least made secondary to the development of the intellect, and this rapidly bore its fruits. Instead of men of great spirituality, and of intellectual ability but humble with it all, came leaders who, proud of their scholarship and of their own views, entered into controversy with others like-minded. And so the church was led into endless disputes on speculative theology; factions and schisms arose, the church forgot her message to the world, lost her power, and the fire of her zeal burned low in northern Africa.

Then came division, excommunication, anathemas of one faction against the other and all the attendant evils which cause angels to weep and devils to smile. The missionary spirit was dead, and all the energies of the church were spent on her internal struggles, and when her energies were thus wasted, her golden opportunity frittered away, the great trust placed in her hands betrayed and weakened by internal discord, Islamism came armed with the sword and she received a blow from which she has not recovered unto this day. Now all of north Africa, except Abyssinia, is under the sway of the Crescent, and the teachings of the false prophet are rapidly extending southward.

Besides the Abyssinian Christians there are to be found in Africa the Copts, who are without doubt the descendants of the ancient church of Egypt; but theirs is a sadly corrupted form of Christianity. The Copts seem to have accepted, in part at least, the teachings of Islamism. They number barely two hundred and fifty thousand and are the most degenerate and corrupt of all the primitive churches.

Abyssinia has an area of about three hundred thousand square miles, with an estimated population of four million souls, made up of Christians, pagans and Moslems. The ruler, who is nominally a Christian, styles himself "Menelek, King of Kings," and claims to be a direct descendant of Menelek, son of Solomon, and the queen of Sheba who, tradition says, became the wife of the son of the Wise King of Israel. He had some trouble with the British a few years ago, and now Abyssinia is under a protectorate of Great Britain.

At the end of the sixteenth century the Jesuits made a determined effort, under Portuguese authority, to bring the church of Abyssinia under the control of the pope. For a time it seemed as if the effort would succeed and all Abyssinia become Roman Catholic, but later the Jesuitic influence was broken and the Abyssinian church held to its ancient traditions. But the church, like that of the Copts, is in a sadly corrupted state and is badly in need of reform.

The Abyssinian church has twelve bishops, one metropolitan and numerous arch priests. Every priest must be over thirty-three years of age and the husband of one wife. They also have orders of monks and nuns who take vows of perpetual celibacy. Thornton says the ceremonies of the church are very ancient in origin. Several Jewish practices remain, and both Saturday and Sunday are kept holy. Prayers in the ancient Ethiopic are both solemn and sublime, while the primitive custom of having churches without seats is observed. The congregations stand to pray, and the feeble are supported by crutch or staff. Preaching is not commanded and is seldom heard. The elements of the communion consist, as in the Greek church, of ordinary bread and the unfermented juice of the grape. Prayers for those asleep in Christ (not in purgatory) and for absolution are pronounced over the dead. The Virgin Mary has a high office in the church, and some think the work of redemption is attributable to her. There are traces of strict discipline, observed long ago, and public confession of sins. No professing Christians on earth fast so rigidly as do the Abyssinians. They have fasting nine months out of the twelve. Yet immorality is the order of the day, and even priests and monks are guilty of moral obliquity. Marriage is seldom conducted in the churches and is regarded as simply a civil contract. Briefly stated, such is the present religious condition of the Abyssinians.

At the present a railway is in course of construction from Jibutl on the Red Sea to the capital of the state, Addis Abbi. When this is completed ancient Ethiopia will be in closer touch with the modern world. The distance from the capital to the Red Sea is five hundred miles, and two hundred miles of the road is now completed and in active operation. The capital is also connected with the coast by a telegraph line. Under the British protectorate the country is insured the blessings of a stable government and is said to be in a prosperous condition.

In modern times the Dark Continent has become an open missionary field, and now earnest efforts are being made to Christianize and civilize its peoples. In 1897 the entire Bible had been translated into ten different African languages, the entire New Testament into twenty, and a beginning had been made upon some parts of the Old Testament and of the Gospels in no less than sixty of the languages. In this noble work the American Bible Society has taken a prominent and active part. It has published the Zulu Bible, the translation of which was the life work of Robert Moffat.

The Moravians, first of all churches in modern times to catch the missionary spirit of the primitive church, were first to send missionaries to southern Africa. This in 1742. These, with Livingstone, Krapf, Rebmann, Stanley and others, missionaries and explorers, have opened up the Dark Continent so that all parts are now accessible. The governments of Europe have divided the country into zones of influence among themselves and have undertaken to preserve order and establish

"In the Dawn of Civilization."
A Kaffir Family
Converted to Christianity.

In the Dawn of Civilization, an African Family Converted to Christianity.

good government. This they are rapidly accomplishing, and in many parts of southern Africa life and property are as safe and secure as in the United States or in the best governed countries of Europe.

A chain of missions stretches across the country from the Congo to Mombassa, and both the east and west coasts, south of the equator, are dotted with missions. The interior is also being invaded and the results in Uganda are held up as an example of what may be done by earnest endeavor in leading the sons of Ham to accept Christianity.

What are the opportunities for work? Is the field occupied? Let these figures answer the question. In central and southern Africa there is to-day one Protestant missionary to every fifty thousand pagans. North of the equator, and south of the Sahara desert in the great Soudan states, there is but one Protestant missionary to forty-five million Mohammedans, and northern Africa has a single Protestant missionary for each one hundred and twenty-five thousand Moslems. Surely the question is answered and there is a great field, unoccupied as yet, for those who would take part in illuminating the Dark Continent by giving it the light of the Gospel of Jesus Christ.

Some of the existing social conditions among the natives hinder to some extent the success of mission work, but these are not so deeply rooted as is the caste system in India. The dawn of Christian civilization is breaking over darkest Africa and it will grow until the Sun of Righteousness shall rise in his full glory of light.

Polygamy constitutes a barrier in the way of the speedy introduction of Christianity. The rule is that a man adds to his importance and dignity every time he takes an additional wife. It would be necessary at first to make the best of this social condition as was done in apostolic times. Now that stable governments have been provided by the nations of Europe who have parcelled out the country, and tribal wars have ceased, the causes which led to and perpetuated polygamy will disappear and Christian teaching, as in the days of the apostles, will finally correct the evil. But it will take time and patience to overcome a practice so closely connected with all the intricacies of the social system of the natives. It cannot be

Preaching Among the Blacks near Johannesburg, South Africa, in Mining Camp. A Converted Zulu is telling the Story of the Cross.

hoped that the ancient and long-cherished custom will pass away without a long course of Christian and moral teaching.

"Lobolo," a gift for a wife, is also a prevailing custom among the natives quite repugnant to our ideas of the proper method of a union in marriage. It virtually amounts to the giving, by the future husband to the father of the girl, a sum of money or cattle as an equivalent for what he is to receive. While this practice is less objectionable than that of polygamy, it stands in the way of a speedy reformation of the social conditions now obtaining among the natives. It has deteriorated to the sale and purchase of the girls of South Africa for wives. The practice of making a gift to a future wife, or her parents, is as old as the history of the race. Abraham sent rich presents when he would secure a wife for his son Isaac, and Jacob wrought at hard labor fourteen years for Rachel. The custom prevailed in Germany until recent times and may still be found in Christian Norway. It is not a matter of surprise that a father who has tended and cared for his daughter till womanhood, and who has been cheered by her presence in his home, should be quite willing to accept from the stranger a present for the bestowal of his daughter's hand. It would in some way compensate the father for his loss, and show, to some extent at least, the appreciation of the future son-in-law for what he was to gain by the marriage. In time this practice became so fixed among the people that it is now a fixed part of their social fabric. Perhaps in the best sense of the term the contract is not to be regarded as the sale and purchase of the daughter. The woman does not become the slave of the husband. He may not sell, injure, prostitute, maltreat, or misuse her, all of which he might do if she were his slave. In case he misuses her beyond all hope of reconciliation she may return to her father's house and claim his protection, and the husband loses both his wife and his "lobolo." On the other hand, if the separation results from the wife's misbehavior, the "lobolo" is returned to the husband. Thus the gift becomes an element in cementing the union. No woman so separated from her husband may remarry except from her own village with the consent of her father or guardian. The consent for a girl under twenty-one years of age must be obtained before she can be married. After that age she may be married without the consent of parent or guardian. The giving and taking of gifts in securing wives, like polygamy is so interwoven into the social fabric of the people that it would be unwise to attempt an immediate change.

The Witch Doctor with Face Smeared with Lime Determining the Fate of his Victims.

It will finally give way to Christian teaching and higher civilization. It is not nearly so difficult a problem as is child marriage in India.

The natives are, for the most part, densely ignorant and as a result are full of superstition. They are firm believers in witchcraft and the witch doctor is an important personage in the village. He is perhaps the most feared among all the people. When death occurs it is believed to result from the malign influence of some person possessed of an evil spirit. The witch doctor at once enters upon his duties and he accuses some one, often an entire family or families, and these are at once put to death. The death rate is thus largely increased among the natives. Every one who dies from a natural cause brings about the death of one or more at the instance of the witch doctor. In dealing with these people they must be used as overgrown children. The physical has been fully developed, but the intellectual dwarfed until it is scarcely more than embryonic.

The greatest hindrance to mission work in India is caste, which is entirely unknown among the natives of South Africa. Neither are they idol worshipers. Their ideas of religion are very limited and crude as a result of their ignorance. But they learn rapidly. They are well built, strong limbed and capable of great endurance. Some of them would make excellent models of fine physical development for the sculptor's chisel. In their home life but little clothing is worn. In the cities a blanket is sufficient to cover their nakedness, and it will take time to teach them to dress themselves in modest clothing. They are generous, independent and always willing to divide their substance with their fellows in need. It seemed strange to us to have a native Christian refuse a small sum of money for carrying our heavy hand luggage to the station. It was entirely different from all previous experience not only in the Orient but in Europe and America as well that it has not been forgotten.

Here one may hope to build up a self-supporting church, which is the unusual in India. The people insist on helping. They build their own churches and schoolhouses and in many

Kindling Fire. The Stick is Whirled Between the Hands until the Friction Ignites the Wood and the Fire is Kindled.

A Native Christian Teacher with His Bible Class.

cases not only support their own workers but send money to
carry the Gospel to others.

Among the missionaries in South Africa there is some
uneasiness as to a movement on the part of the Ethiopian
Christians to be entirely free from the control of the European
and American churches. The Methodist African Episcopal
church is the prime mover in the " Ethiopian movement," and
it seems to be gaining ground. To the writer this is a hopeful
sign. The independent spirit which seeks to control its own
work and support its own churches is to be commended. But
the whites here have much the same feeling toward the blacks
as is found in our own Southern States. It is the opinion of
those who have given the most careful study to this important
question that ultimately the negro himself must be the prime
factor in the regeneration and uplifting of his race. The example of Mr. Booker T. Washington in the United States is
attracting the attention of the entire civilized world, and he is
giving an object lesson that is influencing thought and methods in South Africa. It is coming to be felt that with sending
out the missionary to preach the Gospel, must also come the
industrial and intellectual training, so that the people may
reach the highest possible religious and moral development.

The need of workers in this great missionary field will be
seen at a glance, when it is known that in central Africa there
is but one missionary to eighty thousand natives and in South
Africa one to every fourteen thousand negroes. The area
embraced in the territory named is larger than the United
States, and there is no question as to the fruitfulness of the
field. The people appear to be willing to accept Christianity,
and, with fewer hindrances than in India, it would seem that
South Africa is a promising field in which to labor.

A serious drawback to living in Africa is the prevalence of
fevers. The African fever is a serious disease and much more
to be dreaded than the malaria fever of India. Among the

Group of Native Girls and Women Clothed for the Occasion.

fatal fevers in many localities is that known as the black water fever. A remedy for this form of disease has not been
found. The average length of life service among the missionaries in the interior has been eight years, and the death rate
is unusually large. In British South Africa health conditions
vary as to locality. Away from the river marshes, conditions
are such that these localities are recommended as health re-
sorts. The climate is also pleasant as one goes south, re-
sembling in some places that of southern California and at
others that of Virginia and South Carolina.

And now we turn our faces toward " Dear Old India "
again, for the time being our homeland. The German East
African steamer *Somali* had been selected for the voyage, and
we found her a good, seaworthy boat. Going north we landed
at Parapet and went out among the natives. There are but
two whites living in the port, and a short walk from the seashore brought the travelers to a native village where whites
seldom appear. The people, men, women and children, came
out of their dome-shaped huts and showed themselves very
friendly. They were especially interested in our kodak, and
picture-taking was to them a source of great curiosity. They
are also very observant. One of our party had dental bridge
work in his mouth and two gold teeth showed up rather prom-
inently in front, and these at once attracted the attention of
the observant blacks. The wonder to them was how such
teeth should grow in the mouth of the white man. Then Stover
Sahib, who is provided with an upper set of teeth on a dental
plate, excited the greatest degree of surprise by allowing these
to drop out of place. After a series of facial contortions and
a slight pounding on the top of the head, the eye of every
native fastened intently upon him in the meantime, the teeth
dropped down and there went up a great shout from the
crowd. To them the thing was little less than a miracle, and

Harbor of Dar-es-Salaam.

from that time until we left for the ship, we had a crowd following us and there came repeated requests that the performance should be repeated. I secured, at a nominal cost, several of the native spears used in warfare and also a large knife employed for the same purpose.

At Parapat the natives are engaged in the culture of peanuts, and large quantities are produced annually. Several times a year ships put in at the place to carry away the product. We took on board the *Somali* six thousand sacks, each containing about three bushels of the hulled nuts. The natives carried them from the village down to the seashore and into the water to the lighters, which brought them alongside the ship. They were consigned to Hamburg, Germany, where they are made into a first-class grade of olive oil. The hulls are removed by hand and then they are laid out in the sun to dry. While lying on the ground the natives crawl over them and pick out the imperfect kernels, after which they are placed in sacks ready for shipment. The harbor at Parapet is good after entrance is gained, but the entrance is obstructed by a bar formed by the river that flows into the sea at this place. The *Somali* struck the bar and we were compelled to wait for the rising tide, when the boat floated again.

In German East Africa the best harbor is found at Dar-es-Salaam. The harbor is not only good, but it is a beautiful spot. A large German Protestant and also a Roman Catholic church stand close to the water. It is the seat of the German governor and has a white population of several hundred. Here our Boer fellow-passengers armed themselves with rifles and also secured a heavy stock of ammunition.

We visited the native villages in the vicinity and found the people peaceable and friendly, but within a few weeks after our visit there occurred an uprising among the natives and the Catholic bishop and several missionaries were murdered. The German government is at present sending soldiers to

East Africa to quell the disturbance, for it seems that the uprising among the natives has become general and a strong force will be required to restore order and to insure the safety of the whites in the territory.

From Dar-es-Salaam our course lay by Bagomayo, where Stanley emerged from the dark continent, crossing from west to east and successfully rescuing Emin Pasha. Thence we ran to Zanzibar and lay at anchor while we took aboard three hundred and fifty tons of cloves for Bombay, the great central distributing point for the spice. The opportunity to revisit the city was taken advantage of and an interesting day was spent ashore.

Our homeward cruise brought us again to Mombassa, the gateway to British East Africa. The city lies on an island and has two good harbors, one to the north, the other to the south side of the town. The *Somali* entered the south harbor first, where freight was discharged and passengers disembarked for the interior. This was hastily done, as the captain, in order to save time, wanted to reach the north harbor and anchor there for the night, and at the same time discharge cargo for that place, for he must have daylight to pass the dangerous coral reefs lying at the entrance of the harbor.

The sun was sinking below the western horizon when we lifted anchor and turned the prow of our ship to the sea. Even before we passed out of the south harbor it began to grow dark, for there is but little twilight so near the equator. The moon had not yet risen and the sky was overcast with storm clouds. A heavy sea was running and the roar of the waves as they rolled landward and broke on the " coral strand " could be plainly heard. Steaming northward we soon reached the entrance to the harbor on that side of the city. It was now quite dark and the lighthouse gave out its warning beams telling of the dangers of the reef. It also marked out the line of safety on one side of the entrance; but it was so dark

A Zanzibar Woman.

Hair Dressing.

that the buoy on the other side could not be seen. I was standing at the rail of the ship at the moment and saw that we were approaching dangerously near the surf breaking over the hidden rocks. Suddenly the ship's engines were reversed and the sound of rattling chains told the story that the anchor had been cast. It was found that instead of passing between the lighthouse and the buoy the ship had actually been steered outside the buoy and had been stopped within fifty feet of the reef. It was a narrow escape. Fortunately the anchors held firmly and we escaped the threatened danger of shipwreck and loss of life. Soon after casting anchor the ship veered around and fell into the trough of the sea. Then there came a record-breaking experience in the rolling of a ship. Everything movable on the boat moved, and the first lurch broke all the unsecured crockery and glassware on board the *Somali*.

What was now to be done? This question concerned officers and passengers alike. The captain said: " It is entirely too dangerous to lie at anchor for the night. There is a heavy sea and we may be cast on the reef. I must either get inside or run the ship out to sea and steam up and down the coast for the night and make the entrance in the morning." He determined to make another attempt to enter the harbor. A boat was lowered and four sailors, provided with a red lantern, took their places in the boat and were instructed to find the buoy and place the lantern on top of it. We watched the little boat until it was swallowed up in the darkness and then the red light until that too disappeared. Then after waiting what seemed a very long time we again saw the gleam of the red light and knew that the sailors had fastened it to the buoy. With the light to steer by the captain made another attempt and at length brought the ship safely to anchor in the harbor.

In my notebook for July 1, 1905, I find written: " I realized this day as never before how good it is to have a light by which to steer in the darkness of the night." The captain kept the red light in his eye, steered the boat by it, and soon brought us in safety into our desired haven. So amid the darkness and storms of life when temptations assail and dangers encompass us, it is so good to have the " Light of the world " to guide us and by which to steer our tempest-tossed boats. There can be no mistaking the red light of the cross of Jesus Christ.

After leaving Mombassa and crossing the equator we steered north to Cape Guardafui and from thence took a straight course for Bombay. The southwest monsoon had now set in, and for twelve days we were rolled and tossed on the Indian Ocean, but through it all the Lord safely brought us, and to him be all the praise, the honor and the glory.

END OF PART ONE.

The Other Half of the Globe

PART TWO

Australia and China.

CHAPTER I.

The Coming of the Monsoon—The Mango, King of All India
Fruit—Off for the Other Half of the Globe—A Long Sea
Voyage—Seasickness and Chronic Gastritis—Ceylon the Is-
land of Spices—Crossing the Equator—The Doldrums—Hot
Weather and the Prickly Heat—The Man of Many Corks—
Eating Snails—The Stormy Coast of Australia.

THE life-giving monsoons had come and gone again when
we bethought us that the time had come for our voyage to
Australia. After months and months of cloudless skies, of
hot, thirsty days, spent in waiting and watching for the expected downpour, with old mother earth parched and cracked
as if her millions of open mouths were pleading with piteous
cries for rain, how glorious were the refreshing showers that
came down, soaking the ground and changing all the face
of the landscape from the brown and sere to a living, livid
green. The rain came down so steadily, so gently and so
quietly that one felt like going out and standing in it and
thanking the Lord for it. It had not rained for nearly nine
months, and here was contrast strong enough to give the
keenest edge to the sense of enjoyment. The farmers rejoiced,
and we rejoiced with them. Here so much depends on the
coming of the rains, so much is at stake, for surely there
is but a step between the poor in India and sufficient food on
the one hand to keep soul and body together, and famine and
death from starvation on the other. If there be a generous,
plenteous downpour from the clouds of heaven there will be
work and food; if not, gaunt famine will stalk through the
land, bringing suffering and death to millions. So the rains
come to mean so much to these poor people, and you cannot

live among them and work with and for them without entering into their joy when the rain comes or their sorrow when it is withheld.

And then there also comes the time of the mangoes, not the tasteless, stringy seedlings sometimes found in the New York markets, but the great, yellow Bombay kind, as full of juicy, pulpy, nutritious sweetness as an egg is full of meat. The mango is easily the king of all the fruits of India, as the mangosteen is, for delicacy of flavor, the queen of all tropical fruits. The natives feast on the mango for a month or more, and rich is the feast. They eat them before they are ripe and many a little brown skin is afflicted with a pain in that part of his anatomy usually covered by the little shirt, where shirts are worn, from overeating green mangoes. Then comes the doctor with an iron heated to a cherry red, and the little one bears a deep scar ever afterwards. The fruit is found everywhere in India, and in the height of the season it may be bought as low as thirty cents the hundred. The government has wisely planted mango trees on both sides of the public highways, making a continuous shade from the heat of the sun, and yielding immense quantities of the luscious fruit. When in full bearing the trees of the best varieties look as though they were covered with a mass of gold.

And now we are to have the mango in the United States, and the very best of the fruit too, for our Agricultural Department has taken hold and will be content only with the very best. In 1889 the first East India mango trees were planted in Florida. Only one of these escaped the hard freeze of 1895. When this tree, saved by Prof. Gale, of Mangonia, Florida, came into full bearing it was a revelation to the fruit-growers of our country. An eight-year-old tree bearing five thousand mangoes of large size and of the finest quality was a sight worth seeing. The fruit was fit for the table of a king. From this one tree thousands of grafted mango trees are now growing in Florida south of the frost danger line. To meet the demand for the very best mangoes in the world, the department has taken to America young plants of the very best varieties from every region where they are grown, and there is assembled in the various greenhouses of the department the largest and best-selected collection of mangoes in all the world. These are being fruited in Florida and California, and the best will be propagated as rapidly as possible for distribution. Before many years mangoes, better than the average fruit of India, will be as plentiful in our home market as oranges, and as cheap too.*

There are about one hundred and fifty varieties of the mango grown in India. The tree is an evergreen with spreading branches, a dense foliage, leaves narrow and from six to eight inches long, of a shiny dark green color. It is of rapid growth, attaining a height of over forty feet, while its undivided trunk never reaches a length of more than ten to twelve feet. In blooming season it is densely covered with small white, tinted with red or yellow, blossoms. The fruit varies in size and color as to different varieties, from a greenish yellow to a deep golden hue. It is somewhat kidney shaped and contains a large flattened stone nearly as long as the fruit. The stone is covered with stringy fibers which are also found in the fruit of the poorer quality. It also has a very strong taste of turpentine, while the best varieties are entirely free from this taste and are without the strings of fiber, the pulp being luscious, sweet or with a slight taste of acid. The unripe fruit is used for pickles, sauces, jams and jellies, and the kernels are roasted and eaten as food in a time of scarcity.

And now we are off again for the other half of the globe, with Australia, the Southland of the world, as our objective point. It is two-thirds as large as the United States without

* " National Geographic Magazine."

Alaska, the Hawaiian and Philippine Islands, with a population of but four million souls. Australasia, meaning South Asia, includes the continent island of Australia, New Zealand, Tasmania and the Fiji Islands. Its native population has interested students of anthropology for more than a century, and many of the mysteries connected with the strange and interesting people remain unsolved as yet. Their boomerang throwing, their writing sticks, their corobboree dances and strange marriage customs are full of absorbing interest to all who give time to the study of God's crowning work of creation—man. But more of this in a succeeding chapter.

From our note book. We were three, Maijee, Sister Eliza Miller, of Bulsar, India, and the writer, and what a pleasant time we did have cruising down the old globe. It's only a memory now, but one that makes the heart warm when recalled. September 16, 1905, we left our India home for a sea voyage, going and coming, of nearly fifteen thousand miles, and when we landed at Sydney, New South Wales, the farthest limit of our tour of the world was attained. In reaching it we had traveled, geographically speaking, thirty-eight thousand three hundred and seventy-two miles. This included all our journeyings for the year, and had we followed the equator closely there would have been miles enough to have taken us around the globe one and a half times. When we leave Australia some months hence we shall gladly turn our faces homeward by way of China, Japan and Honolulu. These days bring to the pilgrims and wanderers in far-away lands among strange peoples and unfamiliar scenes longings for the old home and heart yearnings for old friends.

If you will take a map of the world and draw a line along the coast of India from Bombay to Colombo, on the island of Ceylon, and thence directly southeast to Freemantle, on the western coast of Australia, following the sinuosities of the coast and crossing the great Bight to Adelaide, Melbourne, and Sydney, you will have the course of the voyage from India to the Austral continent. The distance in common miles is seven thousand four hundred and eighty-seven, a voyage long enough to satisfy one's desire for the sea. We covered the entire distance in twenty-two days, including the stops at the several ports en route.

Breakwater at Colombo.

We considered ourselves fortunate in having secured passage on the fine French steamer, the *Ville de la Ciotat,* commanded by Captain Etienne, a very courteous gentleman and a splendid sea captain. We had a good ship, good officers, good, well-cooked food, good service, good company, good staterooms, good beds, good weather for the most part of the time and as a matter of course a good, enjoyable time. There was sea enough on part of the voyage to test the staying qualities of the passengers, of whom we had but few, twenty first and second class, of whom only a few succumbed; but these had but little to say about the *mal de mer*. Very few travelers like to admit that the sea does not agree with their inner anatomy. It must be prompted by a false pride, for very few people escape the fell malady of the sea. It may also arise from the fact that no one gets much sympathy when seasick.

Once upon a time a friend was taking his first sea voyage. He was a good sailor and stood the rolling and pitching of the ship very well indeed, and was justly proud of his staying qualities. He even grew a bit boastful, saying that after all seasickness is largely imaginary and that all a man has to do is to have the will power to make up his mind not to allow the malady to overcome him, and he is safe. The next day we had a storm at sea and the "waves rose up to the heavens and sank again into the depths, and men staggered to and fro and were at their wits' ends." Our friend appeared on the scene later with a sad look on his face. He was making a desperate effort to suppress and hide his feelings, but was making a dismal failure. After he had made the usual offering to the sea he explained that when at home he was often subject to attacks of acute gastritis and that he felt he was having a slight attack of it now. The French call it *mal de mer,* the Germans *seekrankheit,* we say seasickness, but our friend invented a new name for the malady, acute gastritis.

The third day out we reached Ceylon and cast anchor in the commodious harbor of Colombo. Ten years ago we spent some weeks visiting the "Pearl of India," and a revisit shows that it has lost none of its gorgeous, tropical beauty. On shore we found the 'rikishas ready for us, and we rode out to our old home at Galle Face by the sea. The smooth road, as level as a floor, reddish-brown in color, hugging the sands of the sea where the crested billows break, with the rich beauty of the tropical vegetation about us, confirms the opinion expressed a decade ago that Ceylon is one among the most beautiful islands in the world. At Colombo we were detained a day awaiting the arrival of a steamer from Marseilles for China and Japan. She had passengers for our steamer, and we for her. This made the wait necessary. Steamers do not

Ceylon Fishing Boat.

as a rule make as close connection as do railway trains, but on the morning of the second day the delayed vessel steamed into the harbor, transfers were made and in the afternoon we were off again for the Austral lands. Looking back at Ceylon in the evening we had a most beautiful sight. Between ship and shore was the expanse of blue water sparkling and dancing in the light of the setting sun; shoreward it turned into a rich emerald, skirted with a long stretch of white fringe where

the waves lost themselves in the sand. The background was
the spice island itself, and it made a picture unsurpassed by
the efforts of the world's greatest masters.

At Ceylon our steward laid in a supply of the delicious
tropical fruit known as the mangosteen. In the whole range

Ready for a Race.

of the world's fruits there is not a single one that surpasses
the mangosteen in flavor or in the beauty of the delicate
morsel covered with a purple-brown rind a quarter of an inch
thick. Remove this and you have a small mass of beautiful
white pulp, more delicate in flavor than the best plum, indescribably delicate and delicious. The only way to know
how the fruit tastes is to eat of it, and then you will have only
one feeling of dissatisfaction, that there is not more of it.
An authority on fruits says of this queen of the tropics that
the tree rarely reaches twenty feet in height, has an erect,

tapering stem, and a regular form, somewhat like that of the fir. The leaves are seven or eight inches long, oval, entire, leathery and shining; the blossoms are large, with corolla of four deep red petals. The fruit, which is orange-like in shape, dark reddish-brown, spotted with yellow or gray, has a thick rind and is divided internally by thin partitions into segments like the orange. The pulp is soft and juicy, cooling, with a mixture of sweetness and acidity, and is delicately flavored.

Mangosteen.

South of Ceylon we plunged into the intense heat of the equatorial regions. · Here the sun is master of the situation and the rays come down with full force. The officers of the ship laid off their regulation uniforms and appeared in white cotton suits. Everybody on board put on the lightest clothing, and so prepared for the great heat.

We crossed the equator at a slant, and if the captain was correct in his reckoning I saw one end of the great circle. He said we would cross it at six o'clock in the morning, and as the sun rose from its watery bed at that hour the next morning the eastern end of the notable circle was clearly marked by the rim of the sun as it rose above the waves. Looking back, as we sailed down the southern half of the globe, the equator looked like a ribbon of blue touching sea and sky on the line of the horizon north of us. It is said some people have tried to photograph it. I didn't.

Some one has said there isn't a degree of latitude north or south but that believes if it had its rights it would have been an equator itself and could have done the work quite as well and fully as satisfactorily as the great circle itself about which so much fuss is made. Whether this be true or not, it is certainly very human. A man working on a farm without special preparation for editorial work had the opinion that he could edit all our church papers, and do it as well as it was being done, for half the money paid for the work.

And it was hot while we lingered around the equator. A kind of steamy, sticky, humid heat that made you feel uncomfortable all over; a kind of heat that makes one long ardently, and without ceasing, for a cold breeze from the north—no, that is a mistake. On this half of the globe the cool breezes and the wintry blasts and storms come from the south. And a few days later it came to us over a rippling, sparkling summer sea, a sea cool now.

And now we are on that portion of the tropical sea known to sailors as the doldrums. It is characterized by calms, light, baffling winds, hot sultry air, local squalls and thunderstorms. It is the dread of all sailing ships. Caught in this belt the sailing ships crossing the equator often beat about for weeks and months before escaping from calms and contrary winds. Here one finds the highest temperature and the greatest amount of moisture with the gentlest winds to be found anywhere on the ocean. Here the surface of the sea is glassy in its smoothness and often bears a thin coating of oil and waste dropped by passing ships and floating for a long time on the bosom of the unruffled ocean. For years the doldrums were the great dread of the sailing ships, but in these days of steam one may plough through the glassy sea and suffer only from the inconvenience of the great heat and excessive moisture.

And it was hot, hot day and night, and got no cooler until we were well clear of the doldrums and away from the equator. Did you ever suffer from the effects of the prickly heat? I had it for two months and it's a prickly nuisance. Also I had boils at the same time, not as many as afflicted Job, but I really believe I could have made a good second to that pious, godly, patient, perfect man, in the way of boils at least. I had the aftermath coming down this side of the globe. One morning I counted twenty-three, all of them in a painful state of activity. They were decidedly unpleasant company, but not serious, except one with five openings, a regular carbuncle. The dictionary says a carbuncle is a kind of a jewel. I know better. You can't always put your trust in dictionaries. At least, so says Mark Twain.

We had on board a cork man from Spain, not a man made of cork but a man who makes and sells cork. In a fifteen-minute talk he told me more about corks than I had heard before in sixty years. Spain has a monopoly of the cork business, the man said, and he knew, for he was a member of the firm of the largest cork makers in the world. He had just come from San Francisco, where he had been selling the finished article to the wine producers of California, and they use millions and millions of corks. He had also been in Milwaukee, Chicago and St. Louis supplying the beer bottlers with corks. He said his firm sold the Busch brewery eighty million corks annually and that the Schlitz people took twelve hundred and fifty bales, with one hundred and fifty gross to the bale. Also he sells corks in Russia. The Russian government has a monopoly on vodka, the national intoxicant of that people. It is all sold in bottles, little and big, holding from a couple of ounces to a quart, and every bottle must have a stopper. The man said it takes five billion corks annually to supply the demand. He seems like a truthful man, but I confess his figures appear a little extravagant. The price for first grade corks is from sixty to seventy cents per gross.

After giving all this information about corks he told of a vineyardist in Sonoma county, California, who, when he planted his large vineyard forty years ago, also planted ten cork trees. "And now," said the Spaniard, "they are as large and fine as any grown in my country." If that man had planted a hundred thousand cork trees when he planted the ten he would be a multimillionaire now. The bark is stripped from the trees carefully, so as not to injure the inner covering under which the sap flows, and then it grows again, and in ten years is ready for another stripping. The shavings and refuse from the cork factory are packed in bales and shipped to the makers of the floor matting called linoleum, the largest manufactory of which is located in the United States.

And what glorious sunsets we did have as we sailed south of the equator. These are only memories now, but memories that stay by one. To see the sun sink into the western sea overhung by a curtain of clouds, is to have a scene of such transplendent and regal beauty that pen cannot describe it. "The vast plain of the sea is marked off in bands of sharply contrasting colors; great stretches of dark blue, others of purple, others of polished bronze; the billowy mountains show all sorts of browns and greens, blues and purples and blacks, and the rounded velvety backs of certain of them made one want to stroke them, as one would the back of a sleek cat. Then the clouds were flooded with fiery splendor, and these were copied on the surface of the sea, and it made one drunk with delight to look at it."

The other day I saw hundreds of flying fish. The sun shone brightly and the sea was exquisitely tinged with a deep Mediterranean blue. The fish darted from the waves and flew a hundred yards, skimming the surface of the sea like flashes of silver light. They are graceful creatures and their flight across the waves is a thing of beauty. Once one came aboard the ship. It was ten inches long and its fin-like wings reminded me of the flying squirrels that used to interest me in the woods of Maryland a half century ago.

There is much French and but little English spoken on the *Ciotat*. The stewards all speak French and some of them "Angleese" according to the French way.

Maijee's bathroom steward is a friendly fellow and not averse to talking. He has been in New York and knows the United States quite well. She told him that we lived near Chicago and he said, " Oui, oui, Madam, I know ze Che-caw-go vair well! He is vone big cittee, vone World's Fair cittee. He is in ze New Orleans! "

We have an attentive and most polite table waiter. He speaks and understands about as much English as I do French, and our vocabulary is very limited. One of the best appetizers at our meals is his effort to translate the French bill of fare into English and our efforts to understand him. He always goes to Maijee first and her face is a study during the process. Sometimes she understands and sometimes she doesn't. When she doesn't she says, " O yes, thank you, that will do." Eliza gives assent and I nod approval, and then we wait with ex-pectancy the surprise in store for us. Once we were looking for roasted chicken and got mushrooms. Again Eliza under-stood the waiter to say " Snitz." Now every well-regulated

Pennsylvania Dutchman knows that the word is used to indicate dried apples. We all said, "Yes, if you please," and
presently the waiter came with a dish of French snails and
they are considered a dainty morsel by epicures. Maijee took
none, Eliza took three and I five, and I ate mine and found
them very palatable. After a few days we got on better, but
we missed the surprises. Think of ordering string beans and
getting fried kidneys, or having a dish of boiled tripe when
you were expecting mutton chops. It made dining exceedingly interesting.

We have a fine promenade deck, and if one walks around
it eight times he has a mile to his credit. One evening I
walked around it twenty-four times, and felt as if I had walked
from Mount Morris to Silver Creek and back. I used to do
that twenty-five years ago.

We are now in the region of the trade winds and a steady
to strong breeze blows from the southwest. The sea is rough
and choppy, which gives the ship a drunken, wobbly motion
and makes walking rather uncertain. Also it rains, and after
the tropical downpour the clouds assume a dull leaden hue,
and this was photographed on the waters, and instead of the
deep blue that fades away into the sapphire the sea looks like
a great pool of ink. If one could dip a pen into it, it would
make fairly good writing fluid, so black it looks. Along the
Australian coast one finds storms that lay the Atlantic variety
in the shade.

The days are growing longer, and for the moment it is
rather puzzling. According to all our former experience the
days always grow shorter from June to December. Here the
whole thing is reversed.

To-day the ship passed through heavy rainstorms and
squalls of wind. Sea rough and choppy. With a small ship
great discomfort would have been felt, but the *Ciotat* is a
large boat and has every possible comfort. Latitude at noon

to-day, 8 degrees and 51 minutes south; distance made in last twenty-four hours, 327 miles.

The lifeboats impress one with thoughts of their possible use. There are ten strung along both sides of the ship. Should a serious accident occur, collision or fire, these frail-looking boats, capable of carrying fifty passengers each, would be our only means of safety or escape. And what an escape, here in the most unfrequented part of the Indian Ocean, fifteen hundred miles from the nearest port. To take to the boats and drift and drift until exhaustion and death come is not a pleasant thing to contemplate. Let us go down to our cabins and get out of sight of them. But thousands of lives are saved by these same lifeboats. Often our only means of help and safety are not pleasant subjects for reflection.

This Lord's Day morning, September 24, we have a high wind and a rough sea. The heavens are overcast with black, threatening clouds. The blue waters have taken on the hue of the clouds and resemble nothing so much as a great pool of ink. It looks black enough to write with. Presently the rains come down, gently at first, but then faster and faster the drops beat on the angry, crested waves. These kept up the struggle for a time and then gave it up. The little drops of water had stilled the angry ocean and there was a calm, smooth sea. So powerful is the force of little things in this world. So, too, little words of kindness still the angry waves of passion which stir the human soul. We had some days of steaming hot weather when we lingered around the equator. Now we are far south of the great circle and are entering the south temperate zone. We are getting a breeze from the south pole. It has traveled a good many thousand miles to get to us, but it comes laden with a suspicion of ice and has a snap and vigor about it that makes it very welcome indeed after the tropical heat of the torrid zone.

Ten days from Colombo we sighted the southwest coast of Australia, and soon after entered the harbor at Freemantle and cast anchor for a day after our long voyage. From this port the distance is 2,500 miles to Sydney, and the sea was rough the entire distance, and part of the time very rough. But we came through without serious inconvenience. Neither Maijee nor I suffered from seasickness. Sister Eliza is of age and can speak for herself. The captain said we had a fine voyage, and we believed him. On the return voyage on her last trip to Australia the *Ciotat* was caught in a hurricane off the coast here and both her great masts were snapped off like pipe stems. She escaped, but finished her voyage without masts. The day we landed at Bombay after our African trip the mastless, battered ship also entered the harbor. Since then she has been fully repaired and is as fit as ever for storms and hurricanes.

CHAPTER II.

Sydney Heads—Entrance to the Harbor—A Dangerous Place—
Wreck of the Duncan Dunbar—Springtime in October—Syd-
ney's Beautiful Harbor—Government Ownership of Street
Railways—Captain Cook's Discovery—The Convict Colony—
The Rabbit Pest.

OCTOBER 8, in the morning, we sighted the Heads, as
nature's great, rocky fortresses which guard the entrance to
the harbor of Sydney are called. We passed Botany Bay,
where Captain Cook landed a hundred and fifty years ago and
where England's exported criminals and convicts were landed
for so many years. Then we steamed along the great wall of
rock with no visible opening. Presently the ship's engines
slowed down and the pilot boat *Captain Cook* came steaming
toward us. The pilot was soon on board, and then we discovered the entrance to the harbor.

Sydney harbor is the boast of Australia and is said to be
among the finest in the world. It is shut in behind a great wall
of rocks facing the sea without visible opening from the distance. There is a break in the middle affording a safe entrance to the harbor, but it makes so little show that navigators often sail by without noticing it. Not far from the entrance is another break in the wall of the precipice, so much
like the first one that it has been mistaken for the real entrance. This caused the wreck of a vessel and a great loss of
life some years ago. The story has been often told, but it
will be new to many of our readers and it cannot be better
told than in the words of another:

South Head, Sydney Harbor. Where Indentation is Seen in Picture, the Duncan Dunbar was Wrecked.

" The *Duncan Dunbar* was a sailing vessel; a fine, favorite passenger-packet, commanded by a popular captain of high reputation. She was due from England, and Sydney was waiting, and counting the hours; counting the hours and making ready to give her a heart-stirring welcome, for she was bringing back a great company of mothers and daughters, the long-missed light and bloom and life of Sydney homes; daughters that had been years absent at school, and mothers that had been with them all that time watching over them. Of all the world only India and Australasia have by custom freighted ships and fleets with their hearts, and know the tremendous meaning of that phrase; only they know what the waiting is like when this freightage is trusted to the fickle winds, not steam, and what the joy is like when the ship returning this treasure comes safe to port and the long dread is over.

" On board the *Duncan Dunbar,* flying towards Sydney in the waning afternoon, the happy home-comers made busy preparation, for it was not doubted that they would be in the arms of their friends before the day was done. They put away their sea-going clothes and put on clothes meeter for the meeting, their richest and loveliest, these poor brides of the grave. But the wind lost force, or there was a miscalculation, and before the Heads were sighted the darkness came on. It was said that ordinarily the captain would have made a safe offing and waited for the morning, but this was no ordinary occasion; for all about him were appealing faces, faces pathetic with disappointment. So his sympathy moved him to try the dangerous passage in the dark. He had entered the harbor seventeen times, and believed he knew the ground. So he steered straight for the false opening, mistaking it for the true one. He did not find out that he was wrong until it was too late. There was no saving the ship. The great sea swept her in and crushed her to splinters and rubbish upon the rocks at the base of the precipice. Not one of that fair and gracious company was ever seen alive again.

"The tale is told to every stranger who passes the spot, and it will continue to be told to all that come, for generations; but it will never grow old, custom cannot stale it, the heart-break that is in it can never perish out of it.

"There were two hundred persons in the ship, and but one survived the disaster. He was a sailor. A huge sea flung him up the face of the precipice and stretched him on a narrow shelf of rock midway between top and bottom, and there he lay all night. At any other time he would have lain there for the rest of his life, without chance of discovery; but the next morning the ghastly news spread through Sydney that the *Duncan Dunbar* had gone down in sight of home, and straightway the walls of the Heads were black with mourners; and one of these, stretching himself out over the precipice to spy out what might be seen below, discovered this miraculously-preserved relic of the wreck. Ropes were brought and the nearly impossible feat of rescuing the man was accomplished."

As we entered the harbor on this beautiful Lord's Day morning we thought of the story of heartache which is here set down. It was a long time ago, but it still stirs the human heart and will continue to do so as long as there are human hearts to be moved by sorrow and sadness.

We landed at noon and our long voyage was over, and when we spoke of it all, and had thanked the Lord for his goodness in caring for us, Maijee said: "Yes, but we have it all to go over again; and yet the Lord who has brought us in safety thus far on our way can take us safely home again."

The quiet October days have come, spring days they are on this half of the globe. And there is no mistake about it's being spring. Everybody tells us it is springtime and we are compelled to believe them. The seasons seem to have got mixed up and turned wrong end to. Here, when we at home

Entrance to Sydney Harbor.

have the frosts of coming winter, they have the warm sunshine, the richest profusion of flowers, the rose queen of
them all, the early spring vegetables and the mating time for
birds and all that tells one that springtime has come. Outside
our door come the flower and fruit sellers calling to would-be
purchasers, in the lingo of the street peddler, impossible of
translation and unprintable.

The windows of our rooms at Dawes Point overlook the
beautiful harbor with its numerous inlets and the Circular
Quay, where great ships from all parts of the world find safe
mooring and from which ferry boats leave every few minutes,
day and night, carrying passengers from the city of Sydney
to and from the suburban homes which crown hilltop and
ridge for miles on both sides of the harbor. There are fifteen
ferry boat companies and the boats, brilliantly illuminated at
night by electricity, glide noiselessly through the water, illuminating the bay and making a beautiful sight. Often a
dozen of these illuminated boats are in sight at the same time.

The harbor is " the darling of Sydney and the wonder of
the world." The Sydneyite, first of all, asks the stranger but
one question and that is, " Have you seen the harbor? " Here
he rests his case. If you have seen the harbor you have looked
upon the finest bit of sparkling blue water and natural scenery,
beautified by man, in the world. Sydney, he will tell you, is
a fine city and good enough in its way; New South Wales is
the best province in Australia, and with her natural resources
is destined to become a great state, but the harbor stands first
of all in the estimation of the patriotic Sydneyite. And in
part his pride is excusable. As your boat makes its way
through the crooks and turns of this marvelous waterway,
at places two miles wide, you are filled with admiration and
delight and are quite willing to accord the palm to Sydney
harbor.

Circular Quay, Sydney Harbor.

Mr. Clemens has this to say about the harbor: "It would be beautiful without Sydney, but not above half as beautiful as it now is with Sydney added. It is shaped somewhat like an oak leaf—a roomy sheet of lovely blue water, with narrow offshoots of water running up into the country on both sides with long fingers of land, high wooden ridges with sides shaped like graves. Handsome villas are perched here and there on these ridges, snuggling among the foliage, and one catches glimpses of them as the ship swims by toward the city. The city clothes a cluster of hills and a ruffle of neighboring ridges with its undulating masses of masonry, and out of these masses spring towers and spires and other architectural dignities and grandeurs that break the flowing lines and give picturesqueness to the general effect. The narrow inlets which I have mentioned go wandering out into the land everywhere and hiding themselves in it, and pleasure launches are always exploring them with picnic parties on board. It is said by trustworthy people that if you explore them all you will find that you have covered seven hundred miles of water passage."

Mr. Anthony Trollope finds it impossible to describe the beauties of the place and says: "I despair of being able to convey to any reader my own idea of the beauty of Sydney harbor. I have seen nothing equal to it in the way of landlocked scenery—nothing second to it. The sea runs up in various bays or coves, indenting the land all around the city, so as to give a thousand different aspects to the water; and not of water, broad, unbroken, and unrelieved, but of water with jutting corners of land beyond it, and then again of water, and then again of land." And so one might quote from hundreds of authors who have described the harbor of Port Jackson, as it originally was called, and yet the half would remain untold.

Neutral Bay, Sydney Harbor.

The commonwealth of Australia has a population of a trifle less than four million, and one-fourth of these dwell in two of its largest cities, Sydney and Melbourne, each with a half million souls. The people have the energy, enterprise and push so characteristic of the Chicagoans that it seems as if a part of the Queen City of the Lakes had been set down at the side of Sydney harbor. They are wide-awake, aggressive and up-to-date, and in some things are far ahead of our American cities. They have effectually solved the problem of rapid transit in their cities.

The tramways are owned and operated by the government, and there are none better in the world. The cars are roomy, clean, well ventilated, properly heated in cold weather and enough of them are run so that there is no strap hanging, bumper riding, or side rail clinging on the trolley cars in Sydney. Time tables are issued, the cars plainly marked, and a system of graded fares prevails. You pay two, four, six or eight cents for a ride, the amount being determined by the distance you ride, and the plan seems eminently fair. If one wants to ride say two miles he pays two cents, and double that amount for twice the distance. It cannot be considered a square deal to charge the man who rides half a dozen blocks as much as the one who rides five miles.

The street railways are well managed and produce a handsome revenue to the municipality even at the minimum of a two-cent fare. The cars are models of comfort. You enter the compartments at the sides through glass doors hung on ball rollers which open and close at the slightest touch. At both ends of the cars are compartments for smokers. These are cut off with a glass partition so that the smoke is enjoyed only by the smoker. The cars are run on a fast schedule of time and the people of Sydney have learned to give the tram car the right of way. If the city of Chicago is in earnest as to municipal ownership of her city railways it might be well for the authorities to appoint a commission to go out to Australia and study the system inaugurated there. The commonwealth gave us the Australian ballot and is also able to give us lessons in rapid transit and city ownership of street railways.

Sydney has many fine public buildings, splendid cathe-

Moonlight Scene, Sydney Harbor.

drals and churches and beautiful parks and gardens. The post-office building is a fine structure and makes an imposing appearance. Sydney is a beautiful city and to me it had much that was interesting. I found the public library one among the best arranged and best supplied with books, magazines and papers that I had found in any city of its size. A hundred years ago a poet wrote this prophecy concerning Sydney which was then in its infancy:

"There shall broad streets their stately walls extend
The circus widen, and the crescent bend;
There, ray'd from cities o'er the cultured land,
Shall bright canals and solid roads expand;
There the proud arch, colossus-like, bestride
Yon glittering stream, and bound the chafing tide,
Embellished villas crown the landscape scene,
Farms wave with gold, and orchards blush between,
There shall tall spires and dome-cap't towers ascend,
And piers and quays their mossy structures blend;
While with each breeze approaching vessels glide,
And northern treasures dance on every tide."

St. Mary's Cathedral, Sydney.

In 1770 Captain Cook sailed by the great sea wall, rising perpendicularly to a height of over three hundred feet, without observing that there was an opening leading into a great harbor. A few miles farther on he cast anchor in Botany Bay, so named by Joseph Banks, the botanist of the expedition, because of the rich and varied flora of the place. Thus the poetical name became associated with all penal colonies and with the worst of the criminal classes. The British flag was raised and the country claimed, by right of discovery, as a province of Great Britain. Of course the consent of the aborigines was neither asked for nor wanted. In those days no one gave a thought to the rights of the natives of a newly discovered country. Might made right and the black fellows of New South Wales did not have a single right which the white usurpers were bound to respect. It was a goodly country with great possibilities before it, the natives were weak and the whites strong, and it was only another illustration of the strong coveting and taking from the weak their belongings and then killing them off in the bargain.

Following Captain Cook's important discovery the British government determined to establish a penal colony in this far-away part of the world. They would thus be able to rid themselves of this most undesirable class of their population. Prior to this Great Britain had been sending her worst criminals to the American colonies, but the little misunderstanding of 1776 put an end to the business. The door being closed in America, she found what was wanted in Australia, and the discovery of New South Wales seemed to be a very timely one for the purposes of the government.

In 1777 Captain Phillip was appointed governor of the new land and was sent out with a fleet of six transports and three supply and store ships. On board these vessels were seven hundred and fifty-seven convicts, of whom one hundred and ninety-two were women, and two hundred and eight soldiers with forty of their wives and children. What a collection of humanity to form a colony and found a state! And yet from this colony of criminals and those who had them in charge grew the commonwealth of Australia.

Phillip with his fleet anchored in Botany Bay January 20, 1788, and proceeded to select a site for the new town. It was found that fresh water was deficient on the shores of the

Post Office Building, Sydney.

bay, and this led to an exploration resulting in the discovery
of Sydney harbor, into which flows a river of fresh water.
Here it was determined to land the convicts and found the
strange colony. The landing was effected on the 25th of
January, 1788. From this time on the natives were compelled
to give way before the whites who occupied their country.
It was not without some show of resistance that the usurpers
were permitted to land. They greeted the little fleet with cries
of ' Wara, wara," " Go away, go away." But the whites had
come, and come to stay. A canvas tent was erected for the
use of the governor and the site of the town marked out.
Says Collins, the historian, " The site chosen for this purpose
was at the head of the cove, near a run of fresh water which
stole silently through the very thick wood, the stillness of
which had then, for the first time since the creation, been interrupted by the rude sound of the laborer's axe, and the
downfall of its ancient inhabitants—a stillness and tranquillity
which, from that day, were to give place to the noise of labor,
the confusion of camps and towns, and the busy hum of its
new possessors."

Upon landing a roll call of the colonists showed that
the new population numbered one thousand and thirty. The
following list, which has become historical, was made at the
time and shows the property, both public and private, belonging to the colony:

2 bulls.	5 rabbits.
3 cows.	74 pigs.
1 horse.	18 turkeys.
3 mares.	29 geese.
3 colts.	35 ducks.
29 sheep.	210 chickens.
19 goats.	

In this list of public and personal property are named five
rabbits. One can easily imagine that these were the pets of
some of the colonists. Rabbits were scarce in Australia in

those days, and so far as is known these were the first ever seen there. Bunny found the country and climate suitable for his purpose, and he proceeded forthwith to multiply and replenish the earth. Since then Australia has spent millions to rid the land of the rabbit pest, but has most signally failed. They are in evidence here to-day by the billion. Poisons, traps, wire netting, contagious diseases, and all sorts of things were devised and resorted to in order to bring about the destruction of "Brer Rabbit," but he is in Australia to stay.

On our return voyage an old Australian told me how he set poison in wooden troughs around his place and the result. It was during a drought. He mixed the fatal stuff with water and filled the troughs and the thirsty rabbits came for miles to drink. The next day the man declared there were forty thousand dead rabbits in his neighborhood. The man appeared to be truthful, but somehow I doubted the statement. I said to him the next day, "Are you sure about that rabbit story you told me?" "Absolutely sure," he said. Then I wrote it down in my notebook and asked other Australians about it, and they said the rabbits were thick enough to give the story the semblance of truth. The man may not have estimated carefully, but if he did miss it by a few thousands, still there would be enough left to show that rabbits are plenty in the land.

And nowadays the cottontail is turning out to be a real wealth producer to Australia. Shiploads of frozen rabbits are sent to London every year, from where they are shipped to find a ready market in other parts of Europe. The local consumption is also large, and is rapidly increasing. We had rabbit on our table at least four times a week at Sydney and the meat was white, tender and as savory as any flesh I have ever eaten. Many people eat no other meat, and the rabbits are a Godsend to the aborigines and the poorer whites. The skins are shipped in large quantities to Europe and America and furnish the stock for the best hats in both countries. Many rabbit skins of the best quality, beautifully colored, go into the high-priced furs worn by fashionable ladies at home and abroad. It is now seriously proposed to improve the breed of the animals both for the table and for the production of a better class of fur. "The mutton and wool industries have long been regarded as among the best in New South Wales, but it is no exaggeration to say that there are districts in this state where the rabbits provide employment for more families and pay more revenue to the railways than do sheep and cattle; and these are not districts where the so-called pest has obtained sole control of the country. Altogether the potentialities of the rabbit as a wealth producer are being rapidly realized."*

*Editorial in local paper.

Aboriginals of New South Wales.

CHAPTER III.

Growth of the New Colony—Discovery of Gold—The Hard Life of the Convicts—Mark Twain Describes their Sufferings—"New South Wales Corps"—Evils of Monopoly—Spreading Intemperance—Farming and Wool Growing in New South Wales—Products of that Province.

THE new colony grew and flourished. The criminals were sent out in large numbers, so that up to 1840, when the penal colony was abolished, not less than ninety thousand convicts had been transported from England to swell the population of New South Wales. In addition to these, thousands of Englishmen seeking to better their fortune sought homes in the new colony. Later came the discovery of gold, and then a rush from all parts of the civilized world was made for the gold fields, and population increased by leaps and bounds.

The convicts were poorly fed, badly treated and severely punished for the slightest infraction of the rules. For the most part they wore chains to prevent their escape, and even this precaution did not prevent numbers from escaping and taking up their abode with the aborigines, and thus becoming the wild men of the bush. The gifted author of " Following the Equator " tells the old-time story so well that we have adapted it, giving him due credit at this place for what he has so well told.

English law was hard-hearted in those days. For trifling offenses which in our day would be punished by a small fine or a few days' imprisonment, men, women and boys were sent to this other end of the world to serve terms of seven to fourteen years, and for serious crimes they were transported for life. Children were sent to the penal colonies for seven years for stealing a rabbit.

When I was in London twenty-three years ago there was a new penalty in force for diminishing garroting and wife-beating—twenty-five lashes on the bare back with the cat-o'-nine-tails. It was said that this terrible punishment was able to bring the stubbornest ruffians to terms; and that no man had been found with grit enough to keep his emotions to himself beyond the ninth blow; as a rule the man shrieked earlier. That penalty had a great and wholesome effect upon garroters and wife-beaters; but humane modern London could not endure it; it got its law rescinded. Many a bruised and battered English wife has since had occasion to deplore that cruel achievement of sentimental humanity.

Twenty-five lashes! In Australia and Tasmania they gave a convict fifty for almost any little offense; and sometimes a brutal officer would add another and another fifty, and so on, as long as the sufferer could endure the torture and live. In Tasmania I read the entry, in an old manuscript official record, of a case where a convict was given three hundred lashes for stealing some silver spoons. And men got more than that sometimes. Who handled the cat? Often it was another convict; sometimes it was the culprit's dearest comrade, and he had to lay on with all his might, otherwise he would get a flogging himself for his mercy—for he was under watch—and yet do his friend no good: the friend would be attended to by another hand and suffer no lack in the matter of full punishment.

The convict life in Tasmania was so unendurable, and suicide so difficult to accomplish, that once or twice despairing men got together and drew straws to determine which of them should kill another of the group—this murder to secure death to the perpetrator and the witnesses to it by the hands of the hangman.

The incidents above quoted are mere hints, mere suggestions of what convict life was like—they are but a couple of details tossed into view out of a shoreless sea of such; or to change the figure, they are a pair of flaming steeples photographed from a point which hides from sight the burning city which stretches away from their base on every hand.

Some of the convicts—indeed, a good many of them—were very bad people, even for that day, but most of them were not noticeably worse than the average of the people they left behind them at home. We must believe this; we cannot avoid it. We are obliged to believe that a nation that could look on, unmoved, and see starving or freezing women hanged for stealing twenty-six cents' worth of bacon or rags, and boys snatched from their mothers, and men from their families, and sent to the other side of the world for a long term of years for similar trifling offenses, was not a nation to whom the term "civilized" could in any large way be applied. And we must also believe that a nation that knew, during more than forty years, what was happening to those exiles, and was still content with it, was not advancing in any showy way toward a higher grade of civilization.

If we look into the character and conduct of officers and gentlemen who had charge of the convicts and attended to their backs and stomachs, we must grant again that as between the convict and his masters, and between both and the nation at home, there was quite a noticeable monotony of sameness.

Four years had gone by, and many convicts had come. Respectable settlers were beginning to arrive. These two classes of colonists had to be protected, in case of trouble among themselves or with the natives. It is proper to mention the natives, though they could hardly count, they were so scarce. At a time when they had not yet begun to be much disturbed—not as yet being in the way—it was estimated that in New South Wales there was but one native to forty-five thousand acres of territory.

People had to be protected. Officers of the regular army did not want this service—away off there where neither honor nor distinction was to be gained. So England recruited and officered a kind of a militia force of one thousand uniformed civilians called the " New South Wales Corps " and shipped it. This was the worst blow of all. The colony fairly staggered under it. The corps was an object lesson of the moral condition of England outside the jails. The colonists trembled. It was feared that next there would be an importation of the nobility. In those early days the colony was non-supporting. All the necessaries of life—food, clothing, and all— were sent out from England, and kept in government storehouses, and given to the convicts and sold to settlers—sold at a trifling advance upon cost. The corps saw its opportunity. Its officers went into commerce in a most lawless way. They went to importing rum, and also to manufacturing it in private stills, in defiance of the government's commands and protests. They leagued themselves together and ruled the market; they boycotted the government and other dealers; they established a close monopoly and kept it strictly in their own hands. When a vessel arrived with spirits, they allowed nobody to buy but themselves; and they forced the owners to sell to them at a price named by themselves—and it was always low enough. They bought rum at an average of two dollars a gallon and sold it at an average of ten. They *made rum the currency of the country*—for there was little or no money—and they maintained their devastating hold and kept the colony under their heel for eighteen or twenty years before they were finally conquered and routed by the government.

Meantime they had spread intemperance everywhere. And they had squeezed farm after farm out of the settlers'

Natives Wrestling.

hands for rum, and thus had bountifully enriched themselves. When a farmer was caught in the last agonies of thirst they took advantage of him and sweated him for a drink. In one instance they sold a man a gallon of rum worth two dollars for a piece of property which was sold some years later for a hundred thousand dollars.

When the country was about twenty years old it was discovered that the land was specially adapted for wool culture. Prosperity followed, commerce with the world began, by and by rich mines of the noble metals were opened, immigrants flowed in, and capital likewise. The result is the great and wealthy and enlightened commonwealth of New South Wales.

It is a country that is rich in mines, wool ranches, trams, railways, steamship lines, schools, newspapers, botanical gardens, art galleries, libraries, museums, hospitals, learned societies; it is the hospitable home of every species of culture and of every species of material enterprise, and there is a church at every man's door and a race track over the way.*

A new century has come and since the days of which Mr. Clemens wrote great changes have been wrought in all the world. Sixty-five years ago New South Wales ceased to be a penal colony. Many of the convicts, who had been sent out for a short term of years, never returned to England. At heart they were not bad men, and when their terms of penal service ended they found homes in the new colony and became honest men and useful citizens, and their descendants are among the best in Australia to-day. Some of them engaged in farming, others in sheep raising, and made fortunes in their ventures. So the old penal days have passed away, leaving only a memory as of an unpleasant nightmare of things that were. Nowadays one finds no trace of the old conditions, and you would have to travel far to find a more

*"Following the Equator," Mark Twain, pp. 119-124.

hospitable, enterprising, law-abiding people than those who welcome you to Australia to-day.

Farming in Australia is not carried on to a very large extent. Only in New South Wales and Victoria is there sufficient rainfall to assure a crop of corn. A very small portion of the country is covered by mountains and thus rendered uncultivable. But the absence of mountains is a loss to the country, for it is no doubt responsible for the light rainfalls in a very large portion of the continent and also for the destructive hot winds. In the western half of Australia the rainfall is too scanty to produce crops save at a few favored places along the coast. The population of the country is to be found fringing the coast. The interior is as our own western plains were fifty years ago, a great expanse of pasture lands. And it is not likely that it will ever be otherwise. A lack of water in many parts will render farming impossible. In those parts where a sufficient amount of rainfall is had to insure crops, wheat, corn, barley, oats, potatoes, hay, and other crops are successfully raised.

The wool industry is by far the greatest source of wealth known to the inhabitants of Australia. She has more than twice as many sheep as the United States, and the colony of New South Wales at one time, 1891, outranked us, having sixty-two million head of the wool producers, or three-fifths of the total of Australia. There were at that time one hundred and six million sheep in the country.

The vast pasture fields, the climate and the peculiarities of the soil make Australia, with a single drawback, the greatest wool-producing country in the world. The one drawback is the drouths which at times become so severe that the pastures dry up and millions of sheep die for want of food and water. A few years ago a drought occurred resulting in a very large decrease in the number of the sheep in the country. Since then the number has been increasing slowly, and the

Aboriginal Boys.

sheepmen have been carefully improving the breed of sheep. They are also coming to better understand conditions of climate and are giving better care to their flocks. In many places artesian water has been found and wells are being bored, and when the droughts come they will be better prepared to meet them. The improvement in the quality of the stock is shown by the increase, in the annual clip, from four pounds per head to six.

The discovery and application of cold storage has opened up a profitable market for Australian mutton in Europe. The better grade of sheep makes it possible for the sheepmen to put on the market the very finest quality of mutton. The carcasses are slightly frozen and are then placed in cold storage rooms especially prepared on board ship and arrive in London in prime condition. The meat is all the better for the treatment it receives, and some of the best mutton found on English tables comes from New South Wales. The possibilities of wool-producing in the Southern Continent are limited only by the amount the world can use. With improved breeds of sheep, with better methods of caring for the animals, with artesian wells and a better water supply, Australia can easily outstrip all other countries in this industry and produce the wool and mutton supply of the world.

New South Wales is the favored state of Australia, agriculturally. The province has an area of three hundred and ten thousand square miles, or nearly two hundred million acres. If in some way ten inches could be added to the annual average rainfall it would be the most favored agricultural district in the world. As it is, large crops are raised annually and the country is prosperous. The following table, compiled from the latest statistics, gives a fair idea of what is being done by the farmer and stock raiser of the province:

Wheat, ...14,809,000 bushels
Oats, ...687,000 bushels
Barley, ...103,000 bushels
Corn, ...3,845,000 bushels
Potatoes, ...39,000 tons
Butter, ...39,931,000 pounds
Cheese, ...3,839,000 pounds
Wool, ...310,075,000 pounds
Oranges, ...604,500 cases
Sheep, ...41,857,000 head
Horses, ...486,700 head
Cattle, ...2,047,500 head
Hogs, ...265,700 head
Honey, ...2,259,000 pounds

From the foregoing array of figures it will be seen that there are great possibilities in New South Wales. When all the land that will produce crops is farmed, the increase in the yield of grain will be very great. Australia needs and should have her farming population increased many fold. Smaller farms and better farming, smaller herds and better attention given to them, will increase the wealth of the country very rapidly. At all the ports at which our ship cast anchor she discharged thousands of cases of Nestle's condensed milk. I said to an Australian gentleman, " It seems strange indeed that you must import milk into a country where you have millions of acres of the best pasture land lying untouched." " Yes," was the reply, " we ought to be exporting instead of importing milk, and would be were it not for our immigration laws which shut out many good people who would take up and improve our land."

When men with little means are encouraged to settle in the country, when better methods of farming are introduced, when the great tracts of fertile land now lying waste are brought up to the highest state of cultivation, Australia will be able to support and make prosperous and happy thirty million people.

CHAPTER IV.

Double Seasons in 1905—The American Flag and American Shipping—A Great Navy Without a Merchant Marine—Wastefulness of Building Great Ships for War—The Aboriginals of Australia—An Interesting People—Description by a Local Writer—A Mass of Contradictions—Babies—Religious Customs—Circumcision and Sub-incision—Betrothal and Marriage —Unfaithfulness to Marriage Vows Punishable with Death.

NOVEMBER has come, and with it more of the glad springtime of the year. This morning I sat on the veranda overlooking the blue waters of the beautiful bay and wrote until I was driven in by a warm spring shower. In the sun it is as hot here now as it is at Elgin in midsummer. And it gets warm here in December. One man told me that the mercury sometimes rises to 106 in the shade. But now we are in the midst of spring. The spring birds, the spring hats, the spring dresses, white and fluffy, and the spring poets are in the land.

Here I am reminded of a peculiar experience that has come to us in this year of 1905. We have two winters and two springs. India furnished rather a weak sample of winter in January and February, with a mere touch of ice in the Baroda district. She made a much better showing of spring-time in March and April. Then came June, and we found ourselves enjoying midwinter, with ice and snow and sleet, in South Africa. It was a real winter and there was no mistaking it. And now we are having our second spring in Australia, thirty-eight degrees south of the equator. And it is a real, genuine spring weather even if it does come to us in November. This is crowding seasons enough into one year to suit anyone unless he be very hard to please.

The other day the good ship *Sierra,* from San Francisco, came into the harbor flying the American flag and anchored and moored in full sight of our windows. She was twenty-three days out from her starting point and brought us a heavy mail from home. We are far enough around the world now to receive our letters direct from the United States. It gave me a thrill of joy to see Old Glory waving in the air again. It's a heartsome sight and one not often seen in foreign lands and waters. There also came a feeling of sadness that one sees the American flag so rarely on the shipping of the world. Within the year we have voyaged more than twenty-five thousand miles on the high seas and this is but the second time in all the journey that we have seen the stars and stripes floating from the masthead of a ship. With a population approximating a hundred million, with unlimited resources and wealth piled upon wealth, with a coast line extending over thousands of miles, supplying the world with nearly two billion dollars' worth of our home products annually, we are practically without a merchant marine. Our ships are so rarely seen in foreign ports that the coming of one is a matter of surprise. In this respect even little Japan, the Giant of the Pacific, is far ahead of us.

For the last twenty-five years we have been spending money, and worse than wasting it, in building great steel-armored warships which before another quarter of a century shall roll around will be obsolete and ready for the iron scrap heap. If but half the money spent on these machines, built for the destruction of human life, had been spent in building up a merchant marine for the peaceable and helpful pursuit of carrying the world's trade, the American traveler's eye would be gladdened by the stars and stripes on every sea and in every port on the face of the earth. Ship subsidy bills have been defeated for political reasons while millions are voted at each session of congress for more warships. President Roose-

Ferry Boats and Shipping, Milsori's Point, Sydney Harbor.

velt could use his great influence to no better purpose than to encourage the building of ships to carry the products of our own country across the seas. Trade follows the flag and ships must be built to carry the flag as well as the trade.

The aborigines of Australia are an interesting study. They are set down by some authorities as the lowest of the human race, and as having been found without the instinct for worship common to all the peoples of the world. But a more careful study of the natives of the southern continent has shown that the earlier estimate placed on the black fellows, as they are called, was wrong.

A local authority refers to the aborigines as a very low rank of the human race, both in form, feature and in general intelligence. In the face, almost without exception, the nose may be described as flat and broad, the forehead receding, the lower portion of which projects in a most pronounced manner, giving the expression a constant frown. As might be expected they are a hairy people. The hair is plentiful, not only on the head, but on the whole body, especially the chest and back; most of the men have beards, whiskers and mustaches, and any beardless member of the tribe is looked upon with contempt by his comrades.

The aboriginal population of New South Wales has now dwindled to about 6,000, including half-bloods. Since the advent of civilization, the race has gradually been dying out, despite a certain amount of protection and an annual distribution of clothing, blankets, etc., afforded by the government. In many places in the more outlying portions of Australia the blacks still go about almost naked at all periods of the year, although the seasons experience a considerably greater change than they do in the coastal districts. The natural food of the natives consists of the marsupials for animal food, with yams and the many indigenous berries for vegetable diet; snakes, birds, eggs, lizards, etc., are also con-

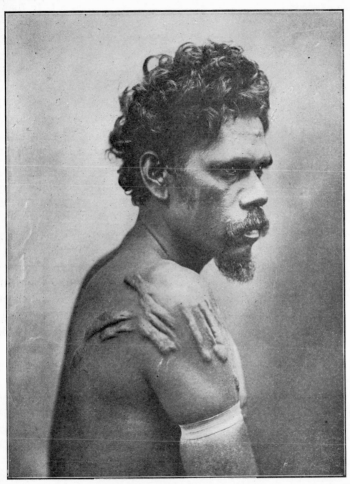

Aboriginal with Scarred Arm.

sumed. No form of agriculture whatever is known among the blacks, and no flocks or herds are kept. Fish are of course used plentifully, and the coastal and river tribes are thoroughly expert in spearing them in the shallows.

Cannibalism was at one time a frequent occurrence, but is now never heard of, although it is still believed to exist in isolated instances in the interior. The weapons used are principally the spear, stone-headed tomahawk, heavy wooden clubs and the boomerang, which latter is peculiar to the Australian native. The boomerang is a flat piece of hard-wood, generally from two to three feet long, bent in the middle at an obtuse angle. When thrown with skill it will change its course in the air, and describing almost a complete circle, return, revolving also on its own axis, to the thrower's feet. A bird may be brought down, or a serious wound inflicted on an enemy, with this weapon at a considerable distance.

Periodical tribal meetings are held which take the form of what is known as " corrobboree ; " at nighttime, during one of these meetings, which generally last from two days to a week, grotesque dancing round huge fires is indulged in by the men, who paint themselves over the face, head and body with light-colored clays, the women meanwhile supplying the music, such as it is, with a monotonous chant in chorus and by beating sticks of different thickness together. During the day, hunting, spear, and boomerang throwing competitions are entered into with as much vim as the naturally lazy native can muster, and should game be plentiful, feasts are partaken of until the whole tribe are thoroughly gorged.*

Here is sentimental gush over the aborigines. The writer evidently is not noted for his sympathy for the blacks, but there are others who find in them many noble characteristics. After reading much that has been written on the subject I find

---

*Dymock's " Guide to Sydney."

myself in a state of uncertainty as to these strange people. Mr. Clemens makes the following list of what they are and are not: " In his history, as preserved by the white man, he is everything—everything that a human being can be. He is a coward—there are a thousand facts to prove it. He is brave —there are a thousand facts to prove it. He is treacherous— oh, beyond imagination! He is faithful, loyal, true—the white man's records supply you with a harvest of instances of it that are noble, worshipful, and pathetically beautiful. He kills the starving stranger who comes begging for food and shelter —there is proof of it. He succors, and feeds, and guides to safety to-day the lost stranger who fired on him only yester-day—there is proof of it. He takes his reluctant bride by force, he courts her with a club, then loves her faithfully through a long life—it is of record. He gathers to himself another wife by the same process, beats and bangs her as a daily diversion, and by and by lays down his life in defending her from outside harm—it is of record. He will face a hundred hostiles to rescue one of his children, and will kill another of his children because the family is large enough without it. He is a sociable animal, yet turns aside and hides behind his shield when his mother-in-law goes by. He is childishly afraid of ghosts and other trivialities that menace his soul, but dread of physical pain is a weakness which he is not acquainted with. He knows all the great constellations, and has names for them; he has symbol writing by means of which he can convey messages far and wide among the tribes, he has a correct eye for form and expression, and draws a good picture; he can track a fugitive by delicate traces which the white man's eye cannot discern and by methods which the finest white intelligence cannot master; he makes a missile which science itself cannot duplicate without a model—if with it; a missile whose secret baffled and defeated the searchings and theorizings of the white mathematicians for seventy years ·

and by an art all his own he performs miracles with it which the white man cannot approach untaught nor parallel after teaching. Within certain limits this savage's intellect is the alertest and brightest known to history or tradition; and yet the poor creature was never able to invent a counting system that would reach above five, nor a vessel that he could boil water in."

Here you have the native as he appears from the records, and under certain conditions all these things are true of him. Recently a more careful and extended study of the aboriginals has been made. Men have gone among them where they have not come under the influence of modern civilization and have given us many interesting facts concerning these remarkable people. "The Northern Tribes of Australia," a work by Spencer and Gillen, supplementing an earlier work by the same authors, the "Native Tribes of Central Australia," gives a vast amount of information concerning the natives. They spent a year among the northern tribes and their books are the latest and best on the subject. The writer is indebted to these excellent works for part of the information concerning the aborigines of Australia.

At birth the native child is red and copper colored, but in the course of a few days it darkens, and in a short time assumes the chocolate color of the adult. In the southern tribes the color of the women is slightly lighter than that of the men, but in the north there is a more general sameness of color. The only clothing worn by the women is an apron made of strings twined together which hang down from a string passing around the waist. The men wear even less clothing than the women, and in the north are entirely naked. It is a strange thing that the natives have never learned to use the fur of the marsupials, which is plentiful in Australia, especially the kangaroo and the opossum, to protect themselves

One of Australia's Little Ones.

from the cold of winter. Often the mercury falls below the freezing point and yet they wear no clothing.

Some of the religious practices of the natives of Australia remind one of the Jewish religion of the olden time. One cannot help but wonder whether at some time, in the remote past, some wandering Jewish teacher did not find his way to this far-away end of the earth and influence these people in their religious beliefs. The law of blood revenge, and eye for an eye and tooth for a tooth, he that sheddeth blood shall have his blood shed, is found among the aborigines. If a man of one tribe kills one of another, reprisals are made and the difficulty can be settled only by the killing of some one of the same tribe who did the killing in the first place. It matters not whether the individual aggressor is slain or not, so long as one of his tribe pays the penalty. Blood revenge was so strongly imbedded in the national life of the ancient Israelites that cities of refuge were founded to which the slayer might flee and find safety until legal investigation determined whether the slaying was accidental or otherwise. The Australians have no city of refuge and the law of blood revenge keeps up a continual warring among the wild tribes.

Circumcision and incision are practiced among the aborigines. These rites are performed when the boys are initiated into the secrets and mysteries of manhood and its religious ceremonies. This occurs at about the age of fourteen, and is an important event in the life of the youth. He now leaves the camp of the women and joins that of the men, he goes to war and assumes the duties of manhood. A circle is formed and the boys to be initiated enter one by one. " The old men put armlets of kangaroo skin upon their arms, a fillet round their heads, and a band around the waist crossed back and front, and they pass out as accepted braves. But before and after the rite there are ordeals to be undergone, they must live apart for a time in the bush, abstaining from food, and

must not look upon a woman." During this period of in-
itiation the rite of circumcision is performed.

Peculiar customs prevail among the natives as to be-

Bora Ceremony.

trothal and marriage. These vary among different tribes, but
a similarity is to be seen among them all. In many of the
tribes the woman is given away by the father. He tells the
man to whom he has determined to give his daughter that

when the girl has grown to womanhood he can take her as his wife. At the same time he places the girl's hand in the hand of her future husband. The proposed son-in-law then presents the father with boomerangs, spears, tomahawks and

Type of Aboriginal.

food, and after this they do not look at one another. At intervals the bridegroom makes more presents of boomerangs, etc., always giving them to his future wife and telling her to take them to her father. The girl makes out of her own hair a girdle which the youth receives at her hands and wears around his waist when he is fully entitled to take his place among the men of his tribe.

In the marriage and betrothal among these people one recognizes the " lobolo " referred to as existing among the negroes of South Africa, the purchase of wives in North Africa and the old Bible custom of giving presents as in the case of Isaac and Rebecca.

When marriage is proposed by men the way is not so smooth, and very often a deadly conflict takes place before the question is decided. The gifted author of " My Australian Girlhood " gives the story as it came to her from a native woman who had long been a member of the household: " There did not seem to be a great deal of sentiment about the way in which the young braves conducted their courtship, it being the custom for a young man in search of a wife to walk up to a camp where, among her kindred, squatted some girl who had taken his fancy, and to throw his boomerang into the midst of the family circle. Then, if it were picked up and returned to him he had to fight a rival for the possession of the fair one, who was delivered over to the best man ; but if the boomerang were allowed to lie he might step in and claim his bride without further preliminaries. No doubt, however, there had been ogling and sighing, and perhaps tremors, fears, and heart burnings before this culminating point was reached. It is only in the setting, after all, that the eternal drama alters. The main motive is the same."

The social and marriage relations among the aborigines are full of intricacies and it would require a volume to enter into details. Here we can merely glance at them in passing. What is known as group marriage is practiced among many if not all of the tribes. In this peculiar relation the wives and husbands of the so-called group, under certain conditions, are the wives and husbands of the entire group. And inside the group the law of marriage is held inviolate and infidelity to the marriage vow with one outside the group is punished with death as was the sin of adultery under the law of Moses. The same native woman to whom reference is made in the preceding paragraph would relate how she had seen an unfaithful wife speared to death in the camp by her husband, the elders applauding, and another frail woman taken out by her brother and beaten with a nulla nulla,—fighting club,—till she was almost dead, while the injured husband, who had a tender heart, sat by and wept at her shrieks, but dared not interfere. There is nothing in the group marriage relation approaching polygamy. It is simply a question of a certain group of men and women who may lawfully sustain marital relations to each other. There is nothing abnormal about it, and in all probability this system which is called group marriage, serving as it does to bind together, more or less closely, groups of individuals who are mutually interested in one another's welfare, has been one of the strongest and most powerful agents in the early stages of the upward development of the human race.

CHAPTER V.

Death and Burial—Mourning and Cutting the Flesh—The Tree
Graves—Burial of the Bones—Eating Certain Kinds of Flesh
Prohibited—The Nose Bone—Aboriginal's Ability to Suffer
Great Pain without Murmuring—Amputating a Leg with
Fire—The Trackers.

DEATH and burial among the natives of Australia are
attended with much mourning, great lamentations and horrible
lacerations of the body. Spencer and Gillen give a graphic
account of a scene witnessed in the Warramunga tribe. I
abridge it somewhat to serve the purpose of this volume.

Late one afternoon we were startled by a sudden, loud,
piercing wail in the direction of the men's camp. Every one
knew that the end of some one was near at hand. With one
accord all the men ran toward the camp as hard as they
could, most of them howling at the same time. Between us
and the camp lay a deep creek, and on the banks of this men
were sitting with heads bowed between their knees, weeping
and moaning. Crossing the creek we found that, as usual,
the men's camp had been pulled to pieces. Some of the women
who had come from all directions, were lying prostrate on
the body, while others were standing or kneeling around,
digging the sharp ends of yam-sticks into the crown of their
heads, from which the blood streamed down over their faces,
while all the time they kept up a loud, continuous wail.

Many of the men, rushing up to the spot, threw themselves
upon the body, from which the women arose when the men
approached, until in a few minutes we could see nothing but
a struggling mass of bodies all mixed together. Others sat
together with their backs turned toward the dying man,

wailing loudly. In a minute or two another man of the same class rushed on the ground yelling and brandishing a stone knife. Reaching the camp, he suddenly gashed both thighs deeply, cutting right across the muscles, and, unable to stand, fell down into the middle of the group, from which he was dragged out after a time, while he lay exhausted on the ground. Gradually the struggling mass of dark bodies began to loosen, and then we could see that the man was not dead, though the terribly rough treatment to which he had been subjected had sealed his fate. The weeping and wailing still continued, and later the sun went down, leaving the camp in darkness. Later in the evening when the man actually died, the same scene was reënacted, only this time the wailing was still louder, and the women, apparently frantic with grief, were rushing about cutting themselves with stone knives and sharp-pointed sticks and striking each other with fighting clubs, no one attempting to ward off a blow. Then, without more than an hour's delay, a small torchlight procession started off across the plain to a belt of timber a mile away, where the body was left on a platform built of boughs in a low gum tree.

Next morning there was not the sign of a habitation on the side of the creek where the man had died. The only trace left was a small heap of earth piled up on the actual spot where the death had occurred. The cause of this removal was because no one was anxious to meet the spirit of the dead man which was believed to be hovering about the spot, or that of the man who had brought about the man's death by evil magic. These people do not regard death as coming from natural causes, but associate it with the evil influence of some enemy.

Now there came more laceration of the bodies, cutting the scalps of the nearest relatives of the man and searing the wound with a red-hot fire stick, the division of the dead man's

Aboriginal with Scarred Breast and Arms, from
Cuts made when Mourning.

property, the visit to the place where the man died, a visit to
the tree grave where they march around and around the tree,
singing and mourning loudly, then another and another visit
to ascertain if possible by some signs the murderer of the
dead man. Often the various mourning ceremonies are kept up
for an entire year. Later the bones are taken down and
buried in an ant hill with the exception of the arm bone which

Man with Lacerated Thigh.

is buried at another place with elaborate ceremonies and with
more wailing and cuttings of the flesh.

Laws, or rather customs, regulating what kinds of flesh
shall and shall not be eaten as well as those prohibiting the
eating of certain kinds of flesh at certain seasons are found
among the aborigines and remind one of the prohibitions
found in Leviticus. Mrs. Campbell tells of a legend, held as
true by the blacks, in which it is related how a young girl
went out with her father to hunt and ate the flesh of the

iguana, a large lizard eaten by the natives, in a forbidden season; whereupon the Great Spirit was angry and a storm arose and frightened the girl so that she at once confessed her crime. The Great Spirit was not appeased by her confession, for while she was making it the earth toppled over

Tree Grave.

and buried her, and the mountain which covered the place is called Murran, the native name for iguana, and may be seen unto this day.

Kindling fire is done very much as in South Africa. There are two distinct methods in common use. The one is by rubbing a piece of hard wood very rapidly, as if sawing, over a softer piece, and the other is by twirling one stick on another. In the first method two men sit on the ground and hold an old wooden shield, or other piece of very dry wood, between them with their feet. Then taking hold of a spear thrower, one at each end, they draw it back and forth with great rapidity. Very soon a groove is worn into the dry wood, and the dust-like powder resulting from the friction soon begins to smoulder and smoke, and by carefully blowing it the tinder in which it has been placed ignites and a flame is produced.

The other method is more commonly used. In practice a hard and soft stick are required. At one end the hardwood stick is rounded off to about an inch in diameter and is about two feet in length. This is held upright between the palms of the hands, and pressed down firmly on the horizontal piece of wood held firmly in place by the feet of the operator. At the one side of this a notch has been previously cut at the spot where the upright stick is to be twirled to allow the smoulder-ing powder to fall down among the dry tinder so placed as to receive it. Usually two men sitting opposite each other take part in the operation. The object is to twirl the upright stick continuously and so rapidly as to produce the smoulder-ing powder. This result is usually attained in a minute or two at most. The powder collects in the hole and falls through the notch into the tinder when it is carefully blown into a flame. The process is simple enough to look at, but not so easy to accomplish. A trial of this may be made and the skeptical will soon be convinced that producing fire in this way requires patience and skill. Usually a little fine sand is dropped into the hole in the horizontal stick to increase friction.

A tradition common among the people, and held by many tribes, tells how fire was first made. In ancient times two brothers were wandering over the country and the younger said to the elder, "How shall we make fire? Shall we twirl two sticks together?" But the elder brother said, "No, but

Kindling Fire.

we will rub two sticks together." They did so and fire was made, for up to that time they had none. The younger brother carried the great fire stick, but not being used to fire burned his hands badly.

Reference has already been made to dress or rather lack of dress among the native tribes of Australia. One of the customs peculiar to them is that of boring a hole through the septum,—the partition between the nostrils,—of the nose, through which a nose bone or stick, decorated with figures, is thrust and worn as an ornament. It must be much more inconvenient to wear than the nose rings of India. It is disgusting enough in appearance and must cause the wearer no little trouble. But it's the fashion in the swell society in the bush, and it is presumed that like the people in more civilized countries the aborigines feel that one might as well be out of the world as to be out of the fashion.

All savages are able to bear great physical pain without flinching, but the native Australian is a past master in this. Upon the death of a husband the women lacerate their bodies in a most cruel manner and the men submit to the same kind of torture uncomplainingly. The Rev. Dr. Willotson, of Melbourne, a surgeon as well as a minister, records several remarkable cases that came under his observation. I give them here somewhat abridged. He was traveling across the country, and, after camping for the night and cooking and eating his supper, noticed one of his native guides, who had not spoken to him of his injury, collect the hot coals of the fire, and deliberately place his right foot in the glowing mass for a moment, then withdrawing it suddenly he stamped the ground, uttering a long-drawn guttural sound of mingled pain and satisfaction. He repeated the operation several times. Upon being asked the meaning of all this his reply was, " Me carpenter-make 'em " (I am mending my foot). He then showed his charred great toe, the nail of which had been torn off by a tea tree stump, in which it had been caught during the journey, the pain of which he had borne with stoical indifference until the evening when he proceeded to cauterize it in this primitive manner.

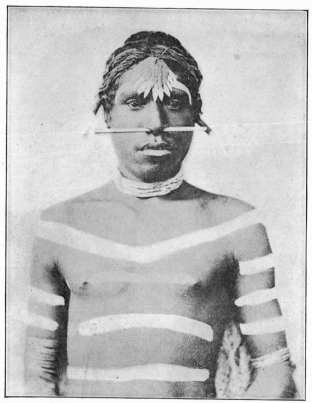

The Nose Bone. Up to the Latest Fashion. Nose Bone, Necktie, Armlets, Painted Body and All.

He also tells of a native applying to him to extract the wooden barb of a spear which, during a fight in the bush four months previously, had been thrust into his chest by his enemy, just missing the heart. He had cut the spear off, leaving the barbed head in his body, which by muscular action gradually forced its way to the back and when the doctor examined the man he could feel a hard substance between the ribs below the left shoulder blade. A deep incision was made and with a pair of forceps the barb, made of hard wood about four inches long, was taken out. The wound made by the spear had healed, leaving only a small scar, and the man bore the operation, without an anæsthetic, without flinching.

A native once came to the doctor with but one leg, asking him to furnish him with a wooden limb. He had come nearly a hundred miles for the purpose. The doctor says: "I examined the limb which had been severed just below the knee, and found that it had been charred by fire, while about two inches of the calcined bone protruded through the flesh." This was removed with a saw and a presentable stump covered with flesh was made. The man was kept until the wound made by amputation was healed, after which he went away happy with a wooden leg. It seems the man had the bone of his leg below the knee pierced with a spear. Finding the wound serious, he had literally burned his limb until the lower part dropped off. The cauterization checked hemorrhage, and in a few days he was able to hobble to the station, with the aid of a long stick; and he spent a week on the road.

Other cases might be referred to, but these are sufficient to show how these people are able to endure great pain. In this respect their powers of endurance are far beyond those of the civilized peoples of the world. Sensitiveness to pain and highly strung nerves are the price we are compelled to pay for our civilization.

On our return voyage from Australia we had on board ship, as fellow-passengers, Mr. Anning and his daughter, of New South Wales, on their way to England. Mr. Anning had spent his life among the natives of Australia, and his daughter,

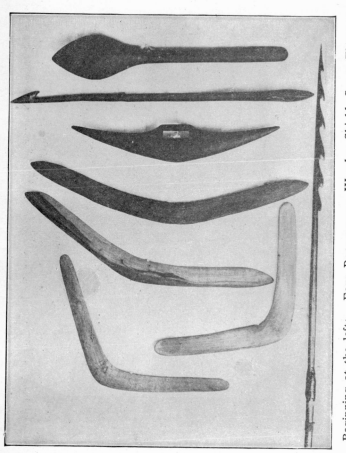

Beginning at the left: Four Boomerangs. Wooden Shield, Spear Thrower, Club; at bottom, Wooden Spear.

Group of Aboriginal Trackers.

a young lady of more than ordinary intelligence, was born there. They gave us much reliable information as to the country and the aborigines. As already noted, they are the most unerring trackers in the world. Mr. Anning said that without failure they could tell by the scratches on a tree made by an opossum whether the animal had gone in and remained or had come out again. Given the footprints of a white man who had been lost in the bush, the tracker would unerringly follow the trail until the lost was found.

The following incident will illustrate the ability of the native to follow a trail with the unerring instinct of a blood-hound. It was proposed to make a test of one of the best trackers among the natives. A white man was to drive a cow across the country, unseen by the black fellow, hide her and then the tracker was to find the animal. The native was shown the tracks of the animal and familiarized himself with them. He was then taken away and the owner drove the cow away. He was careful to drive her among other cattle where her tracks would be crossed and recrossed, and after reaching a point some two miles from his home he drove the animal back by a circuitous route and hid her away in one of his outbuildings. Then the tracker was brought on the scene and started on the outgoing trail. This he followed unhesitatingly and rapidly until he arrived at the building where the animal was hid away. Surely king " Billy " told the truth when he said, " White man's eye no like black man's. Black man see much better."

As soon as the children are old enough they run about, imitating their mother whom they accompany in the brush in her search for the daily food for her family. All the children learn the art of tracking at a very early age. They soon learn to recognize the footprints of their playmates and to distinguish them from others. Out in the bush with their mothers they learn the tracks of every animal, and at an age

Native Tree Climber.

when civilized children would just be learning to read books, the savage child is busy, though he scarcely knows it himself, in learning to read nature, and in acquiring the knowledge which will enable him to obtain his food supply and to guard himself against the attacks of enemies.

Their ability to follow a trail far exceeds that of the American Indian. Mr. Chauncy, in speaking of the alert intelligence of the native in tracking the emu, kangaroo or opossum and other game says: "As he walks through the bush his step is light, elastic, and noiseless; every track on the earth catches his keen eye; a leaf, or a fragment of a stick turned, or a blade of grass recently bent by the tread of one of the lower animals, instantly arrests his attention; in fact, nothing escapes his quick and powerful sight on the ground, in the trees, or in the distance, which may supply him with a meal or warn him of danger. A little examination of the trunk of a tree which may be nearly covered with the scratches of opossums ascending or descending is sufficient to inform him whether or not one went up the night before without coming down again."

Mr. Clemens says that from reading Australian books and talking with the people he became convinced that the aboriginal tracker's performances evince a craft, a penetration, a luminous sagacity, and minuteness and accuracy of observation in the matter of detective work not found in nearly so remarkable a degree in any other people, white or colored. In an official account of the blacks published by the government of Victoria, one reads that the aboriginal not only notices the faint marks left on the bark of a tree by the claws of a climbing opossum, but knows in some way or other whether the marks were made to-day or yesterday.

CHAPTER VI.

A Doomed Race—What Might Have Been—The Wilds of the Bush—The Beginning of the Trouble—Murder and Bloodshed—Dr. Roth's Report—Harsh and Unjust Treatment of Natives To-day—Among the Aboriginals at LaPerouse—Harry the Boomerang Thrower—King Billy with War Club and Shield—Message Sticks—Good-bye to the Aborigines—The Platypus—Kangaroos and Opossums—The Dingo and the Australian Bear.

AND now these interesting people are rapidly disappearing from off the face of the earth. Like the American red men, they melted away at the approach of the whites. Statistics are wholly unreliable in dealing with them. The difficulty arises from the fact that they are nomads, wandering from place to place and have no settled habitation in all the wild land they inhabited for who knows how long before the coming of the whites. It is estimated that there are from fifty to one hundred thousand now. There are also a number of half breeds, for the white man has not always been careful as to the selection of the mother of his children. Some of the half breeds are partially educated and have made such rapid advance in education that they are now numbered with the whites. Also many of the aborigines are in camps under control of missionaries who are educating and civilizing them. Pity 'tis that in the first place this plan had not been adopted by the whites in dealing with these untutored men of the bush. A different story would adorn the page of history instead of the record of rapine, outraged womanhood, blood and murder and treachery that stains all the history of the dealings of the whites with the blacks.

" Had the white man, when he came among the blacks,

A Bush Home in the Wilds of Australia.

but realized the native ideal, who knows that there might not have been a new kind of divine dynasty after that of the children of the sun! They were brave, honorable, and reverent of the higher human qualities, those original barbarians. They did not become mean and false and cruel till civilization set them the example, and their women were not unchaste until white men taught them immorality," writes Mrs. Praed, and she knew her subject, for she was born and spent all her childhood and girlhood days among the blacks, whom she learned to love, for they were her playmates and she felt sure that they did not deserve their fate, nor the evil that has been spoken of them, for it was mainly the fault of the whites that they learned treachery, and were incited to rapine and murder.

The scene where the great tragedy was enacted was in the wilds of the bush, and Mrs. Praed knows so well how to paint the surroundings in words that we let her speak. Words fail to paint the loneliness of the Australian bush. Mile after mile of primeval forest; interminable vistas of melancholy gum-trees; ravines along the sides of which the long-bladed grass grows rankly; level, untimbered plains alternating with undulating tracts of pasture, here and there, broken by steep gully, stony ridge or dried-up creek. All wild and utterly desolate: all the same monotonous grey coloring, except where the wattle, when in blossom, shows patches of feathery gold or a belt of scrub lies green, glossy and impenetrable. I know nothing so strange in its way, as to travel for days through endless gum forests. Surely there never was tree so weird as a very old gum, with its twisted trunk, the withes of grey moss which hang from its branches, and the queer protuberances from its limbs in which the wild bees hive.*

In the wilds of the country, unmolested by the whites, the aborigines lived and filled their destiny, such as it was; then

---

* "My Australian Girlhood," page 9.

came the whites. Many of them were convicts, and it was not long until in the black homes there was mourning because some dusky maiden had fallen a victim to unbridled lust, and the white man who had been welcomed as a friend was regarded

On the Warpath. Fighting Men.

as an enemy. So the trouble began. The blacks were quick to learn in the school of treachery, and in tracking and in all the art of woodcraft they were far ahead of the whites. The latter had cattle, and in times of great scarcity of food, when starvation stared the little camp of blacks in the face, it is not to be wondered at that once in a while they killed a calf and had a feast. Then came the killing of the blacks, and so the trouble began. Mrs. Praed tells how on a dark night the natives crept into a hut at Nie station, and left a white man behind them with his head battered in.

Then the white squatters of the north rose in their fury. They surrounded the camp of the blacks and surprised them and shot them down like wild animals. They went mad with the killing as men do when they catch the fever of slaughter and shot down men, women and children. building up a great pyre of wood and burning the bodies upon it, and some said that not all the bodies were voiceless.

This was a half century ago, and in all the years that have passed since then the aborigines have been, from such like causes, growing fewer each year. In some parts of the country they are entirely extinct, and it seems now only to be a question of time when they shall have gone from the face of the earth. And the injustice to the black fellows of Australia is still being carried on. In a recent issue of the *Review of Reviews,* published by Mr. W. T. Stead, of London, England, the editor contrasts the actions of the British government in their dealings with the aborigines of Australia with that of the Belgians. He is giving an extended notice of the report of Dr. Roth, and says: " The report of Dr. Roth, who has been employed in the treatment of the aborigines of West Australia, suggests a tale of horror only less horrible than that of the Congo because it is on a small scale, and because the system is not deliberately instituted by the government for the purpose of extorting dividends, but is incidental as an incident in the development of the making of dividends by private speculators. The treatment of the Australian black fellows has long been a scandal and a reproach. Whereas in New Zealand the Maori is preserved,

and in South Australia the aborigines promise to multiply and
increase so as to leave no room for the white colonist, the

Aboriginals Painted and Marked for One of Their Ceremonies.

Australians stand accused before the rest of mankind as the
exterminators of the aborigines. In Tasmania there is not a
specimen left and in the other colonies the black fellow appears

to be marked down for destruction. In West Australia water is scarce, but without water even a black fellow cannot live. When the white settler comes he seizes the well and declares that the black fellow must suffer first. The thirsty aboriginal whose water has been stolen retaliates by stealing the white man's ox or his sheep, and then there is trouble in the camp. Forays take place in which no mercy is shown. A whole camp will be wiped out.

"What Dr. Roth reports as existing at this hour is that in some districts there prevails a system that is a most abominable travesty of justice that man can conceive. Whenever any cattle are reported killed by black fellows, a company of policemen is mustered for the capture of a lot of the aboriginals. The first requirement of this police force is chains for the purpose of chaining their captives. These chains weigh from two pounds to five pounds. Once fixed they are never removed night nor day, and cases are mentioned in which they were worn for two years:—

" 'Chains in the northern, not the southern, portion of the State are fixed to the necks instead of to the wrists of native prisoners. . . . Children of from fourteen to sixteen years of age are neck-chained. There are no regulations as to the size, weight, mode of attachment, or length of chain connecting the necks of any two prisoners. When the prisoner is alone the chain is attached to his neck and hands, and wound round his body; the weight prevents him running away so easily. . . . The mode of attachment of the chain round the neck is effected with handcuffs and split links.'

"Sometimes the distance between one chained neck and the other is only twenty-four inches.

"Having provided themselves with chains, the next thing is to seize a number of black fellows. It does not matter in the least whether they are innocent or guilty. The quota of seizures must be made up, chained and carried off. The captives are divided arbitrarily into accused and witnesses. But for this it might be difficult to find excuse for carrying off women and children, although Dr. Roth does mention a case in which a fourteen-year-old-boy was sent to two years' hard labor for cattle killing. There is often no difference in the treatment of witnesses and prisoners. They are all alike, chained and driven in a slave gang through the bush at night. The women are violated by the police.

" ' Numerous charges of immoral conduct are made against the police and their assistants in connection with the women who are herded together and driven through the bush as witnesses, and chained to the trees at night. And that there is much truth in these charges was admitted by everybody who gave evidence on the subject.'

" When the miserable wretches arrive at the court of justice the legal proceedings are a farce. The station manager does not take the trouble to prosecute. Why should he? He is busy, and it is enough that the police and the magistrate should see to the punishment of the blacks. The prisoners do not know why they have been seized. The trial is a perfect farce. The evidence is procured on the principles described in the following statement made by a boy convicted on his own confession of cattle killing.

" ' I was caught by Jack Inglis and Wilson (policemen) . . . Wilson asked me if I killed cattle. I said, " No." Wilson and Inglis then talked together, and they said they would shoot me. Inglis put a cartridge in his rifle, pointed it at me, and said he would burn me at a rock. It frightened me, and I then said I did kill a bullock. Many of the natives undergoing sentences of punishment have no idea what they are imprisoned for, but suppose that they have been gathered together merely for the purpose of making roads.'

" The police are allowed from 1s. 6d. to 2s. 5d. per head

to ration the prisoners.   As of this sum they keep a liberal
allowance for themselves, the more prisoners the more profit.
So works in certain districts the sacred principle of the pre-
dominance of race in Western Australia in this year of grace
1905."

One more incident by Mrs. Praed, and this fearful record
of man's inhumanity to man must close.   Volumes have been
written and more volumes might be written and the subject
still left unexhausted.   She tells how the settlers were at first
received with open arms by the blacks.   Then came the wrongdoing of the whites, followed by reprisals by the wronged
aborigines, and so the trouble began.   There were killings and
murders on every side.   An Englishman who had settled near
the natives was fearful that they would attack his home.   It
was the glad Christmas time when gifts are made and there
is joy in every heart at home because of the happy memories
connected with the natal day of our Lord.   He told the black
men that it was customary in England at this season of the
year to make a great feast and give the people plum pudding
and cakes.   Would they come to the feast at his house on the
morrow?   They said they would, and were lost.   They came
and ate to repletion, as only hungry men can eat, and that
night there were groanings and moanings and weepings.
There had been death in the pot.   The host had mixed
arsenic with the sugar with which his cakes and puddings had
been sweetened.   In the morning the camp of the blacks was
hushed with the stillness of death.   Every man, woman and
child was dead.   It is supposed that the squatter had rest after
this, but how about his conscience?   The very worst part of
this horrible story is its absolute truthfulness.

But why continue the record of the outrages perpetrated
by the whites in their dealings with the aborigines of Australia?   It was not a one-sided affair.   After the trouble began
the blacks did their part in killing.   They were apt learners

and did their lessons well. The whole story is only a repetition of what has taken place wherever and whenever the dominant race, in its inordinate thirst and ambition for power and enlarged territory, has come in contact with the colored races of the world. In our own country we are shamed with the record of a century's dishonor in our dealings with the red men. In Africa, beginning with unchristian slave trade and continuing down to the twentieth century in the atrocity of the Belgian government on the Congo, it is the same old story of rapine, outraged womanhood, murder and bloodshed. All the nations of Europe, claiming to be Christian nations too, have taken a hand in this work of the devil. The daily papers of to-day tell how the Zulus and other African tribes are being hunted down like wild animals and shot in their tracks. So the white man bears the burden of elevating the barbarous and half civilized peoples of the world. Instead of elevating and civilizing them he is decimating them and taking their territory.

I talked with the aborigines at Botany Bay and found them ready to tell their story. And they told it well. With sadness they said their race is rapidly dying out and will soon cease to exist. It might all have been different had the spirit of Christ pervaded the hearts of the white men who came into contact with them. It would all have been different had the law of love, taught by the Master, instead of the law of hate and war, and bloodshed,—emanations from the prince of the pit,—been sown among these wild children of the bush. But it was a repetition of what has been going on among men ever since sin came into the world,—the strong taking what they want from the weak and then killing them off into the bargain. And the very worst part of the whole business is that it has been and is being done by governments posing before the world as Christian.

And so the name of the blessed Christ, the Prince of

What might Have Been under Christian Influence.

Peace, he whose coming into the world was heralded by an angelic choir singing " Peace on earth, good will to man," is tarnished with the base actions of those who profess to follow Him. So our Master has been grievously wounded and put to an open shame in the house of his friends. The poor heathen cannot discriminate between the missionary who comes to him teaching the way of Christ and the soldiers of the same Christian (?) government who come and shoot them like wild animals and exterminate them like vermin. In his mind the two are associated together and give the people of China, India, Africa and Australia the strongest possible argument against the missionaries. " You bring the Gospel of peace," they say, " then why are you followed with soldiers and war and murder and bloodshed? " And who will answer?

And now when the harm has been done, the several colonial governments are housing and feeding, and caring for the remnants of the aborigines, especially in south Australia. But there are but few of them left now to house and feed. To show how they have gone, the statistics of a single state are given. When the whites first came into Victoria there were possibly twenty thousand aborigines in the province. In 1851 they had dwindled down to two thousand six hundred and ninety-three, and according to the returns of the census of 1901 there were but two hundred and seventy-one to tell the story.

At La Perouse, on Botany Bay, near where Captain Cook landed, there is a large camp of aboriginals under the care of missionaries supported by the various churches in Sydney. I visited them twice and found them to be bright and intelligent and many of them able to read and write and speak English fluently. Here is an illustration of what might have been had the black fellows received different treatment at the hands of the dominant race.

I was anxious to see an exhibition of the skill of the boom-

La Perouse, on Botany Bay.

erang thrower and had my curiosity gratified. I found more
than a hundred natives, young and old, little and big in the
camp, some full bloods and others half caste. Many of them
spoke English quite fluently and were ready to talk with the
stranger who came among them to seek information. King
" Billy," once a noted chief and warrior of his tribe, was among
the number. He is straight, well built, alert and is an expert
with war club, spear and boomerang. His skin is a dark choca-
late color with full beard and straight hair. Both hair and
beard are now white with age.

Inquiry was made for the boomerang thrower, and Harry
Simmons, an expert at the business, put in his appearance, and
with him a ten-year-old boy, Harry's youngest son. They both
had boomerangs, and it was hard to determine which was the
more skillful in throwing the crooked stick. I was told the boy
began throwing when he was three or four years old. With a
strong grip Harry grasped one end of the boomerang and threw
it from him, and it darted through the air with the swiftness
of a bird flying in a straight line until it reached a point about
a hundred feet from the thrower, when it made a graceful turn
and came back and fell at Harry's feet. Then he threw it again
with tremendous force and it went whizzing through the air
like an arrow in a perfectly straight line, made the curve at the
regulation distance, came back to a point over the head of the
thrower, described a circle about twenty feet in diameter above
his head and then settled down into the outstretched hand of
the wizard. Again and again the boomerang was thrown, and
always seemed to obey the will of the aboriginal.

I had heard many stories of the skill of the boomerang
throwers, how they could throw the weapon from them and
have it come back and strike a man in the rear and it was
always just a little hard to believe it all. But now I was convinced. Harry asked me to try the throwing. An effort was
made, resulting in a dismal failure. Then he gave a few les-

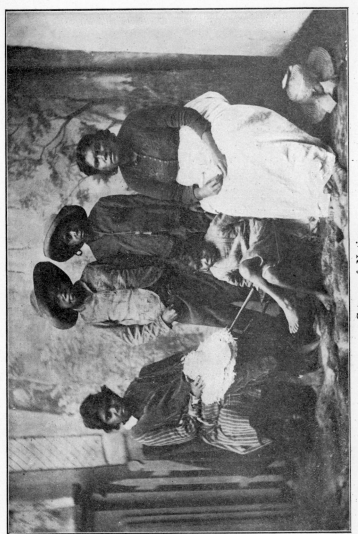

Group of Natives.

sons, and trying again and again the weapon actually made the curve, but failed to return to the thrower. With a good knowledge of human nature Harry said, " By and by you make a very good boomerang thrower." He makes them for sale and does a prosperous business selling them to tourists. I came away with boomerangs, spears, war-clubs and shields. They will be objects of interest to friends at home, and may serve to keep in order any who are disposed to be unruly.

Before leaving the camp Maijee asked King " Billy " to show us how he used the spear, war-club and shield. The old warrior grasped the old-time weapons, and as he flourished them there came into his aged eyes the fire of youth. He seemed to imagine himself in the bush again meeting an armed foe for deadly conflict, and he gave us a splendid exhibition of the skill with which the weapons are used. It requires a trained and skillful hand to ward off the blows of an enemy with the narrow piece of wood which serves the purpose of a shield. The old warrior bared his head and showed us a deep indentation in his skull, crushed in by a blow from a boomerang, which would have finished an ordinary man, but the hardy aboriginal recovered from the wound without the aid of doctor or surgeon. He said with a smile, " Billy's head too high and shield too low that time." We paid several visits to the camp and interviewed the missionaries in charge and they gave flattering reports of the advance the natives were making in educational and religious lines.

As already intimated, the aboriginals do not have a system of notation and are able to count only up to the number five. If they have occasion to speak of a greater number than this it is expressed with the word " metanoly," meaning literally, many, or very many. In counting they say " kimmeroi " for one, " bulla " two, " bulla-kimmeroi " three, " bulla-bulla " four, and " bulla-bulla-kimmeroi " five, and then " metanoly " to express a greater number. It seems strange that they have not acquired a knowledge of numbers and have been able to make use of a kind of a symbol writing with which messages are sent from tribe to tribe. In practice, carved pieces of wood are used, called message sticks, on which various marks are carved. Some writers have concluded that these sticks are used only as a means of friendly recognition, while others hold that messages are sent from place to place by means of the message sticks. It is a fact, recognized by all, that they are

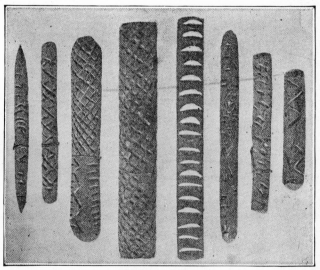

Message Sticks.

used to summons the various tribes to a general meeting, and this would seem to indicate that the symbols used are well understood by those who send and those who receive them.

I am sorry to say good-bye to the aboriginals of Australia. They stand in a class by themselves, and their story is so unique, and so full of interest that the remaining chapters of this book might be filled with merest mention of their manners and customs, their peculiar history, and their strange doings. In their strange way they have filled their place in the world's history and seem now doomed to utter extinction. They deserved a better fate and better things, and in the day of all days those responsible for the evil thrust upon them will be called to account where might does not make right.

But there are other things of interest to write about, and

The Duck-Billed Platypus.

among some of these are the strange animals that make their habitat among the aborigines. First of all and most curious and remarkable of all known animals is the duck-billed platypus, which puzzled the naturalists for many years. When they came to classify the strange being it was hard to determine whether it was a bird or an animal. It has the fur of the seal, the bill and webbed feet of the duck, dives and swims like a fish, lays eggs and when they are hatched nurses the young with the milk of its breasts. I saw but one specimen of this strange aquatic species and it is a peculiar combination of fish, bird and animal.

The platypus, called by the naturalists ornithorhyncus, is aquatic and amphibious in its habits, and when full grown is about twenty inches long. Its legs are short, the toes being joined together with webs and armed with strong sharp claws which serve the animal a good purpose in making burrows. It is covered with a short thick fur, soft to the touch and dark brown in color. The mouth is small and has a striking resemblance to the bill of a duck. For a sleeping and breeding place the animals make deep burrows in the banks of the lakes and water holes which they frequent. The tunnel has two openings, one below the surface of the water, and the other hid away among the grass and weeds just above the water level. Starting below the surface of the water the burrow extends up into the bank as much as fifty feet. At the end it expands into a living chamber, the floor of which is covered with dry leaves and grass. Here two eggs are laid and hatched by the warmth of the animal's body, and the young are reared.

When Captain Cook reached Australia in 1770 he noticed a peculiar animal with small head and short front limbs, an immense tail and long, strong hind legs, which the natives called "kanguroo," and with a slight variation in spelling, this name has passed into all the European languages. The kangaroo belongs to the great marsupial family distinguished by the pouch in which the mother places her young at birth, for protection and nourishment. One branch of the family is found largely distributed in the United States, in the opossum. There are some forty varieties of the animal found in Australia, varying in size from the kangaroo rat, wallaroo, brush and rock wallabies, and the large red and grey kangaroos. The large grey kangaroo when sitting erect on the tripod formed by its great tail and hind legs, is seven feet in height.

Large Gray Kangaroo, Female.   Note Opening to Pouch
where Young are Carried.

The kangaroo is a timid, harmless animal, depending upon the keenness of its senses and the rapidity of its flight to escape from its enemies. In running, it makes peculiar eccentric boundings with its fore legs and great tail flapping in the air, and when going at full speed covers from twenty-five to

Group of Wallabies.

thirty feet at a single leap. When closely pursued by hounds, it defends itself by striking out with its hind foot. The powerful claw of the fourth toe cuts like a knife, and a single blow will kill a dog. The fact that there are very few flesh-eating animals in Australia accounts for the large number of kangaroos found in that country.

From one to three young are produced at a birth, and the little fellows are very small, not more than an inch in length, and are entirely helpless. With her lips, the mother places

Red Kangaroo.

them in the pouch which nature has provided for them. They are unable to suck the mother's milk and this is injected into the mouth and down the throat by the action of the muscles of the mother. They remain in the pouch for weeks and even months until they are able to run about and help themselves. Then they leave the pouch, but keep near the mother's side and return to their closed home whenever danger threatens them. Frequently you may see a little fellow with his head thrust out of the pouch in which he is being carried.

Nowadays they are hunted for their skins, which are sent to the United States where they are made into a fine quality of leather. When it was discovered that good leather could be made from the hides, immense numbers were killed and there was danger of the total extinction of the species. A single firm in Sydney,—Winchcombe, Carson & Co.,—shipped in one year nearly two hundred thousand kangaroo skins to the United States, and for the same period, over half a million opossum pelts. Finding that these animals were being rapidly decimated, the colonial government passed a law of absolute protection for two years, and after that a closed period from August 1 to January 1, each year. During the closed period none of the animals named are to be killed. The large grey kangaroo skins sell at Sidney at from ninety cents to a dollar and a quarter each, the smaller wallaby sell at from ten to fifty cents each, while the best quality of opossum pelts may be bought at about three dollars and fifty cents a dozen.

Another of the marsupials very common in Australia is the opossum. That they abound and that the country would be a sort of an opossum paradise for the negro of the South, is apparent from the fact already given of the shipment of over half a million pelts annually by a single firm. The Australian variety has a bushy tail and the fur is highly prized for robes and also for lining greatcoats to be worn in the cold regions of the northern hemisphere. A robe made of twenty-four opossum skins of the best grade of fur, sells for from forty to fifty dollars. The aboriginals feast on the flesh of the opossums, and they are a source of considerable income to the trappers and hunters.

Australia also furnishes the only specie of dog in the

The Australian Opossum.

world existing both in the wild and domesticated state. It is also the only flesh-eating, placental mammal in the country. It is known as the dingo, and some writers regard it as an example of the domesticated dog having answered the call from the wild and returned to its natural state. This, however, is not accepted by most authorities. The fact that the bones of the animal have been found in old strata of the country shows that it has lived there for many centuries. It may have been brought to Australia from Asia by the aborigines when they migrated to the country before the dawn of history. The dingo is about two and a half feet in length and two feet high, with sharp, pointed ears and a bushy tail. In color it approaches the yellow dog.

The Dingo, or Wild Dog.

Like the aboriginal, the dingo is rapidly disappearing from off the earth. The sheep men wage an unremitting warfare against them, for they are very destructive to their flocks, killing very many more animals than they eat. It is altogether likely that in time they will become extinct. When the puppies are taken young, they are easily tamed and domesticated. They are cunning, courageous and affectionate to their native masters, who treat them very kindly. They are good hunters and assist in tracking opossums, rats, snakes and lizards,

The Australian Bear.

all of which are used for food by the natives. The flesh of the dingo is also used for the same purpose.

The so-called bear of Australia is the only species of its kind in the country. It is much more like the sloth in its habits, than the bear. The animal is peculiar in shape and has strong, sharp claws. It carries its young on its back as seen in the illustration. The little fellow clings fast and is removed only with difficulty. The silver-tipped skins are in demand in our own country, where they are used to make fur clothing for the intensely cold climates of Canada, Alaska, and the Klondyke goldfields.

CHAPTER VII.

The Religions of Australia—Ninety Per Cent Christian—The Melbourne Cup—A Nation of Gamblers—Mark Twain's Description of the Races—A Plague-Stricken Ship—A Nervous Passenger who Could Drink or Let it Alone—The Little Girl and Her Father—A Burial at Sea.

STATISTICALLY, Australia is one among the most religious countries in the world. Ninety per cent of the white population are called Christians. When Mark Twain said there is a church at every door and a race-track across the street, he spoke within the ordinary limit of truth as seen by the humorist. There is a place of public worship for every four hundred of the white population of Australasia. This is far above the general average in our own country. It appears to be a healthy atmosphere for the propagation of sects. All religions—the Christian, Jewish, Mohammedan, Buddhist, Brahman and all others—are absolutely free, and state aid is given to none.

The Church of England has the largest number of adherents. In Tasmania and New South Wales about one-half the entire population are members of this organization, while in Western Australia forty-two per cent profess its doctrines. The different denominations have adherents as follows:

Church of England,	1,811,603
Roman Catholic,	965,221
Presbyterian,	602,608
Methodists, all branches,	587,928
Baptists,	108,705
Congregational,	80,405
Lutheran,	79,854
Salvation Army,	39,099
Unitarian,	3,097

Other Christians, ... 85,795
Jews, ... 16,851

Among those classed under the head "Other Christians" are to be found Christians or Disciples, Bible Christians, Christian Brethren, Church of Christ, Society of Friends, New Jerusalem Church, Believers in Christ, Calvinists, Christadelphians, Christ Chapel, Christian Israelites, Christian Socialists, Church of God, Evangelists, Exclusive Brethren, Free Church, Free Methodists, Followers of Christ, Gospel Meeting, Greek Church, Huguenot, Hussite, Mennonite, Moravian, Plymouth Brethren, and Seven Day Baptists. Other religions are made up of the following list:

Jews, ...16,851
Mohammedan, ... 3,247
Buddist, ...18,837
Hindoos, ...   848
Free Thinkers and Agnostics, ...13,897
Indefinite, ...   856

There is also at least one member of the Brethren church in New South Wales, a Greek brother, Nicolai Narroney, of Smyrna, Asia Minor. He was much pleased to meet us, as we were to meet him. He says he would like to work for the church in Sydney, but there is such poor opportunity. There are so many priests and preachers to be supported, that it is not much use to ask more to come. He has a prosperous business, a fine restaurant, and insisted on our dining with him. After the meal I offered to pay, but he would receive nothing and said, " So long as you stay in Sydney you eat at my table. Cost you not anything." While we could not conscientiously accept the kind offer, I liked the spirit in which it was made. The brother is a bright, intelligent man and is exceedingly liberal. A few days ago he set aside the proceeds of his business for the city hospital and turned over to that institution fifty dollars.

The various denominations in Australia sustain missions in India, China, Africa and other of the unchristianized parts of the world. A few days ago six missionaries left Sydney to join the Inland Mission of China. Missions are maintained among all the aborigines where they can be reached.

As already noted and from the statistics here given,—and these are official, as I copied them from the government report, 4,381,166, or over ninety per cent of the entire population of Australia are members of some branch of the Christian church. Since there are churchhouses and meeting places where religious services are held for every four hundred of the population, and the churches are active in supporting missions among the unchristian people in the world as well as among the aborigines of their own country, it would seem there are better opportunities at home for reaching non-church-members and non-church-goers and for supplying places of worship for the people than there are in Australia.

Ninety per cent of the Australasians are church members, nominally; if we are to believe common report, a hundred per cent of them attend horse races. Not all the people go to the races all the time, but all of them attend at sometime. Big and little, great and small, high and low, men, women and children, even children in arms go to the races and with few exceptions all who go engage in betting. Every town and city has its race course, and these are most liberally patronized. Betting is the universal rule. Boys of ten may be found on the streets hawking chances on the races as our newsboys sell papers at home. And the chances are so arranged that the lad with a few pennies may take a chance to win money. The Australians are a race of gamblers and the evil is so serious that thoughtful men are interesting themselves as to the best methods of dealing with the evil.

The one great race of the year is held at Melbourne, and is known as the Melbourne Cup. On our return voyage we reached Melbourne the day after the great event. Both houses of parliament adjourned, and in a body with the premier, attended the races. The city of over a half million souls had been in a state of nervous excitement for weeks, ships and railways had been bringing in the people by the tens of thousands. New Zealand, thirteen hundred miles away by sea, was represented and Tasmania was there. Hotels and boarding houses were crowded to the utmost and we were told that some failed to get lodgings. We went into some of the shops to make purchases, but found shopkeepers and assistants listless and indifferent. They were in a state of relaxation after the great event of the year. The multitudes were leaving the city, going home to get ready for the next race, a year hence. Some were poorer because of their losses, others richer on account of their winnings. The whole crowd took much less money away with them than they brought. All were poorer spiritually, for all this mass of betting, gambling, horse-race-attending crowd were professedly followers of the lowly Nazarene. None of them received a spiritual uplift at the races, none were made better morally by the performance, but all had fastened upon them, stronger than ever before, the habit of gambling and of trying to get something for nothing. It's a picture of a race gone mad on horse-racing, sporting and gambling.

Lest it be thought I overdraw the picture, let another tell the story: "Melbourne spreads over an immense area of ground. It is a stately city architecturally as well as in magnitude. It has an elaborate cable-car service; it has museums and colleges, and schools, and public gardens, and electricity, and gas, and libraries, and theaters, and mining centers, and wool centers, and centers of the arts and sciences, and boards of trade, and ships, and railroads, and a harbor, and social clubs, and journalistic clubs, and racing clubs, and a squatter club sumptuously housed and appointed, and has as many

churches and banks as can make a living. In a word, it is
equipped with everything that goes to make the modern
great city. It is the largest city of Australia and fills the post
with honor and credit. It has one specialty; this must not be
jumbled in with those other things. It is the mitred Metropolitan of the horse-racing cult. Its race ground is the Mecca
of Australasia. On the great day of annual sacrifice—the fifth
of November, Guy Fawkes's day—business is suspended over
a stretch of land and sea as wide as from New York to San
Francisco, and deeper than from the northern lakes to the
Gulf of Mexico; and all men and women, of high degree
or low, who can afford the expense, put away their other duties
and come. They begin to swarm in by ship and rail a fortnight
before the day, and they swarm thicker and thicker day after
day, until all the vehicles of transportation are taxed to their
uttermost to meet the demands of the occasion, and all hotels
and lodgings are bulging outward because of the pressure from
within. They come a hundred thousand strong, as all the
best authorities say, and they pack the spacious grounds and
grand-stands and make a spectacle such as is never to be seen
in Australia elsewhere.

"It is the ' Melbourne Cup ' that brings this multitude together. Their clothes have been ordered long ago, at unlimited
cost, and without bounds as to beauty and magnificence, and
have been kept in concealment until now, for unto this day
are they consecrate. I am speaking of the ladies' clothes; but
one might know that.

"And so the grand-stands make a brilliant and wonderful
spectacle, a delirium of color, a vision of beauty. The cham-
pagne flows, everybody is vivacious, excited, happy; everybody
bets, and gloves and fortunes change hands right along, all
the time. Day after day the races go on, and the fun and the
excitement are kept at white heat; and when the day is done,
the people dance all night so as to be fresh for the race in the

morning. And at the end of the great week the swarms secure lodgings and transportation for the next year, then flock away to their remote homes and count their gains and losses, and order next year's cup-clothes, and then lie down and sleep two weeks, and get up sorry to reflect that a whole year must be put in somehow or other before they can be wholly happy again."*

And so year after year these worldly, pleasure-loving people, who count the excitement of the race-course, and the winning or losing of a fortune on the chance of a favorite horse passing under the winning wire a second or two ahead of all competitors, as real happiness, spend a good portion of their lives. Some of their ministers preach against it and others go to the races. No voice in all the so-called Christian church in Australia is strong enough to call the people away from the races and the gambling with all their attendant evils. After all, it might be well to send missionaries out to convert these nominal Christians and win them to the Christ-life. They probably need conversion more than do the heathen in some other countries.

Aside from racing, Melbourne has other claims for distinction. With a population of slightly over half a million, probably a trifle ahead of Sydney in numbers, the Capital of the Commonwealth of Australia, a parliament-house costing five million dollars and a town hall costing a little less, a dozen converging railroads, a large, land-locked, commodious harbor, an immense shipping trade and a progressive, wide-awake, energetic lot of business men,—all these easily give the place a rank above all important towns and cities in the southern hemisphere. It is the seat of an archbishop of the Roman church, has a bishop of the Anglican church, a consul-general of the United States, and other dignitaries of more or less note. It exports much gold and silver, wool, and large numbers of

---

*" Following the Equator," pp. 162-164.

hides, cattle and sheep. About six-sevenths of the entire commerce of Victoria is carried on by Melbourne.

It may be a matter of surprise to some, as it was to the writer, that in trade, according to population, Australia leads the world. With her small population of four million whites, she buys and sells annually about six hundred million dollars worth of various products. The entire export trade of the great British Empire, with all her dependencies, is placed at three billion dollars annually. Australia claims one-tenth of the entire amount. India has a population of nearly three hundred million and exports annually five hundred million dollars in products. Australia with her four million people sends out to the world at large, three hundred million dollars worth of goods of various kinds. By way of comparison, the people of India sell to the outside world products to the amount of one dollar and seventy-five cents per individual, while the Australian sells seventy-five dollars worth for each man, woman, and child in the commonwealth. Melbourne is the chief center of this wonderful commercial activity.

" There are trustworthy statistics furnished by Sir Richard Hemple and others, which show that the individual Indian's whole annual product, both for export and home use, is worth in gold only seven dollars and fifty cents; or, thirty-seven dollars and fifty cents for the family aggregate. Ciphered out on a like ratio of multiplication, the Australasian family's aggregate production would be nearly sixteen hundred dollars. Truly, nothing is so astonishing as figures, if they once get started."*

From the census reports of 1901 I copied the following statistics concerning these wonderful people. Their energy and productiveness are unequalled in the world.

---

*" Following the Equator," page 174.

	Whites	Aborigines
New South Wales,	1,362,232	3,656
Victoria,	1,199,692	271
Queensland,	502,892	5,537
South Australia,	354,001	26,433
Western Australia,	182,533	5,261
Tasmania,	172,000	
Totals,	3,773,370	40,880

If we add to the above totals the population of New Zealand it will be increased by seven hundred and seventy-two thousand; seven hundred and nineteen thousand whites and forty-seven thousand Maoris, the natives of that far-away island. This makes the entire population of Australasia over four and a half million and the aboriginals in round numbers, a hundred thousand.

Lines of railroads connect both Sydney and Adelaide with Melbourne, and after a long sea voyage many passengers leave the steamers at Adelaide and travel across country by rail. The railroad companies offer as a special inducement to such travelers, tickets at half fare. The same is true of returning tourists. They prefer to take the cars at Sydney and join the ship later either at Melbourne or Adelaide. As for our little party we decided to stay by the ship. It is much safer and decidedly more pleasant to travel on a good ship than by rail. Figures show that more people lose their lives on railroads than on the sea in comparison with the numbers who travel by land and sea. The pleasures of a sea voyage are augmented when its advantages are considered. You are free from the dust and smoke of the railway, you have your hotel with you, you eat, sleep, rest, or take exercise as suits your convenience. And then you have a good library on board affording the best reading matter, and I know of no better place to enjoy reading a good book than a quiet corner on deck where unmolested you may delve into the riches of your favorite author.

No one could have desired a more beautiful day or a smoother sea than that which favored us when we said good-bye to Sydney and sailed away from Australia on the 9th of November, 1905. Again we had opportunity to enjoy the beauties of the famed harbor, and as we glided over its smooth waters and passed through the great, rocky gateway, out upon the bosom of the placid sea we congratulated ourselves on the auspicious beginning of the twenty-three days of sea-faring life that lay before us until we should reach our desired haven at Bombay. The fine weather continued two full days, and then came one of those sudden changes for which the Australian coast is noted, and for a week we had storms and high seas. The great ship rolled and pitched so that it was almost impossible to walk about the deck, and the sailors staggered to and fro like drunken men.

In the center of our ship an indicator is placed that marks the rolling of the boat. A pendulum swings in front of a half circle divided into degrees, and as the ship rolls from side to side the pendulum swings and indicates the extent of each lurch from the perpendicular. I stood at the indicator when the storm was at its worst, and could stand only by holding on to an iron railing, and found that the pendulum swung from side to side over forty-four degrees, or from twenty-two degrees on one side to the same on the other. Trying to walk erect on deck was something like trying the same performance on a house roof with a quarter pitch.

Maijee and the writer escaped without seasickness, but we were far from being comfortable and it wasn't a good time for reading a book in a quiet nook on deck. Sister Eliza Miller did not escape so well, but we all pulled through in the best of shape, thankful that it had been no worse. The storm was soon over and forgotten when fine weather and smooth

sailing came again, and we enjoyed it all the more because
of the howling winds and unruly sea which preceded it. Our
sense of enjoyment is much increased by contrasts. If there
were never a storm or a rough, boisterous sea, the calm would
never be half so attractive, nor the smooth sailing nearly so
enjoyable as it is after the tempest is over; if there were no
clouds, the sunshine would become monotonous and almost
unbearable; if there were no winter cold, who could endure
the intense summer heat? Even the zest and pleasure of the

Street Scene in Adelaide.

activities of life are intensified when contrasted with the quiet
sleep of death.

After a short stay at Melbourne we took ship again for
Adelaide. By rail the journey between the two cities is made
in seventeen hours; by sea it takes nearly forty-eight hours.
Adelaide is the prosperous capital of the vast province of
South Australia, an empire within itself in extent. The city,
including suburbs, has a population of a hundred and sixty-
two thousand souls. Its streets are broad and well laid out,

and it has fine public buildings and a good harbor. It is connected by rail with Broken Hill, famous for its fabulously rich silver mines. The city owes much of its importance to these mines which have made millionaires of many poor men.

Post Office, Adelaide.

At Adelaide one of our number was taken ashore because of illness, we were told, but the fact that the bubonic plague had broken out on the ship was wisely kept from the passengers. When we reached Freemantle the disease had gained such headway that it could no longer be kept secret. We had twenty-five passengers on board for that port. The health officers made an examination and at once placed the ship in quarantine. Four men stricken with the plague were taken ashore and placed in the plague hospital, where two soon after died. The passengers were taken to an island five miles away, to the quarantine station where they were to remain a number of days.

When it became generally known among the passengers that we had the real bubonic plague on board the *Ville de Ciotat* there was a good deal of anxiety and nervous excitement among them. Some of them had spent the week at Melbourne at the races, and doubtless their experiences and their life at that place had not prepared them to meet the dread disease so fatal when it once seizes its victims. One of the passengers, a man of bright intellect and of fine address, with whom I had spent a good deal of time in social interviews, was almost overcome by the news. He had told me that he was in the habit of taking a glass of strong drink occasionally and that he was quite able to take it or leave it alone, for he was master of the situation. It was pointed out that not all men were able to do this and many who had the same confidence had fallen into drunkenness and were filling drunkards' graves. The gentleman was strong in his conviction that he was secure in his strength to take or leave alone strong drink at his will. When he heard about the plague he was thrown into an extreme condition of nervous excitement. He was to land at Freemantle to look after some business which was intrusted to his care. The quarantine officials decided that those who landed, as well as the plague-stricken patients should go into the quarantine station and remain there until all danger of spreading the disease was over. My friend, whom I had learned to admire very much, was wonderfully wrought upon when he was told what was in store for him. Soon after this he disappeared from deck and later I learned that he had been drinking heavily. When I next met him he was under the influence of strong drink, and how I did pity the poor fellow. His strength had left him and he was drunk. Only another illustration of the cruel deception of strong drink. A man is led on by the specious argument that he can take it or let it alone, and then when a crisis comes, down he goes. Not in many years have I witnessed a case that appealed more to my sympathy than did the one here related. The last I saw of my friend was on board the tug which took the Freemantle passengers to the quarantine station.

One among the stricken men who was landed at Freemantle and who died a few days later was one of the ship's engineers. He was past the prime of life and had earned a pension and retirement. He was making his last voyage and intended to settle down with his wife and children at home, when the ship reached Marseilles, France. But he never reached the old home. Wife and children watched in vain for the return of father and husband. He was buried ten thousand miles from home.

Among the passengers for Freemantle was a mother with a dear, sweet-faced little girl of three years. She looked so bright and happy and said she was going to see her papa. The husband and father was on shore anxiously waiting the coming of his loved ones. When little bright eyes was told that no one on shore could come on the ship and no one on the ship go ashore she cried for her papa and sobbed as if her little heart would break. That night she sobbed herself asleep over her great disappointment. The next morning when the Freemantle passengers had gone down the side of the ship and were seated in the steam launch that was to take them to the quarantine station a little boat came alongside and the mother held out her darling to the father who took his little girl in his arms and she threw her arms around his neck and hugged and kissed him, while he tenderly and lovingly pressed her to his heart. Then as the boats separated he handed her back to her mother again. There were a good many dim eyes among the onlookers, for it was a pathetic, heart-touching scene. Will there be such separations in the day of judgment?

After leaving Freemantle we had a time cleaning up the ship. Everything about the boat was renovated, disinfected, chlorided, sulphur-fumed, soaped, scoured, rubbed, scrubbed and polished until ours was the cleanest ship afloat. Mattresses, blankets, pillows, sheets, hammocks, boxes, bags, bunks, life-preservers, sailors' clothing and everything in which bacterii or germs might find a hiding place were put through the great disinfectant boiler on the fore deck. The doctor was the busiest man on the ship. He not only gave orders, but saw that his orders were implicitly carried out. It was no doubt due to the care exercised by our doctor and the precautions taken that we escaped with as little loss of life as we did.

When I reflected on the care and anxiety of the doctor, how he was absent from the table for days, how he neglected his usual recreation on the deck and how assiduously he looked after the cleaning up of the ship and putting her in the very best possible sanitary condition so that the health of the passengers might not suffer, I gave him, as did all of the ship's company, praise. We all thought he was doing his duty and doing it well, and heartily commended him for it. Then came the thought that if so much care is taken of a ship that makes but a few voyages across the sea, comparatively speaking, and then is broken to pieces and is forgotten, how much more careful ought we to be to keep our souls pure and clean and unspotted from the world, for we are to live forever.

The Great Australian Bight, dreaded by sailors and passengers alike, notwithstanding Tennyson's line, " The spangle dances in bight and bay," is, not too accurately speaking, a great stretch of water between Adelaide and Freemantle. It is formed by an irregular, semicircular indentation of the coast line of South Australia, and is somewhat like a bow in shape. The string of the imaginary bow is two thousand five hundred miles in length and is the course always followed by ships sailing between the two cities. Here the sea is nearly always rough, and even in calm weather there is constantly

Breakers on the Rocky Coast of South Australia.

a heavy rolling sea. Then when the storms come, as they frequently do, there is a rough time in store for the luckless voyagers. Here ships are dismantled, masts snapped like pipe stems and many a good boat is tossed at the mercy of the waves, finally to be cast a helpless wreck on the rocky coast.

Both coming and going we escaped without heavy storms. Indeed, the captain said the voyages were the smoothest he had ever made, and we were delighted and thankful for our good luck.

After sailing away from the Headlands of Australia we had a beautiful sea, a sea so calm, and peaceful, and blue that one wondered if it were ever ruffled by storms, or tossed by tempest. One by one the hours passed into days which were spent in reading, walking, eating and sleeping. Then in the far-away distance the island of Ceylon came into view like a mere speck on the horizon, and we felt that our long voyage would soon be over. In the early morning we reached the famous island of spices and cast anchor in the harbor at Colombo. But we were much feared and hence unwelcome guests. The cable had brought the news that ours was a plague-stricken ship, also that two of our company who had been landed at Freemantle had died. We were at once placed in quarantine and the passengers for that port were not allowed to land and so were compelled to go on to Bombay. The cargo for the place was also carried by. They would have none of us or our belongings on shore. Here our home mail, forwarded from Bulsar, was brought to us. There were eighty pieces, and we had a feast after a four weeks' famine.

The time for running from Colombo to Bombay is sixty hours. On the way one poor fellow, who had been in ill health for some time, died and was buried at sea. He was traveling for his health and expected to reach his home in Spain in a few weeks. He found a watery grave, and his friends will look for him in vain at his old home. The morning we cast anchor in the outside harbor at Bombay another death occurred from the plague, and we were told that it was the most deadly type. We were quarantined and for a time it seemed as if we were not to be allowed to go ashore, and that the prospects

were good for us to go on to the next port, Aden, at the
entrance to the Red Sea.

Brother Stover, Brother and Sister Berkebile, and Sisters
Quinter, Pittenger and Sadie Miller were in Bombay and
came out to the ship in a small sailboat, but were not allowed
to come on board, nor were we permitted to go to them. We
talked down to them and they up to us, and we had the comfort of knowing that all were well at the various mission stations. Then they left us and we waited patiently and anxiously
for the final decision as to what our fate was to be. Presently a
little tugboat pulled up alongside, an official came on board
and handed the captain a document and we soon learned that
we were free to go ashore. We stood not on the order of
going, but went. In a short time we had our belongings on
a little native sailboat, for the ship was two miles from the
dock, and were pulling for the shore, glad and happy to leave
the plague-infected ship.

That night when we were safely housed we realized how
good God had been to us and we gave him thanks for bringing
us safely back to "Dear Old India" again. He had also
given us peace when we were surrounded with danger, for
there was no time on the journey when we were over-anxious
as to the result. We had fully and unreservedly placed ourselves in the hands of the loving Father, and knew in whom
we trusted. The day in Bombay harbor was the hardest on
our nerves of any on the entire journey. How sweet and
refreshing was the sleep that followed that day. What a
restorer to the weary is rest and sleep. Thank God for
refreshing sleep.

CHAPTER VIII.

Home Again in India—The Little Children—The Flight of Time—
"God be with You till We Meet Again"—Prince Arthur of
Connaught—The Extravagant Expenditure of Money—The
End of the First Stage of Our Homeward Journey—The Chi-
nese New Year—Fears of an Outbreak—Hong Kong to Can-
ton—Boat Houses—Sedan Chair—Singular Street Names.

WE landed at Bombay on the sixth day of December,
1904, and sailed away again from the same port for China,
Japan and the homeland on the twenty-third day of January,
1906. These two dates are deeply impressed on memory's cal-
endar because of the joy of meeting loved ones and of the sorrow of parting with them. The measure of time included in
these dates is full of pleasant memories and sacred associations.
When we landed and thought of the time that must pass before we should leave India again, the parting seemed a long
way off. But when it had all so swiftly passed away, we felt
as if we had not had half our intended stay. We learned to
know all our missionaries better, and to know them better is
to love them more. How all the mission band endeared themselves to our hearts, the workers as well as the little ones God
has given them to cheer their homes in India.

Here are Emmert Stover and Henry McCann growing to
be big boys now, big enough to ride a bicycle which some kind-
hearted friend sent out from America for Emmert. It brought
to him the gratification of a long-time desire, for what boy
is there who is not ambitious to ride a bicycle? And what good
times these boys do have together when they visit at each other's homes! Their being together means much to them, for
they are isolated when it comes to playmates of their kind.

Except when they are together they must seek their associates from among the native boys. And there is little Mary Mc-Cann, her father's only girl, and she clings to him with all of a

Emmert and Henry.

child's love for her parents. Also there is the dear little treasure that came to Brother and Sister Enoch Eby's home to cheer and make glad the father and mother heart in far-away India. We think of them all, of the happy days at Bulsar, and how we did enjoy them, of the evenings spent on the veranda of the old bungalow in social converse and the story telling with little Miriam Stover's oft-repeated request, " Please tell us a story, Grandpa! " How we did enjoy it all, and how it warmed our hearts to know that we had won the love of the children! Gone now are those pleasant, happy hours, gone are the days spent at Dahanu with Brother and Sister Adam Ebey and little Paul and Mary.* How their eyes sparkled with pleasure in their childish railroad play, and for that matter we had as much pleasure in it all as they. All these children entered into and became a part of our life in India, and now we have these memories to treasure up in our heart of hearts.

And so the time for leaving came all too soon, and when it did come, we both felt a strong desire to remain in India. It would have been so easy for us, so far as personal feelings are concerned, to have spent the rest of the days the Lord has for us to live in this world with our band of devoted mission workers. We love India, we love the mission work, we love our native brethren and sisters, but more than all we love our noble band of self-sacrificing mission workers. We are loath to leave them all, but home duties were pressing, and then, too, there came a rapid development of a heart difficulty, which has been with the writer for a number of years, and so it was thought best to turn our faces homeward.

Before saying farewell to India we had a most enjoyable love feast with the native members, and a number of the mission band were also present. Two hundred and forty-seven members of the mystical body of Christ sat at the tables of the Lord, and among them Brother James la Personne. We all love to call him " Uncle Jimmy" or " Jimmy Sahib." For years he has been with us in sympathy and in heart, and now

---

*Since then the angel of death entered the happy home at Dahanu and carried little Paul and Mary away to join the angel band in heaven. "Suffer little children to come unto me, and forbid them not, for of such is the kingdom of heaven."

Uncle Jimmie and Family.

he has been received into holy fellowship by the rite of Christian baptism. A few days later we sat down to a meal with more than a hundred of our native members. It was a dinner given by " Uncle Jimmy." It was not an elaborate affair, but it was seasoned with the spice of love, and as we ate the native food, discarding knives, forks and spoons, using our fingers instead, we really felt that it was one of the most enjoyable meals of our lives. Then there was singing in Gujerati and English, and as the sweet songs of Zion sounded out in the night air there was spiritual joy and devotion in all our hearts. The native heathen gathered in large numbers in the roadway and listened and wondered that we should have a feast without drums and the screeching noise which passes for music among them. Then there were words spoken, words of encouragement to the workers, exhortation to the members to lead holy and pure lives, and of cheer to those going away. Then we had prayer together, kneeling on the ground under the starry sky; tears were shed, farewells spoken, and so we parted not to meet again until Christ shall come and take us to himself, where we shall dwell forever.

There came a day when a goodly number of that same mission band stood on the quay at Bombay. Tender and tearful farewells had been said, and the wanderers stood together on board the great ship, which in a few minutes was to carry them away from these loving hearts. Shall we ever meet them again? This question came to us as we stood on the deck of the *Simla,* and as she moved slowly out upon the waters of the great deep there came to us the beautiful words of a parting song from those who were there to see us off on our long journey, the words a benediction and a prayer, " God be with you till we meet again." With bowed heads and streaming eyes stood the wanderers on board the ship, alone, and yet not alone, for even as the words of the song were wafted to us on the morning breeze the prayer was answered and God was with us and sustained us as he was with those who stood on the shore.

Yes! beloved in Christ, we shall meet again. It may not be in India, it may not be in America; if not, then it will be in that better land where tears of parting are never shed. And until then God will be with us all to keep what we have committed to him unto that great day.

And so we left them and left India, and again we were impressed with the thought of how quickly all the days and months had fled away, and our stay in India was all too short for us. But time never hangs heavy on one's hands when he is interested and busy in good work. There is no single phase of the mission work in which we were and are not deeply interested, whether it be the evangelistic, the orphanage, the medical, or the educational, for each of these has for its ultimate object the conversion of the heathen. We were moderately busy, too. We traveled over four thousand miles by rail, going about from station to station and to Bombay.

And now we are off on our seventeen days' voyage for Hong Kong, China. It was destined to be one of the most pleasant of all our sea voyages. Barring a few hot days and nights, the journey was all that could be desired.

At Colombo, a thousand miles from Bombay, we transshipped on the *Dongola,* a new steamer of the P. & O. line. She proved to be an excellent sea-going boat and offered the passengers every possible comfort.

Prince Arthur of Connaught, nephew of King Edward VII of England, and his party of English noblemen were passengers on the *Dongola* from Colombo to Hong Kong. We also had Prince and Princess Dhulip Singh, of India, on board as far as Singapore. Prince Arthur goes to Japan to confer the highest order of honor within the gift of King Edward on the mikado.

At Colombo, Penang, Singapore and Hong Kong, all British colonies, Prince Arthur received royal receptions. Royal salutes were fired, triumphal arches erected, cities illuminated and flags and banners were everywhere displayed. At Hong Kong a part of the British fleet assembled to do him honor. The roar of the heavy guns on the great battleship was deafening and we were heartily glad when it was all over. The Chinese quarter of the city was brilliantly lighted up with Chinese lanterns, and presented a grand sight.

I have no fault to find with the prince. The accident of birth has placed him in a position for which he is not responsible. He appears to be a sensible young man, and has a fine, intellectual face and is twenty-two years old. But I do find fault with a system that spends millions in display, burning and worse than wasting money, while paltry thousands go to feed the starving in the empire. There will be more money wasted on these royal tours,—three are in progress at this time, the Prince of Wales in India, the Duke of Connaught, father of Prince Arthur, in South Africa and Prince Arthur to Japan,— than will be given to feed the quarter of a million subjects of the king who are starving in India. And all this by those who profess to follow the lowly Nazarene.

The following extract from a noted journal, not religious, shows how the secular press to some extent regards these royal tours:

" In India they are giving the Prince of Wales a grand send-off. Millions on millions of rupees are being shot away, and eaten away, and drunk away, and squandered on banners, and triumphal arches, and processions, and costly but worthless gifts. It is almost picturesque. Probably the poet laureate, if he could write poetry, could rhapsodize most thrillingly upon it. In India millions are suffering from hunger, tens of thousands are dying of the plague. During the stay of the Prince of Wales, his father's loyal Indian subjects will be lessened by many scores of thousands from these two causes—for neither pestilence nor famine will knock off out of deference to visiting majesty. If this were really a civilized world, England would not send a prince still further to ravage the depleted resources of the Indian people. It would invest the money his visit will cost in food and sanitary appliances."

At Hong Kong the first stage of our home journey was finished, and we quietly awaited coming events. The unrest among the Chinese, the massacre of missionaries and the general feeling of uncertainty on the part of the officials, made us feel that it would not be best to carry out our plans. We had arranged to spend some time in China, go into the interior and study the mission question at short range. It was said that the American minister at Peking had telegraphed to Washington that he feared an outbreak and a massacre of foreigners. Already several United States battleships and gunboats were lying at anchor in the harbor at Hong Kong, ready for an emergency, and it was authoritatively stated by the English newspapers that the officials at Washington had ordered other large battleships to proceed at once to Chinese waters, and also that a large number of troops were being sent to Manila to be near at hand in the event of an outbreak. Things looked decidedly warlike and made the time of our stay in the Flowery Kingdom very uncertain. But the war cloud happily passed away, and now, six months later, it would seem that all danger of an outbreak, such as was feared when we reached Hong Kong, has entirely passed away.

For an account of our stay and our impressions of China and things Chinese, I refer to my notes, written *en route*. In preparing them I drew largely from personal observation and also from a number of excellent authors. I am especially indebted to the " Middle Kingdom," one of the very best books published on Chinese life. The author, Mr. Williams, spent thirty years in the country and was well prepared to write. I also found " Village Life in China," by Smith; "A Cycle in Cathay," Martin; " Wanderings in China," Cumming; " The Attaché at Peking," Mitford, and " Chinese Characteristics," most helpful, and to these authors the writer acknowledges his indebtedness.

The Chinese New Year, which occurs the last half of January or the first half of February, is the occasion of great festivities and immense gatherings in China. The Great Powers, including America, entertained fears that the assembling of so many people might result in the much-talked-of outbreak against foreigners. A score of warships anchored at Hong Kong and Canton, a hundred miles up the river of the same name, had a deterrent influence. At Canton, a center of foreign hostility, a dozen of these powerful peace compellers lay at anchor with the city under their guns. It was a powerful argument in favor of peace, well understood by the Cantonese. The day passed without disorder. I saw the stars and stripes floating from the mastheads of four armored ships. For good or ill our country has become a great world power. If the principles of the Gospel of the Prince of Peace prevailed in the hearts of all his professed followers, these precautionary demonstrations would be entirely unnecessary.

Having come to China for the purpose of becoming better acquainted with the mission field and to learn more of the ways of the people of the country, it was a grievous disappointment when we were told that the doors would be closed against us. We found a good deal of feeling at Hong Kong and the English papers had editorial leaders on the prevailing unrest among the Chinese and of the threatened outbreak against foreigners. Yet we did not feel that we were taking undue risks in visiting Canton. Trusting in the Lord, we went, had an interesting time, a profitable visit and returned unmolested and unharmed.

The distance from Hong Kong to Canton as the steamers run is about one hundred statute miles. A number of comfortable passenger steamers have supplanted the Chinese sampans of the olden time, and daily runs are now made between the two cities. The fare is from one fifty to four dollars first-class, fifty cents second and still cheaper third-class. We took passage on the steamer *Fatshan* with eleven hundred and twenty Chinese and four white passengers. The boat left the dock at Hong Kong at eight-thirty in the morning and at five in the evening we were in the Victoria hotel at Canton.

The day was heavy with clouds, rain, mist and fog. Once we narrowly missed a collision in the dense fog. The engines were suddenly reversed at full power, the boat trembled and shook as if in the grasp of a great giant, but the danger was happily averted. We saw but little of the country, as the fog was so dense as to hide the shores of the river. This was disappointing, and yet the trip was not without interest. When the fog lifted, as it did several times, we caught glimpses of miles upon miles of rice fields on the shores and of the Chinese sampans, house boats, on the river. At places the stream was literally covered with them from side to side.

Where the river flows into the estuary there are a number of ancient forts of considerable interest to the traveler. They were built centuries ago for the defense of the river. A short distance from the forts the stream has been filled with great stones with only a narrow, unobstructed channel left for the passage of steamers. This is to prevent the ascent of the river by a hostile fleet.

At Whampoon about five hundred of our Chinese passengers disembarked. We cast anchor in midstream and in a few minutes were surrounded by Chinese boats to land the passengers. It was a stirring scene, only to be witnessed on the rivers of China. Here one sees how the Chinese have learned the art of packing themselves away in the smallest possible space. It seemed incredible when we were told that we had over eleven hundred souls on our small steamer, but when I saw them scramble out by the hundreds, filling scores of the small river craft, I was compelled to believe.

Approaching Canton one finds boats everywhere. There are myriads of them and they are to be counted by tens of thousands. As far as the eye can reach one sees them moored along the banks of the river. They are arranged in streets and alleys with space for the passage of the river craft, and are regularly numbered as are the houses of a city. Canton has a floating population of over three-quarters of a million, so it is said. It is a floating population in the fullest sense of the word, and presents a phase of life to be found in no other city of the world. On the house boats all the activities of family life are carried on. Here generations have been born, lived, labored, loved, suffered and died, knowing no other retreat or home than the boats of their fathers. Circumscribed by the limits of a boat from twenty to thirty feet in length and eight or ten in width, covered with a semicircular roof made of bamboo basket work, so closely woven as to be rain proof, people live with their pigs, chickens, ducks, geese and children, and they seem to get on well together. The camera would have revealed some interesting details of this strange life, but the continual rain and mist made the use of the kodak impossible.

We left the steamer at the dock, and entering one of the small boats were rowed and poled to the hotel, passing *en route* through street after street of house boats. Some of these, the flower boats, were handsomely decorated, and looked like floating palaces, with their gaudy colors and superabundance of tinsel,—the abode, we are told, of the least reputable class of society. The hotel was crowded and we slept on bunks in the dining room. No! It was only an attempt at sleep. The policemen passed and repassed the house every half hour, each sounding a small drum which the officers carry, doubtless to

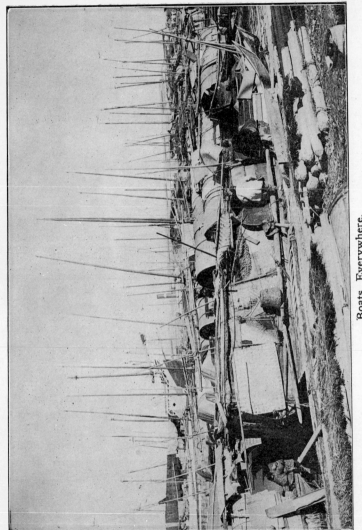

Boats Everywhere.

warn evil doers and to remind others of their presence; also
to keep the newly-arrived traveler awake.

Historians say that Canton was founded B. C. 300. In
those ancient days it bore the name of Nan-Woo-Ching—" The
Martial City of the South." From its start,—it would not be
correct to say from its foundation,—it was a floating town of

Flower Boats.

moored house boats, and its site was moved from place to place
to suit the convenience of its inhabitants. Gradually buildings
were erected on the shores of the stream, and to-day Canton is
one of the most interesting and fascinating cities of its kind
in the world.

The first care of the traveler who wishes to see the old city
is to secure a competent guide, a sedan chair and men to carry

it when he has taken his seat. We secured the service of Woo Chow, a noted guide, whose English was fairly good, and three men to do the carrying. The chair is securely fastened to two long, springy bamboo poles and hangs in the center. The ends of the poles are fastened together by bars wide enough apart so that one rests on each shoulder of the carriers. After you are seated the poles are raised to the shoulders of the men and they trot off with you, apparently with great ease. They are strong, muscular fellows and never seem to tire. And yet my three men had gone only a short distance before complaint was made that " Melican man was too much big," and a fourth carrier was at once secured. I afterwards learned that this was a method they have of securing employment for more of their class. The guide, chairmen and chair cost four and a half taels, or about one dollar and fifty cents, per day.

I had read much of Canton and its environments, I had talked with travelers who had visited the strange city, and had listened to glowing accounts of its wonders, but I confess I never realized what surprises the city had in store for the visitor until I saw it for myself. It was a revelation in more ways than one. I never understood the meaning of the term "density of population " until I was carried through the maze of narrow streets, many of them less than six feet wide, and saw the teeming multitudes thronging the narrow passageways of the old Chinese city.

There are miles and miles of streets in this vast city, with a population estimated as high as three million, so narrow that but a mere strip of blue sky at the tops of the high buildings can be seen, and in many places this is shut out by matting stretched from roof to roof, casting deep shadows and intensifying the mass of rich color below.

The long, broad signboards add much to the quaintness and rich color of the street views. They are not placed horizontally against the walls of the buildings, as in our cities, but are raised perpendicularly, facing the street from both sides of the board.   They are some twenty feet in length and about two feet wide.   Bright colors in deep red, scarlet and yellow, and the use of much gilding, make them really gorgeous in appear-

Street of Heavenly Peace.

ance.   The signs are usually surmounted with the image of some lucky sage or the god of wealth, and at the lower end are spread out two gaudy fans.   Beautifully-colored paper lanterns hang in front of the shops, both for ornament and for lighting at night.

The Chinese are adepts in the use of stilted phrases and are decidedly poetical in the selection of the names of their shops. Here is a weaver of silks, and he has given his shop the name of " Prospered of Heaven," while the ivory carver over the way has chosen the title of " Ten Thousand Times Fortunate." Then there are shops of " Never Ending Good Luck," " Great Gains," and " Market of Golden Profits." In the latter one is left in doubt as to whether the owner gets all the profit or whether the buyer also shares in the streams of gold.

If the names of the shops are peculiar, the names of the streets are none the less so, and if these names indicate the character of the Chinese they must be a peace-loving people. As a matter of history, they did have uninterrupted peace for a space of two hundred years before the Europeans began their encroachments and robberies. You will find such names as these given to the streets of Canton: " Ten Thousandfold Peace," " Everlasting Love," "Accumulated Blessings," " Refreshing Breezes," "A Thousand Beatitudes " and " Heavenly Rest." The love for children's names is manifest in the streets named " One Thousand Grandsons," " One Hundred Grandsons."

CHAPTER IX.

Awakening of a Giant—Through Canton—A Quiet, Orderly People
—Shops and Shops—Ivory Carving—Silk Weaving—Jade
Stone—The Barbers and the Chinese Queue—Curios for Sale
—Outbreak at Nanchang—Massacre of Missionaries.

THE general feeling of unrest prevailing in China to-day
is evidence of the awakening of a great nation from a lethargic
sleep of centuries. The American boycott, the disturbances at
mission stations and the hostility shown to foreigners indicate
the depth of feeling. Many causes are assigned for the
awakening, but the principal reasons are three in number.
The efforts of the missionaries, the contact of the Chinese with
Western peoples and ideas, and last, but by no means least, the
influence of the Russo-Japanese war. For the first time in centuries an Asiatic, heathen nation has been conqueror, on land
and sea, in a series of the most brilliant victories of modern
times, over one of the strongest nominal Christian countries of
Europe. This has made a profound impression on the Asiatic
mind and has awakened a feeling of pride that is sure to carry
the Chinese far in advance of their former conservatism, inac-
tivity and exclusiveness. It is settled that in the future the nations of Europe will not deal with China as they have in the
past.

My last notes closed on the eve of our departure from
Hong Kong for Woosung, Shanghai and possibly Hankow.
We spent a day at Maceo, a port twenty-seven miles from our
starting place, taking on a cargo of thirty tons of opium for
San Francisco. The drug is considered so valuable that a
squad of twenty armed soldiers stood guard over it on the Chi-

nese junk. The stuff will cost the consumers over a quarter of a million dollars, and except the modicum used for medicine, will do no one any good but an incalculable amount of harm.

The opium was produced in India by a Christian(?) government that monopolizes the business and receives a vast revenue from it, shipped to China and prepared by the "heathen Chinee" for use in another nominally Christian country. Strange combination, isn't it, to carry on the destruction of soul and body of hundreds of thousands of opium victims? But there's money in it, and you couldn't run a government without money.

After a pleasant voyage of four days we reached Woosung, where the *Coptic* cast anchor, and we were transferred to a small steamer and came up the river to Shanghai, distance fourteen miles.

Now return we to Canton and its strange sights. Not the least interesting phase of the visit was the skill with which the chairmen threaded their way through the narrow streets, thronged as they were with the vast hordes of people. Crying out continuously the words "Yoh-Hai-Yo," they jogged along at a half trot where open space afforded the opportunity, and squeezing through the throng when necessary, they made rapid progress. At the sound of their cry the people plastered themselves against the walls on both sides of the streets, opening a passageway just wide enough to allow the chair to go through. Once we met a chair coming from the opposite direction and it was only with the greatest difficulty that we passed.

Canton is said to be a center of unrest, but I never saw a quieter or more orderly crowd of people. Everybody appeared to be intent on his own business. There was no lounging on street corners, no drowsiness, no lagging, but a hurrying to and fro, all in the most striking contrast with the movements of the people in India, where energy, push and doing things in the least possible time seem to be lost virtues. The people were kind and courteous, and in not a single instance was the slightest disrespect shown. When I stepped out of the chair to walk through the most interesting places, progress was made at a slow pace. One of the Chinese said to me, " Melican man vely, vely old, no must walk fast." After seeing the city I dismissed the guide and was carried back to the ho-tel, entirely across the town, alone. But the unrest is among the educated and ruling classes, and they control the minds of all others.

In the narrow, dirty, dingy streets are little shops by the thousand where, with the crudest tools, the Chinese workman produces marvels of workmanship and skill in carving, paint-ing, weaving, embroidery and silks ; products surprising to the beholder and astonishing to the world.

The shops are not merely places for the sale of manufac-tured articles and wares, but factories as well, and if you have time and care to wait you may witness the making of the curi-ous things offered for sale. The salesroom is usually in the rear of the workshop and back of this are the family living rooms. At the threshold of the house is a tablet to the earth gods, inside the ancestral tablet, and in the living room the kitchen god. The god of plenty is also in evidence. In front of tablet and image, at stated periods, red tapers and incense sticks are burned. It reminds one of the incense and candle burning of the Greek and Roman churches. The Chinese are said to be a very religious people.

The chair stops in front of an ivory carver's shop. Four men are at work cutting great elephant tusks into suitable shape for their purpose. Others are carefully working on im-ages and figures which when completed will represent years of patient toil. One is working on a ball turned from the tusk. It is about five inches in diameter and has been polished until its surface is as smooth as glass. He cuts fourteen quarter-inch holes to the depth of an eighth of an inch, equally distant, apart, into the surface of the solid ball. Through these openings he proceeds to carve another ball inside the first, and, incredulous as it may seem, continues the process until he has carved nineteen balls each within another, and the last not larger than a pea. Then the outer ball and the larger inner ones are carved into a perfect lace work of the most delicate and perfect figures. He may spend a year on his task and when completed it sells for about forty dollars in gold.

Our next halt is in the street of the silk weaving shops. Here in dimly-lighted, damp, gloomy, filthy rooms weavers are at work with the primitive hand looms,—in use in China when our forefathers lived in caves, wore the skins of wild animals and worshiped pagan gods in northern Europe,—producing some of the finest and most costly silks manufactured. Two men work the loom. One seated above pulls the necessary cords to produce the beautiful figures, while the other seated below thrusts the shuttle through at the proper time and place. It's really all hand work. In America and Europe the machine does the work and the man is simply an auxiliary attendant. Here the man does the work and the machine is auxiliary. They were weaving flowered silk dress goods, the flowers being raised slightly from the surface of the goods. These silks were of the most delicate shades of color and of the most beautiful designs imaginable. The wonder was that such work could be done with such machinery and such environments. It is the perfection of human skill resulting from heredity and continual practice, for the weavers of to-day are the descendants of the weavers of a thousand years ago, and no change has been made in the looms since the days of the fathers.

The street of the jade stone workers is also well worth a visit. Here are rows of shops where this precious stone is cut, carved and polished. It is highly prized among the Chinese and is sold at prices even higher than those secured for diamonds. The stone or mineral is found in the Kuen-lun moun-

Pagoda, Canton.

tains in Turkestan. It is rarely found in any other part of the
world and none has ever been discovered on the American continent.

It is not often found over two inches thick, and when
larger blocks are discovered, if without flaws, they are kept
for the emperor. On such a block an artist may spend a lifetime in producing a sculptured figure to suit the imperial taste.
When, in 1860, the great summer palace of the emperor at
Peking was looted and burned by the English, many of these
priceless art treasures were taken to England and sold at a
nominal price to any who desired to purchase. Mrs. Cumming Gordon in her book, " Wanderings in China," alludes to
this act of vandalism in a paragraph in which reference is
made to jade and the appointment of an artist by the emperor
to work upon a block of the precious stone. She says, " Such
an imperial commission is equivalent to a life work, for although when first broken from its rocky bed the jade may be
easily scratched with a knife, it soon hardens, so as to become the most difficult of all the minerals for the sculptor's
art. Hence, such vases and other ornaments as became familiar to us after the looting of the summer palace, each represented twenty or thirty years of ceaseless toil at the hands of a
faithful and diligent worker. And yet I have seen some of
these priceless art treasures in British homes, where their value
in this respect was undreamt of."

One would think that the purchase and keeping in English
homes of these treasures of art, so highly prized by the Chinese, would bring the blush of shame to the cheeks of the re-
ceivers of looted property. But these things are done in time
of war by Christian nations. A nation may steal and at the
same time have laws that transport a man for life for shooting
a deer. The opening of the present century also witnessed the
looting of the imperial palace at Peking by people calling themselves Christians. Is it any wonder that the Chinese look with

great distrust upon the so-called Christian nations of the world?

A string of beads made of the best jade will be sold to a wealthy Chinaman for about five thousand dollars. Buttons of ordinary size, such as are used to designate rank and scholarship among the Chinese, sell for seventy-five dollars each. The very finest vivid green, like unto an emerald sea, is the most

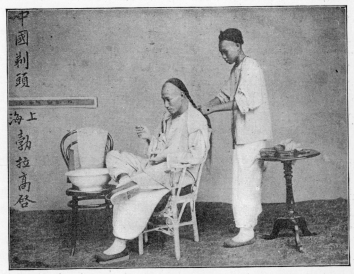

Chinese Barber.

highly prized, and an ornament of moderate size without flaw will readily bring three thousand dollars. Mrs. Gordon may well call the jade ornaments stolen from the summer palace "priceless art treasures."

Many barber shops are to be seen in Canton, and the tonsorial artists all seem to be doing a thriving business. A national and semireligious custom makes it imperative that the hair be allowed to grow only on about two-thirds of the scalp. Draw a closely-fitting skullcap over the head, leaving uncovered a narrow strip of hair all around it, and then shave the uncovered part of the head to the edges of the skull cap, and you have the Chinese cut. The rest of the hair is allowed to grow long, reaching, in some cases, the knees, and is combed smoothly back and carefully braided into the well-known queue, or pigtail, as it is called in ridicule. But why pigtail is hard to tell. It no more resembles the caudal appendage of that animal than do the braided tresses of beautiful hair worn by many Christian women. Fashion dictates that the shaving and hairdressing must be attended to with great regularity; hence the demand for barbers. A man may shave his face, but hardly a narrow swath entirely around his head. Prices for shaving and hairdressing vary as to the rank of the customer. The laborer pays about one cent and others from that up to five and ten cents.

The queue is really a badge of servitude. When the Tartars successfully invaded China and brought the people under subjection in 1615 they imposed the wearing of the queue on the men. Following this imposed custom for centuries has made it the recognized order of wearing the hair, and now no Chinaman would think of making the change to the old way. To lose the queue is considered a great misfortune, only short of death, and one who meets this calamity does not venture to be seen in public until his hair has grown long again. In this respect they somewhat resemble the ancient Jews who placed great store on the beard, and when some of King David's men had their faces shaved by their enemies, they were commanded to remain at Jericho until their beards grew again.

But time and space both fail to tell of all the strange sights of this strange old Chinese city. There are the gruesome execution grounds, where offenders against the law are beheaded or strangled, as the judge may determine; the prisons where instruments of torture are applied, for the stocks and the heavy wooden collar are still in use in China; the temples stocked with idols, one of them has five hundred images crowded into it, where the people worship; the many-storied pagodas of beautiful design and fine workmanship; the homes for aged men and women, for the Chinese show great respect to the aged, where the infirm are cared for; and the palaces and gardens of the wealthy are full of interesting and strange sights.

Then there are the old curios offered for sale at prices beyond the reach of any save the very wealthy, also bronzes, embroideries old and new, silverware, black-wood furniture polished like unto the finest ebony, beautiful screens of rich silk and satin, grass matting of curious design, feather work, fans, paper lanterns, and scores of other things, including the shops where dried rats, dog meat and edible birds' nests are offered for sale, the very mention of which brings a revolting feeling to one's inner anatomy, and the factory of Chy Loong, where the luscious preserved ginger, so well known to epicures everywhere, is prepared. All these and many more, but never a saloon did I see in all the tour through the old town, nor a drunken man in China save three whites who had imbibed too freely. There is a saloon in the English quarter, but if there is a single one in the Chinese city I did not see it.

So page after page might be written descriptive of Canton, and still the subject would not be exhausted. It is a city of ancient ways and ancient days brought into the living present. As we passed and repassed the vast multitudes of human beings we were impressed with the truth of the statement that "these speak of a great nation that has been, a nation that in its day was the greatest, as it is to-day the oldest living nation of the world."

Scott, who visited Canton in 1893, says of it: "Canton is one of the most fascinating and curious cities in the world—a city of the dead ages still alive! Canton with its six-foot-wide streets and dazzling succession of dazzling signboards! Canton with its temples and wondrous idols! Canton with its gruesome execution ground, and mortuaries gay with burial feasts! Canton with its hidden treasures of embroidery in its thousands of unexplored shops! Canton with its life on the river—a city of boats inhabited by mermaidens and mermen, with its flower boats, floating palaces indeed, full of luxury and ease! I am glad I visited China and did not miss Canton."

And now there comes to us at Shanghai news of the outbreak at Nanchang, the burning of the cathedral, churches, schools, missionary property and the cruel murder of ten missionaries. As I write, the wires are carrying an account of the horror to all the civilized world. The leading English papers published here contain particulars of the outrage and the editorial comments seem to place the blame on the missionaries. The *Times* says: "No matter how carefully or gently the onlooker surveys the situation, he is forced to the belief that this is a deliberately-thought-out plan for the extermination of the foreigner. If it should happen that the consummation of such a calamity should take place, it will undoubtedly be due to the missionaries of France, England and America. This is a strong statement to make; but we will give further proof in a future issue."

I shall await with interest the further proof alluded to by the editor. So far as my own observations go, I am decidedly of the opinion that if the Gospel of the Prince of Peace had been brought to China in one hand and the olive branch of peace and love and good-will in the other, none of these difficulties would have been encountered, and China might be a Christian nation to-day. A great statesman once said: "In apostolic days the missionary went out to preach the Word of God. Behind him was the Almighty. Nowadays the missionary goes out, knowing that behind him is a cruiser, a torpedo destroyer, or a battleship." A stronger sermon for the peace principles of Christ could not be written or spoken. If my life is spared I shall revert to this in a future letter.

This recent outbreak precludes all possibility of our going to Hankow, as Nanchang lies between this place and that, and is no great distance from us. The Lord willing, we leave here on the fifth inst. for Japan and home. We feel that there is no occasion for alarm as to our safety. We have long since committed our going and coming into the hands of the Lord, and whatever comes all will be well.

CHAPTER X.

No Saloons at Canton—Opium and Opium Growing in India—
Government Revenue from the Drug—Its Introduction into
China—Efforts of the Emperor to Exclude It—The Opium
War—Effects of Opium on the System—Lord Elgin's Private
Letter—Hindrances to Introduction of Christianity.

ALREADY it has been noted that there are no saloons to be
seen in Canton, and it is to be emphasized that during a stay of
a month in China but three drunken men were seen, and these
were English. But if Canton is free from the curse of the saloon, opium dens abound, and tens of thousands of the Cantonese patronize them. Opium smoking is the great national sin
of China and the dens are to be found in nearly every town and
city in the empire, but perhaps at no other place are there so
many as at Canton.

It may be of interest to the *Messenger* family to read the
story of the introduction of the poisonous drug into the province of Canton. It may also serve as a warning against the
use of this insidious body and soul destroyer, which is making
its victims by the thousands in our own land. Think of the
thirty tons of opium being taken to San Francisco on one ocean
steamer. Look at the rapid increase of the importation of the
drug into America in the last ten years. Unless something is
done to prevent its use we are likely to become a second China
in the use of opium.

First, let us have a brief description of opium growing in
India, adapted from Williams. Practically, opium growing in
India is compulsory. The farmer may want to turn his atten-
tion to raising foodstuff, but is unable to do so. The seed and

361

the money are furnished by the government. The farmers sign the contracts and must turn all the product over to the government agent.

The fields are divided into small beds by ditches running lengthwise and crosswise through the tract to be planted in poppies. A large tank or reservoir furnishes water for irrigating the crop.

The ground is repeatedly plowed and fertilized, becomes mellow and rich, and with proper care produces a large crop. The seed is sown in November, and as soon as the young plants appear above the ground watering begins and is kept up until the flowers are matured. This takes about three months, when the juice is gathered, the gathering covering a period of six weeks.

The opium is contained in the seed pod or capsule of the plant. After the petals have dropped off, the pod is scored or cut with an instrument with four sharp blades. The incision cuts through only the outer skin so as not to damage the pod. The opium juice exudes through the cuts and is allowed to harden for a day and night, and is then carefully scraped off and placed in a dish hanging by the side of the farmer. After it has been gathered it is placed in shallow pans and dried. During the drying process it must be turned over and over in the air until it is ready to take to the factory, where a large quantity is thrown into a large vat and kneaded to a uniform consistency, when it is made into balls and coated with the petals of the poppy. It is then stored in a drying room until ready for packing and shipping. The quality of the drug depends upon the care given it in drying. Covering balls with opium paste also adds to its quality.

When the poppies are in full bloom the fields are surveyed and measured and an estimate is made as to the amount of opium the farmer must deliver to the agent. For this he receives the set price of $1.65 per seer of one pound and thirteen ounces. He has received the money in advance, and if he sells or gives away opium to any one but the government collector, he is subject to severe punishment.

All the opium produced in India is under government monopoly. The government determines each year how much seed shall be sown. The aim is to produce no more than a sufficient supply for the demand so that the price may be maintained. If too much is produced one season, the acreage is cut down the next to even it up. If a farmer should undertake to raise poppies without signing a contract with the government to deliver the product to its collector at a fixed price, his crop would be destroyed unless he could give ample security to deliver the crop to the agent.

As already intimated, the cultivation of the plant is compulsory. Should the farmer refuse the advanced money for the year's crop, the agent throws the rupees into his house, and if he attempts to run away he is seized and the money tied in his dhoty and he is pushed into his house. There is no escape now, and the farmer goes to work to make the best he can out of his bargain, one-sided though it be.

The valley of the Ganges, the best of all the land of India, is given over to opium to the extent of a thousand square miles, and food plants have been crowded out of northern and central India. To some extent at least the terrors of famine would be mitigated if rice and dahl were cultivated on this land instead of the poppy.

The farmer is always anxious to increase the weight of his crop. He does not hesitate, in order to accomplish this result, to adulterate the drug. Sand, clay, cow dung, sugar, molasses, pounded poppy seed, the juice of quinces and other substances are used, and usually the adulteration is detected to the loss of the ryot. When opium is properly dried it is the color of strawberry jam.

All opium grown in India is taken to Calcutta and sold at auction at as high an advance as it will bear. It is rolled in balls with the government stamp affixed and packed in chests each containing 116 pounds. The chests are made of mango wood and closely joined so as to exclude the air. Each chest has twenty partitions so that the balls are partly separated. After the boxes are closed they are covered with rawhide or heavy gunny cloth and seams are closed so as to render it still more nearly impervious to the air.

The government revenue on opium has become so great that a leading Indian editor has said the raising of opium is a matter of life and death to the government of the country. Note the increase in revenue between the years 1840 and 1872. At the first date the revenue amounted to ten million dollars and at the latter it had increased to nearly forty million dollars. Since then I am informed it has gone as high as seventy million dollars. The drug sells at Hong Kong for about $580 per pecul of one hundred and thirty-two pounds.

The Chinese taste has been so carefully studied and the drug is so carefully prepared and of such uniform quality that the inhabitants of the Flowery Kingdom will pay a much higher price for India opium than for any other.

It was at Canton, the one open port in China at the time that the British East India Company first introduced India opium into the Chinese empire. The trade was fostered for the money there was in it, and no thought seems to have troubled the traders as to the result on the Chinamen. When Great Britain took over the East India Company and with it the Indian Empire, she kept up the trade and entered into the business of raising opium, thus securing annually a large revenue for the government.

When the effects of the drug became apparent the Chinese officials, and finally the emperor himself, entered plea after plea and protest after protest against the opium trade. Laws were passed against its use and a number of those who used it were put to death. Finally when plea, protest, and law failed, the emperor caused 20,291 chests of the poisonous drug to be seized at Canton and destroyed. Deep trenches were dug in the earth, the opium balls were broken into pieces and thrown in and covered with quicklime. Then water was turned in upon the mass and the destruction was complete. And so some millions of pounds of the stuff went up in smoke, but poor weak China had to pay the bill. She had a strong, warlike nation, professedly Christian, with which to deal, and what did the protest of the heathen amount to? Simply nothing. England wanted the revenue and the Chinese had to suffer.

The result of this righteous act on the part of the Chinese emperor was the Opium War. Canton was bombarded by the English, some thousands of Chinese were slaughtered by their enemy, who scarcely received a scratch in comparison, the emperor was compelled to pay an indemnity of $21,000,000, to cede the island of Hong Kong to Great Britain and to open the ports of Canton, Amoy, Fuchau, Ningpo and Shanghai to British trade and indirectly for opium. So the dignity of England was sustained and her opium monopoly revenue protected and increased in the end by tens of millions.

The treaty following the one-sided conflict was made on the part of the English by Sir Henry Pottinger, who met the Chinese commissioners. When it came to the discussion of the opium the emperor's commissioner asked this question: " Why can you not act fairly toward us by prohibiting the growth of the poppy in your dominions and thus effectually stop a traffic so pernicious to the human race?" The reply to this plain, simple question, a question worthy the highest possible consideration, was, " If we do not raise opium and bring it to your people the trade will fall into other hands. Some one will bring it to them. If your people are virtuous they will desist from the evil practice. The remedy rests with you and not with us. Quit the use of opium and the demand will cease and the drug will cease to come to your country." It will be noticed that this is exactly the same kind of an argument as that used by the rumseller when the starving mother and children of a drunken husband plead with him not to sell father whiskey.

The English commissioner urged upon the Chinese to legalize the importation of opium at the five treaty ports before named, setting forth that by legalizing it and charging a tariff a large revenue would accrue to the government, that the drug would be brought in any way and they might as well make its importation legal and so secure the revenue. This the Chinese absolutely refused to do, and so for many years the British continued to furnish the Chinese people with opium contrary to law.

History is searched in vain for a parallel of the Opium War. On the one side is the heathen emperor striving in vain to protect his people from a great evil, the curse of the opium habit. On the other a Christian (?) nation forcing the poisonous drug upon them. Then when from sheer desperation the opium is destroyed, a braver act than the destruction of tea in Boston harbor, the strong nation pounces upon the weak, robs it of a portion of its territory, compels it to pay a large indemnity and forces it to open five ports for trade and opium. The Chinese were but as children compared to the English. For nearly two centuries they had lived in peace. They were entirely ignorant of the art of modern warfare. The war was a one-sided slaughter of the innocents. No darker or deeper stain of dishonor rests upon any nation in the world than the Opium War has cast upon the British. Will it not be more tolerable in the day of judgment for the Chinese, heathen though they were and are, than for those professing Christians who engaged in this terrible crime and frightful sin? And what was it done for? Only that the English government might have a little larger revenue.

The enormity of this crime of the centuries will be better understood when the effects of opium on the human system are considered. An eminent physician who has made a careful study of the effects of the drug on the human body says the effects of this habit on the constitution are displayed by stupor, forgetfulness, general deterioration of all the mental faculties, emaciation, debility, sallow complexion, lividness of lips and eyelids, languor and lack of lustre in the eye, and the appetite either destroyed or depraved. To this may be added these words of a Chinese writer: " When first taken it raises the animal spirit and prevents lassitude, but afterwards it exhausts the animal spirit, impedes the regular performance of business, wastes the flesh and blood, dissipates every kind of property, renders the person ill-favored, promotes obscenity, discloses secrets, violates laws, attacks the vitals and destroys life. The smokers doze for days over their pipes without appetites. When the desire for opium comes over them they cannot resist the impulse. Mucus flows from their nostrils and tears from their eyes. Their very bodies are putrid and rotten. The poor victim who has pawned every article in his possession still remains idle, and when the thirst comes on will pawn his wife and children. I knew a poor fellow who smoked away all he had, then sold his wife and child for thirty dollars, smoked that away and then went out and hanged himself."

No wonder the heathen emperor labored so hard to save his people from this worse than living death. Let those who read beware of this insidious habit. The increased importation of the drug into our country tells its own sad story. Physicians prescribe it to relieve pain and in this way the habit is often fastened unwittingly on the poor victim. Could the story of the lives and homes destroyed by opium be written it would cause strong men to weep.

The Opium War led to complications, and in 1860 England was again at war with China to maintain her dignity.

This time she was joined by another Christian (?) nation of Europe, France. The chief actor in the war was Lord Elgin. A private letter to a friend tells how he felt about it. He writes: "On the afternoon of Dec. 20th I got into a gunboat with Commodore Elliott, and went a short way up the river toward the barrier forts, which were last winter destroyed by the Americans. When we reached this point, all was so quiet that we determined to go on, and we actually steamed past the city

Opium Smokers, Canton.

of Canton, along the whole water front, within pistol shot of the town, in front of which were now anchored a line of English men-of-war. I never felt so ashamed of myself in my life. Elliott said to me, 'This trip seems to have made you sad!' There were accumulating the means of destruction under the very eyes and within reach of a population of about one million people, against whom the means of destruction were to be employed! 'Yes,' I said to Elliott, 'I am sad, because when I look at that town I feel that I am earning for myself a place in the litany immediately following after plague, pestilence and famine.' I believe, however, that as far as I am concerned, it was impossible for me to do otherwise than I have done. When we steamed up to Canton and saw the rich alluvial banks covered with luxurious evidences of unrivalled industry and natural fertility combined, I thought bitterly of those who, for the most selfish objects, are trampling under foot this ancient civilization."*

Here spoke the better nature of Lord Elgin, and if he had followed his convictions of right the result would have been different. A soldier's duty, it is said, is to do and die. Elgin did the bidding of England. A furious bombardment was opened on Canton, driving the people like frightened sheep to the western suburbs and destroying a large portion of the city. Canton was again taken, and later on the summer palace of the emperor was looted and burned at Peking, and some thousands of the Chinese were killed. The allied forces escaped without serious loss and the ancient civilization of China was trampled under foot for the most selfish objects of the Christian(?) nations of Europe. Is it to be wondered at that the Chinese distrust and look with suspicion on the nations of Europe and the type of Christianity they represent?

Russia, Germany, England and France have, in turn, by force of arms taken from China large portions of her ancient empire. It was the strong coveting the possessions of the weak and taking them under the false principle that might makes right.

By the treaty of peace following the second war, China was bound over to keep the peace, to tolerate Christianity in

*From "The Middle Kingdom."

the empire, to allow foreign ministers to reside at Peking and the right of foreigners to travel through the land. The toleration of Christianity was forced on China as opium had been by war. Is it to be wondered at that the Chinese are in a state of unrest and that she distrusts Christianity? Every missionary is a reminder of her humiliation, for, right or wrong, the Chinese associate the missionary and the war power of Europe as forming part of the same system from which she has suffered so much wrong in the last sixty years.

One of the great hindrances to the introduction of Christianity into China is the treatment she has received at the hands of nations with whom she associates Christianity. To the ruling and educated classes the missionary is not only a religious teacher but a political propagandist as well. It is probable that the Roman Catholics with France behind them have done more to confirm the Chinese in this opinion than any other power. A few years ago an irresponsible mob killed two German missionaries at Shantung. China did all in her power to make amends, but Germany only satisfied herself by seizing a port and taking a slice of Chinese territory which she holds to-day. The mailed fist, the battleship and the sword followed in the footsteps of the missionary. And the Chinese without noting distinctions look upon the one as the concomitant of the other. The Chinese charge all the outrages of the last sixty years against Christianity. Oh, how the cause of the Prince of Peace has suffered and is suffering because of the wrongs done by his professed followers!

If the Gospel of Jesus Christ had been carried to China in one hand and the olive branch of peace, good-will and brotherhood in the other, if the greed, avarice, and covetousness of professed Christian Europe had been curbed, China might have been won for Christ long ere this. But war, bloodshed, robbery and all attendant evils have followed the advance of the white race, the recognized representatives of Christianity. Our own century of dishonor in dealing with the red man, the murderous wars in Africa, the stamping out of the aboriginals of Australia, and the injustice done the Chinese are all in evidence against the cruelty of the white man's advance and entirely contrary to the teachings of Jesus Christ, the Prince of Peace. If the advance had been made as William Penn sought to make it in America, and as Livingstone made it in Central Africa, without the sword, the name of Christianity would not now be stained with the crimes of modern times. But while the cause of Christ has been made to bleed in this way I rejoice to know that there is a people in the world who protest against this wickedness. I rejoice also that the principles of peace, for which Christ's teaching stands, is gaining ground in the world. May God hasten the day when the swords shall be beaten into plowshares and nations shall no more learn the art of war.

But so many ministers of the Gospel of Peace teach the war spirit from the pulpit. When we were in Sydney we listened to a sermon, and I made the following note of it at the time:

Last night we went to hear the Scotch Presbyterian Rev. Mr. Ferguson. It was to a crowded house he spoke. Even the pulpit steps were filled with hearers. He is a strong man physically, with a fine presence, has a deep, well-modulated voice, enunciates with clearness, is strenuous in manner and matter, has the build and make-up of the orator and carries his audience with him. It was the anniversary of Trafalgar, where Lord Nelson fell mortally wounded, the man whose flag was nailed to the masthead of his ship and could not be lowered. The preacher's theme was " Nelson Our Naval Hero." And how he did laud his hero and condone his bloody deeds, and how masterfully he painted the splendor and glory of his fame. It was a splendid effort, a finished piece of oratory, a masterful presentation of the supposed virtues of a man whose hands

were dyed red with the blood of England's enemies. He said
those were times when it would not do to turn the smitten
cheek to the enemy, but the mailed fist, the sharpened cutlass,
cold steel, and powder and lead. This kind of preaching,—I
thought as I listened, carried away with the eloquence and
earnestness of the speaker,—is doing more to keep up the
spirit of war than any other influence in the world to-day. It is
the pulpit firing the hearts of the young to emulate the deeds
of bloodshed which are held to have made a hero of Nelson.
Were England to cover her fair body in sackcloth and lie with
her face in the dust and ashes upon her head she would more
fittingly observe the anniversary of the bloody man who did
her imperial bidding; a man whose motto was, " Be faithful to
the king," not the King of Peace, but the king of England.
How the Son of God, the Prince of Peace, who came to bring
peace on earth and good-will to men, must be grieved when his
accredited ministers turn their pulpits into lecture platforms
from which to laud the men who have done most to shed human blood and to bring wretchedness and misery to human
hearts. Were this strong man, and all who like him are in the
holy order of the ministry, to lift their voices against war with
all of its hellish cruelty and heartache, wretchedness and sorrow, war would cease from off the face of the earth.

CHAPTER XI.

AT Canton I had the pleasure of meeting Mr. Joseph Lind, General Manager and Superintendent of the Canton and Hankow Railway. A Pennsylvanian by birth, Mr. Lind has spent a number of years in China, knows the people and is well acquainted with things Chinese. Upon comparing notes, we found our native States separated only by Mason and Dixon's line, also Maijee was a Philadelphian; all of which established an immediate acquaintance between us. At home we live in the same town for years with people and do not know them personally, but let us meet in the antipodes and a close relationship is at once established. One feels at times that he would travel miles to meet a fellow-countryman of the right type. So we felt when we met Mr. Lind.

He very kindly invited us to make a tour of the railway in his company, an invitation highly prized and gladly accepted. Mr. Lind is so well acquainted with all the conditions in China, and was so kindly communicative, that it was really a great privilege to travel with him. It afforded an excellent opportunity to see something of the country and to become acquainted with the home life of the people from one who knows. On every hand Mr. Lind was shown the greatest respect by the Chinese. They hold him in high esteem, for he has been just and generous in his treatment of them, and they are as amenable to kindness as any people in the world.

The Canton and Hankow Railroad was surveyed and partly constructed under a concession granted by the Chinese government to a company of American capitalists. Later a large amount of the stock was sold to the Belgians. Now comes the awakening of China with the cry of "Asia for the Asiatics," and the agitation of the question of canceling all foreign concessions and the determination of the Chinese to build and control their own railroads. Here was an opportunity to practice a bit of high finance. China paid six and a half million dollars for the canceling of the concession for building the Canton and Hankow Railway. Only a million and a half had been spent on it. A clear profit of five million to the American company. This deal was carried through by well-known New York financiers, and is said to have done incalculable damage to the good name of our country in China. Business knows no patriotism, and high finance has lost all sense of honor and old-fashioned honesty. We are living under the rule of gold instead of the golden rule.

Leaving Canton, the road passes through a rich alluvial country given almost wholly to the cultivation of rice and the mulberry tree, the leaves of which are fed to the silkworm. So well is the soil cultivated and so careful are the Chinese in saving any and everything in the shape of fertilizers, that two large crops are harvested each year. The water supply of the district through which we passed is superabundant. Instead of droughts, floods are most feared. Instead of acres of rice, here is rice by the square mile, and in this part of China, at least, the people are prosperous.

In many of the fields women were at work turning over the soil and getting it ready for the water. This is hard work. Armed with a long-handled, fork-pronged hoe, the tines of which are driven into the baked earth, the women succeed in pulling clod after clod over until in this slow way the entire field is turned over. Most of the women at work had each a child strapped to her back. The weight of her babe seemed to help her in turning over the ground. After her work is done, water is turned into the field and earth and water mixed to the consistency of a bed of thin mortar, into which the young rice plants are stuck in rows.

The women also do all the work in raising silkworms, gathering the mulberry leaves, feeding them, and, when the worm has spun his cocoon, in winding the silk in skeins and getting it ready for the market. Canton is the center of the great silk industry of China. When our forefathers lived in caves and wore the skins of wild animals for clothing, the Cantonese spun and wove fine silk for their robes. Mr. Lind tells me that the Chinese are the most prolific, industrious, quiet, peaceable people in the world. While the women are turning over the soil of the rice fields or gathering mulberry leaves and rearing silkworms, the men and boys and girls old enough are hard at work in other lines of industrial activities.

Another of the interesting industries carried on by the Cantonese is that of duck farming. Immense numbers of these fowls are reared along the waterways in the district. For hundreds of years the Chinese poultrymen have been using the incubator, not the complicated incubator of our modern civilization, but one of which the man himself is an important part. The eggs are placed in baskets and moved from place to place in a heated room so that the required temperature may be secured. The man has no use for a thermometer to indicate the degree of heat. He has by long usage learned to tell when the eggs are too hot or too cold by the sense of touch, and so finely has this sense been developed that he succeeds in having ninety per cent of the eggs hatch.

After the ducklings have attained the proper size, they are placed on flat boats and taken along the streams to gather their food. In the early morning a plank is laid from the boat to the shore and they march down and out as orderly as a file of soldiers. When the day's feeding is over the plank is again laid down and the fowls march on board to their roosting place for the night. They are so well trained that as soon as the plank is placed there is a rush among them to get on board,

Duck Eggs and Egg Merchant, Shanghai.

and this rush is to be accounted for by the fact that the last ones on the plank always get a whipping. A ready and profitable market is found for ducks and eggs in Canton.

Sam Shui, "Three Waters," so named because of the junction of three rivers at this place, is the present terminus of the Canton and Hankow Railroad. The Chinese are poetically inclined in giving names to their towns and cities. Not far from this place is a station on the railway called Men Shui, "Five Eyed," so called because of a beautiful five-arch bridge which spans the river at the place. To the poetic imagination of the people the arches are five great eyes, hence the name of the town.

The terminus of the railroad is an ancient, walled Chinese city outside the beaten line of travel, hence seldom seen by the world tourist. It is an interesting old place and is well worth a visit. Outside the principal gate of the city is a fine type of the ancient temple of the country. It is centuries old and shows how little change there has been in Chinese architecture in a millennium. At the time of our visit the place was crowded with worshipers, mostly women, making offerings to the god of maternity.

Behind a small counter in one corner of the inclosure stood two fat, sleek-looking priests, who were kept busy receiving " cash," a small Chinese coin worth about a mill, and handing out large sheets of paper and joss sticks. On the counter stood several wooden boxes containing a number of flat strips of bamboo, about three inches in length, on which were written Chinese characters. The women came up to the counter, took the boxes in their hands, shook them so as thoroughly to mix the pieces of bamboo, drew out a strip and handed it with their money to the priest. He at once copied the inscription,—which was supposed to bring to the worshiper the desire of her heart,—on a large sheet of paper, which with a handful of joss sticks was handed back to the woman. The sheet of paper she burned on an altar in front of the god, and the joss sticks, a kind of a candle, she lighted and stuck into holes at the feet of the image. Apparently this completed the act of worship. The burning joss sticks at the feet of the image reminded me of the lighted candles at the shrine of the Virgin at Lourdes in France.

In the temple one heard a continuous clatter of tongues punctuated every few minutes by the discharge of a bundle of firecrackers, which added greatly to the general confusion. The Chinese have a Fourth of July, so far as firecrackers are concerned, every day they worship in their temples, and that is about every day in the week. The people came and went, thronging the place all the time we were there. It was as noisy and at the same time as good natured a crowd as one could wish to see. Many of the people recognized Mr. Lind with a smile, and the words, " Chin-chin," a form of salutation, were heard from many lips. One would never suspect harm from these people, and yet who can forget for a moment the horrors of the Boxer massacres?

At the outer door of the temple, beneath the corridor, a vegetable market was being held. What fine vegetables the Chinese raise, the finest in the world! After seeing their gardens, their methods of cultivation and the vegetables they raise, I no longer wondered why the market gardens of California have been captured by the patient Celestial. As the worshipers came out of the temple they made such purchases as they desired, and so departed to their homes in the city.

Returning to Canton, we had only time to catch a belated boat for Hong Kong. It was late in the evening when our steamer turned its prow down the river. Before proceeding many miles a heavy fog came down and we tied up at the shore for the night. Owing to the great number of small craft on the river, it is unsafe to run in the fog.

At Canton a number of missions are located, and these all report a successful year's work. Indeed, all the missionaries with whom I conversed in China were hopeful of the future. At the Baptist mission I met the manager of the Baptist Publishing House, Mr. Brown, who very kindly gave me information as to their work and showed me over their printing establishment. The Chinese printed from movable type long before the discovery was made in Europe. I was interested in examining a font of Chinese type in which there were eleven thousand different characters. I do not mean to say that I examined the entire eleven thousand pieces of type. But I looked over the collection and thought of our typos at Elgin and wondered how long it would take one of them to learn to set type in Chinese. Here the typesetters were busy at work, not perched on stools, but running hither and thither picking out the required character on the run. All these thousands of ideographs are to be remembered before one can set type in a Chinese printing office. And then, to make the whole thing still more confusing, many of the characters have half a dozen different meanings and uses.

The printing press is not in evidence in the Chinese office. The work is literally done by hand. I watched the real printer at work. He was making a page of the New Testament and making one page at a time. He had the page in type on a table in front of him and a pile of paper cut to the proper size at his right hand. He inked the type with a little whisk broom, then without other gauge or guide than his hand and practiced eye, he laid the sheet on the type and passed a brush over it, and so the printing was done. This is real handwork, and for accuracy of register and evenness of impression it equals some of our best work done at home. We regretted very much that our time was so limited at Canton, for we wanted to see more of the missions. Instead of a month we should have had a year in China.

CHAPTER XII.

Chinese Conservatism—Social Life—Emperor Supreme—Religions —Confucianism—Medicine and Diseases—Strange Remedies— The Horse—The White Wax Tree—The Dog—Rats—Bamboo —Methods of Punishment.

THE closing chapter of things Chinese is to be one made up of such things as fell under my notice in reading and traveling, and which seem to me to be worth setting down, but have not found a place in the preceding chapters.

Strictly speaking, China is the one conservative nation of the world. What was is, and what is was. Except in matters of minor detail, nothing has changed in China for centuries. There is not an institution or a custom but that has its foundations in antiquity and draws its inspiration from the sages of the ages past. In essentials there has been no change for thousands of years. The farmer, the artisan, the merchant follows in the footsteps of his ancestors, and follows the old customs. The plow invented by a Chinese emperor has changed in no whit in twenty centuries. The political and social life is as it was when the sages lived. The reason for all this adherence to ancient custom is to be found in the reverence shown by the Chinese for their ancestors, which has been erroneously called ancestor worship, and also in the belief that the mantle of perfect wisdom had fallen on the sages and wise men who perfected the laws and crystallized the customs of the people. To depart from the ways of the fathers is to commit a sacrilege and to show an irreverence and a want of filial piety and love that is not to be thought of for a moment among the Chinese.

380

So the Chinaman, wherever you find him,—and you may find him in all parts of the habitable world,—is a Chinaman still. He wears his pigtail, and his national costume and clings to the ways of the fathers wherever he may be found.

"If the death of the emperor is announced, it is proclaimed in the words used by Yao, who lived before the time of Abraham. If a mandarin writes a controversial dispatch, he bases his arguments on the sayings of Confucius; if a youth presents himself at the public examinations, he is expected to compose essays on themes from four books and five classics of antiquity; and if a man writes to congratulate a friend on the birth of a daughter, he does so in phraseology drawn from the national odes, which were sung and chanted before the days of Homer."

The society, the social fabric of China is very simple. At its head stands the emperor and his court. These are first in all that pertains to social and political and religious life. Religiously the emperor is the high priest of the Chinese religion, the supreme head of the nation. After the emperor and his court, are the office holders, and then the common people. There are a few families to be classed as aristocracy, but these are limited to half a dozen or more. The farmers, mechanics and merchants form a common level. If there is any difference in these, it is in favor of the farmer.

The emperor reigns supreme; he is the one autocrat of the world; his power is only limited by the endurance of his people, and they are endowed with great endurance. His subjects reverence and worship him. His titles show what he is in the eyes of his people. "The Son of Heaven," "Celestial Ruler," "Lord of Ten Thousand Years," and other extravagantly laudatory titles are given him. He is supposed to rule by direct command of heaven, and he alone of all his people is entitled to worship the azure heaven. This rite is performed in the winter and is attended with the most august ceremony. It takes place in the temple of heaven in Peking, where the emperor kneels and acknowledges that he is inferior to heaven, and to heaven alone.

On the evening of December 20, the emperor goes to the temple where an offering is made to " The Supreme Ruler." After these ceremonies he is dressed in his priestly robes, and fire is set to the whole burnt offering, which consists of a bullock of two years old and without blemish. He then, having invoked the supreme power of heaven, makes other offerings with incense at the sacred shrine and at that of his ancestors. In this way the emperor assumes the authority of the vicegerent of heaven, and by common consent of all his people is acknowledged to have coördinate power of heaven.*

The scholarly class of educated men are those who take examinations and hope at some time to be employed by the government.

Next to these stand the farmers. The tiller of the soil occupies an enviable place among the community. This is because the inventor of the plow was an emperor named Shenung Rhennung, who lived 2737 B. C. The connection between throne and plow has been kept up through all the succeeding centuries, and at the present time the emperor, in the early springtime turns a furrow to inaugurate the beginning of the planting season. This example is followed in every province by viceroy or governor. The empress, to set an example to her sex, as soon as the leaves appear on the mulberry trees, gathers them to supply food for the silkworms of the palace. One of their wise emperors, Kanghsi, wrote, " Give place to husbandry and the cultivation of the mulberry tree, in order to procure adequate supplies of food and raiment. Suffer not a barren spot to remain in the wilds, nor a lazy person to abide in the cities; then a farmer will

---

*" Society in China, " pp. 4, 5.

not lay aside his plow and hoe; nor the housewife put away her silkworms and her weaving."

These maxims are a part of the national life, and perhaps nowhere in the world will you find a more industrious class than the farmers of China. Of course self-interest is also an incentive, but frugality and industry are national characteristics of the Chinese. Those who are familiar with California will recall how the Chinese succeed as market gardeners about the towns and cities of that State.

They toil early and late, are very economical, save every atom of manure that may go to enrich the ground, and with indefatigable labor and with every possible resource they wrest from the soil the utmost that it is capable of producing. In China the laws are against them and they are kept poor by a hard system of taxation, and a low, grinding poverty is the result. The tax is fixed at about $2.50 per acre, but it is stated that often the farmer is compelled to pay six times as much to satisfy the avaricious taxgatherers and those who share in the spoil.

Two of the leading industries in China are rice and the silkworm. The mulberry tree is largely cultivated and the women gather the leaves and feed the worms, while men plant and harvest the crop of rice. The poppy is now also extensively grown and opium is produced in about every province in the country.

The plow, the hoe and the bill hook, which serves the purpose of pruning hook, scythes, sickle, with rakes, complete the farmer's stock of implements. The plow is very primitive. The implement is made by fastening an iron point or share to the end of a bamboo stick of proper length, a single handle at the top and a pole fastened in the center to which the oxen or buffaloes are fastened, complete the rude affair. With this excuse for a plow the ground can be stirred only to a slight depth and the farmer supplements the plow with the hoe, which is made to do duty in getting the fields ready for the seed. As a rule ten acres is the limit of one man's holdings.

The religions of China may be classified under the following heads: Confucianism,—which is hardly to be called a religion; it was rather a system of philosophy,—Taoism, Buddhism, Christianity, and Moslemism.

Confucius was born B. C. 551, died B. C. 479. He was

Taking the Pig to Market.

not a religious teacher, but a philosopher and a thinker. He taught nothing new, but taught men to turn to the counsels of the sages who lived 2,000 years before his time. He found the sayings of Yao and Shan in the book of history and the records of the past, and to him these were the acme of all wisdom and virtue. The central dogma was that all men were born good and that in order to attain to the highest virtue one must only follow his natural strivings for good. Good becomes contaminated when men neglect to follow its strivings. Only in one saying did Confucius rise to the grand level of Christianity, and that was when he enunciated the command to his followers, " What you do not want done to yourself, do not do to others." There was no place in his philosophy for the divine. There was no reward for right doing or punishment for wrong. His teaching was of the earth, earthy. Asked as to the future, he replied that while we know so little of the present it is folly to think of the future.

Laotzu, who lived at the same time with Confucius, although a younger man, crystallized the teachings of a number of men who called themselves Taoists. These teachers had come into personal contact with the Brahminical philosophy of India. Their teachings were vague and shadowy. It remained for Laotzu to bring them into a system that was to have a marked influence over the Chinese.

" His main object was to explain to his followers the relation between the universe and that which he called Tao. The first meaning of this word is the way; but in the teachings of Laotzu it was much more than that. It was the way and the way goer. It was an eternal road; along it all beings and all things walked, but no being made it, for it is being made itself; it was everything and nothing, and the cause and effect of all. All things originated from Tao, conformed to Tao, and to Tao they at last returned. Years after their death the Chinese deified these teachers, and later still manufactured images, and so the philosophy of the teachers was turned into a system of idolatry second only to that of India."

Medicine.

There are no doctors in China who deserve that name. There are many who profess to be able to help the sick. When the doctor is called he feels the pulse of both wrists.

The left indicates the condition of the heart, which is the husband, and the right of the lungs, which is the wife. If these two act in harmony and peace, then good health obtains; if there is a lack of harmony between husband and wife, then evil results. Apapuncture and vaccination for smallpox is practiced. If a joint be swollen or there is rheumatism, the doctor inserts a substantial steel needle and stirs it around. It is said that they do not hesitate to thrust the needle into the stomach and liver. They do not understand anatomy or the circulation of the blood. They have 442 remedies enumerated in their native pharmacœpia. Among these are asbestos, stalactite, fresh tops of stag horn, dried red spotted lizard skins, dog's flesh, tortoise shell, and teeth and bones of dragon. Cholera, diphtheria and smallpox sweep off tens of thousands, and the people are helpless. The late emperor died with the smallpox.

A Chinese author discusses in a very methodical manner, in a great book on science and medicine, the qualities of plants, animals and minerals. The student can turn to the plant, mineral or animal and learn its virtues at once. The horse is referred to at considerable length. The varieties of horses and the best kinds for food and medical use are elaborately set forth for the guidance of the medical practitioner. It is said that the pure white are the best for medicine. Those found in the south and east are small and weak. The age is known by the teeth. The horse reflects the full image of a man. If he eat rice, his feet will become heavy; if rat's dung, his belly will grow long; if his teeth be rubbed with dead silkworms, or black plums, he will not eat, nor if the skin of a rat or wolf be hung in his manger. He should not be allowed to eat from a hog's trough, lest he contract disease; and if a monkey be kept in a stable he will not fall sick. The flesh is treated as an article of food, and it is stated that the flesh of a pure white stallion is the most wholesome. It is recommended that after " eating horse flesh, almonds and rush broth should be taken if the eater feels uncomfortable from his meal. It should be roasted and eaten with ginger and pork; and to eat the flesh of a black horse, and not drink wine with it, will surely produce death." The fat on the croup of the

TEA PACKING.
(Don't look at this picture or study it too closely if you are a tea drinker. The tea is pressed into the chest with the feet, and they are not always clean.)

horse is said to be sweet and good to make the hair grow and the face shine. Reference is also made to the properties of the milk, heart, lungs, kidneys, placenta, teeth, bones, skin, mane, tail, brains, blood, perspiration, and excrements. Eating the liver of a horse is forbidden because of the absence of the gall bladder, which is presumed to remove the poison from the liver of such animals as possess it. It is said that the heart of the white horse, or that of a hog, cow or hen, when dried and grated into spirits, and so taken, cures forgetfulness. If the patient hears one thing he knows ten. Above the knees the books say the horse has night eyes (warts) which enable him to go in the night; they are useful in toothache. If a man be restless and hysterical when he wishes to sleep, and it is needful to put him to rest, let the ashes of a horse's skull be mingled with water and given him, and let him have a skull for a pillow. The hoof of a horse if hung in the house is supposed to bring good luck, as the nailing of a horseshoe is supposed to do by some who should know better.

The white wax tree furnishes nourishment to an insect called the cocus pela, the larvæ of which furnish the wax which is white, translucent and highly crystalline. The department of Kia-ting furnishes the best wax, as its climate is warmer than Chingtu. The eggs of the insect are gathered in Kien-Chang and Ning-yuen, where the tree flourishes on which it deposits them, and its culture is carefully attended to. The insect lives and breeds on this evergreen, and in April the eggs are collected and carried up to Kia-ting by porters. This journey is mostly performed by night, so as to avoid the risk of hatching their loads; three hundred eggs weigh one tael. They are instantly placed on the same kind of tree, six or seven balls of eggs done up in palm-leaf bags and hung on the twigs. In a few days the larvæ begin to spread over the branches, but do not touch the leaves; the bark soon becomes incrusted with a white powder, and is not disturbed till August. The loaded branches are then cut off and boiled, when the wax collects on the surface of the water, is skimmed off, and melted again to be poured into pans for sale. A tael's weight of eggs will produce two or three catties of the translucent, highly crystalline wax; it sells there for five mace a tael and upward. The annual income is reckoned at two million taels. The purposes to which this singular substance is applied include all those of beeswax.

Pills are ingeniously inclosed in small globes of it, and candles of every size are made.

Dogs.

The Chinese dog is very like that reared among the Eskimos and is in all probability the original of the species. They are about a foot high and two feet in length. Pale yellow or black is the color, and this is always uniform. The hair is coarse and bristly, and the tail curves very tightly over the back; so much so that someone has said that it helps to lift the hind legs off the ground. They have sharp, upright ears and bright, black eyes and a peaked head. Those raised for eating are carefully fed on special food and at the markets in all the larger cities command the highest price offered for any kind of meat and are very expensive.

Rats.

If one were to believe travelers in general, it would be said that the Chinese are great rat-eaters, but it is stated on the best authority that this is incorrect. Like the meat of the dog, this meat is too expensive for the poorer classes, and only the wealthy may indulge in the toothsome morsel.

Bamboo.

To see the bamboo grow in its native clime is to see a picture of beauty and grace. A clump of this remarkable vegetable or grass, as it is sometimes called, throws out new shoots from its mass of roots, until the grove is developed. The bamboo attains a height of from fifty to seventy-five feet and in thickness is from that of a pipe stem to twelve inches in diameter.

Its uses are so varied that it would require a volume to give a full description of them. The shoots come out of the ground full grown from six to eight inches in diameter and are cut like asparagus, are pickled or boiled or stewed, and properly prepared make a savory dish. From the joints of the old stems a medicine is scraped which is highly prized for all kinds of disease. The roots of fantastic shapes are carved into umbrella handles or walking sticks and also into unique images and divining blocks.

The long, tapering bamboo poles are seen everywhere in the East, and are used wherever a pole can be utilized; " in

THE COMPRESSED FOOT.
(Many Chinese girl babies have their feet bandaged and pressed into shape seen in photo.)

carrying, propelling, supporting and measuring, for which their light, elastic, tubular structure, guarded by a covering of silicious skin, and strengthened by a thick septum at each joint, most admirably fits them. The pillars and props of houses, the framework of awnings, the lath on which to daub the mud as plaster, the rafters and closer lath work for the tiles of the houses, the ribs of mat sails, and the shafts of rakes are furnished by the bamboo. So also are the fences, and all kinds of frames, coops, and cages, the wattle of the abatis, and ribs of umbrellas and fans. The leaves are sewed into rain cloaks, for farmers and sailors, and thatches for covering their huts and boats, pinned into linings for their tea boxes, plaited in immense umbrellas to screen the huckster and his stall from sun and rain, or into coverings for theatres and sheds. Even the whole lot where a two-story house is building, is usually covered in with a framework of bamboo poles, all tied together by rattan, protecting the workman from sun and rain.

" The wood riven into splints is woven into baskets of every form and fancy, sewed into window curtains and door screens, plaited into awnings and coverings for tea chests or sugar cones, and twisted into cables. The shavings, curled threads, and softer parts are used in stuffing pillows, while other parts supply the bed for sleeping, the chopsticks for eating, the pipe for smoking and the broom for sweeping. The mattress to lie upon, the chair to sit upon, the table to eat on, the food to eat, and the fuel to cook it with are also derivable from bamboo. The master makes his ferule from it, the carpenter his foot measure, the farmer his water pipes, irrigating wheels, and straw rakes, the grocer his gill and pint cups, and the mandarin his dreaded instrument of punishment.

" The paper to write on, the book to study from, the pencil to write with, the cup to hold the pencils, and the covering of the lattice-window instead of glass are all indebted to this growth in their manufacture. The shaft of the soldier's spear and oftentimes the spear altogether, the plectrum for playing the flute, the reed in the native organ, the skewer to fasten the hair, the undershirt to protect the body, the hat to screen the head, the bucket to draw the water, and the easy chair to lounge upon, besides cages for birds, fish, bees, grasshoppers, shrimps, and cockroaches, crab nets, shooting tubes, flutes, fifes, fireholders, etc., etc., are among the many things furnished by this wonderful plant. A score or two of bamboo

poles for posts, joists, rafters and lath with fifty fathoms of
rope made of the same, supply the material for a common
dwelling in the south of China. Its cost is about five dollars.
In India, southern China and Japan the bamboo enters more
largely into the daily life of the people than anything else in the
world or than anything else does in any other part of the
world. The Japanese supply us with fans neatly formed, ribs

Gocart, Wheelbarrow.

and handle, from a single branch of bamboo, and covered with
paper from mulberry bark, while their skill is shown also
in the exquisite covering of fine bamboo threads woven around
cups and saucers."

The Chinese laws are strictly and severely enforced.
Their modes of punishment include torture and are the extreme
of cruelty. Both criminals and witnesses are subjected to the
most cruel torture to secure a confession. It is stated on

authority that the victims often die from injuries inflicted when they are arrested on suspicion of crime.

Certain forms of torture are legalized by law. Three boards with grooves for compressing the ankles, five round

Before the Judge.

sticks for compressing the fingers and the stocks and cangue are among the legalized forms. The latter instrument is a frame for the neck and weighs about thirty pounds. It rests on the shoulders without chafing the neck, but is broad enough to prevent the wearer from feeding himself. Name, residence and offense are written on the frame and the prisoner is attended by a policeman to prevent his escape as he goes about the streets.

The following forms of torture are forbidden by law, but it is said are often resorted to by the judges: Pulling or

In the Cangue.

twisting the ears with roughened fingers, making the prisoner kneel on a chain for a long time, striking the lips with a flattened bamboo stick, putting the hands in the stocks behind the back, wrapping fingers in oiled cloths and burning them, tying the hands to a bar under the knees so as to bend the body double, kneeling on pounded glass, and salt, chaining a stone close to the neck,—these are used to extort confessions, but are forbidden now by law.

In addition to the public exposure in the stocks and with the cangue, whipping criminals through the streets is a common mode of punishment. The guilty man is chained to an officer and another with a heavy bamboo rod inflicts the punishment. A policeman goes before, carrying a tablet on which is written the name, place of residence and the crime for which the punishment is inflicted.

Capital punishment is inflicted by beheading, strangling and ling-chi, the latter the most dreaded of all. The Chinese believe it to be a great disgrace to have their bodies mutilated after death, and hence their dread of ling-chi, in which the body is cut to pieces.

But we must leave China and its most interesting people. Our stay with them was much too short and the space allotted here much too limited to tell all that might be said that would interest the reader in the oldest civilized race on the globe. We are sorry to leave them and regret much that our stay was so limited. But we are on the home stretch now, and when we are safely on board the *Siberia* bound for Japan our regrets vanish in the joy of going home.

Before reaching Yokohama it was discovered that small-pox had broken out on the *Siberia* and the health authorities at the gateway of Japan sent us into quarantine. Our experiences were written at the time in a private letter to a friend from which I quote:

Street Scene in Old City, Shanghai.

"The Japanese do things up in fine shape. This is the way I was treated: A brass ring bearing cabalistic signs in Japanese and the figures 94 in American were handed me, so that I should not lose myself or get somebody's clothing instead of my own. Armed with this and checks with similar figures and signs, I was taken into a small undressing room. I removed all my clothes, placed them in a basket-like tray, attached the check and handed the tray out of the door. Then I went into the bath. And it was hot! Did you ever take a real hot water bath? I mean the Japanese kind. If not, the experience of your life in bathing is before you. You are told to jump in, and in you jump, and jump out a good deal quicker. You say it's too hot. But the attendant says, "No! no! not too hot! Japanese take him hotter yet!" Then you try it again, but cautiously, and by degrees you are immersed in hotter water than you ever were in your life before. When you are in awhile you want to stay in and go to sleep. When I got out I went into another small room and was furnished with soft, woolen kimonos and a pair of slippers, and then with a green belt around my waist I went out into the waiting room steaming hot. There was fire and tea and coffee and such things, and there I lounged and gradually cooled off. Then came a lot of trays with clothing. All there was to do was to show the Jap attendant the ring on your finger, and the next minute you had your clothes smoking hot in a small dressing room. They had been run through a steam fumigator, heated as hot as steam is heated, 212 degrees Fahrenheit. When I took out my undergarments they were hot, so hot as to burn my hands, and they also seemed wet at first, but as soon as exposed to the air they dried rapidly, the heat in the garments drying up the moisture. After dressing we were taken back to the ship and had lunch. The whole process took three hours for each batch, and as we had five hundred people to run through, it took time. But everybody was loud in his praise as to how well the Japanese treated us. It was a good time, well done, and these people know how. When that cholera ship came to New York, some years ago, there was no place to disinfect, and the poor passengers were kept out on the rough sea for nearly a week. Japan does it better than that."

After passing safely through quarantine we lodged pleasantly at the club hotel for several weeks where we found our home mail awaiting us. A hundred pieces gave us plenty to do until the arrival of the *Mongolia,* on which we took passage for the Golden Gate. A stop was made at Honolulu and a day spent with friends there, and then we were off again for the land of the Stars and Stripes. It was a beautiful day when we passed through the Golden Gate and pulled up to the dock at San Francisco. Looking ashore we recognized the familiar faces of Brother Galen B. Royer and wife and Brother Brubaker who had come to meet the returning wanderers. It was a glad, joyous meeting, a delightful home-coming. One night in San Francisco and then we hurried on to Los Angeles and home to Mount Morris. Only a few days after we left the doomed city, came the earthquake and fire which laid it in the dust and ashes, and the town named for St. Francis was desolate.

Through all the journeying the Lord was with us and his blessings are not to be numbered.

> " I lift my heart to-day in praise
> To him who loves me so,
> Whose mercy crowneth all my days
> And makes my cup o'erflow.
> O, have I loved him as I should
> For all his blessings free?
> Praise God who giveth naught but good,
> For he is good to me!"

THE END.